Bareback Porn, Porous Masculinities, Queer Futures

This book analyses contemporary gay "pig" masculinities, which have emerged alongside antiretroviral therapies, online porn, and new sexualised patterns of recreational drug use, examining how they trouble modern European understandings of the male body, their ethics, and their political underpinnings.

This is the first book to reflect on an increasingly visible new form of sexualised gay masculinity, and the first monograph to move debates on condomless sex amongst gay men beyond discourses of HIV and/or AIDS. It contributes to existing critical histories of sexuality, pornography, and other sex media at a crucial juncture in the history of gay male sex cultures and the HIV epidemic. The book draws from fieldwork, interviews, archival research, visual analysis, philosophy, queer theory, and cultural studies, using empirical, critical, and speculative methodologies to better think gay "pig" masculinities across their material, affective, ethical, and political dimensions, in a future-oriented, politically inflected, reflection on what queer bodies may become.

Spanning historical context to empirical and theoretical study, *Bareback Porn, Porous Masculinities, Queer Futures* will be of key interest to academics and students in sexuality studies, film, media, visual culture, cultural studies, and porn studies concerned with masculinities, sex and sexualities, and their circulation across an array of media.

João Florêncio is a Senior Lecturer in History of Modern and Contemporary Art and Visual Culture at the University of Exeter. His interdisciplinary research navigates the intersections of visual culture with queer theory, performance studies, and the medical and post-humanities in order to think how modern and contemporary bodies, subjectivities, and sex cultures have been produced and mediated.

Masculinity, Sex and Popular Culture
Series Editors: John Mercer and Clarissa Smith

Books in the Masculinity, Sex and Popular Culture series promote high quality research that is positioned at the nexus of masculinity, sex, and popular culture. The series brings a media and cultural studies approach to the analysis of contemporary manifestations of masculinity in popular culture. It includes titles that focus on the connections between masculinities and popular culture that extend out from media cultures to examining practices – focusing on forms of participatory action in public spaces (such as bodybuilding and 'Lad' culture), and in more traditionally private arenas of sexual practice acknowledging that cultures of exhibitionism and display and the distinctions between the public and the private are increasingly important considerations in the digital age.

Men, Masculinities, and Popular Romance
Jonathan A. Allan

Bareback Porn, Porous Masculinities, Queer Futures
The Ethics of Becoming-Pig
João Florêncio

Bareback Porn, Porous Masculinities, Queer Futures
The Ethics of Becoming-Pig

João Florêncio

Routledge
Taylor & Francis Group

LONDON AND NEW YORK

First published 2020
by Routledge
2 Park Square, Milton Park, Abingdon, Oxon OX14 4RN

and by Routledge
52 Vanderbilt Avenue, New York, NY 10017

Routledge is an imprint of the Taylor & Francis Group, an informa business

© 2020 João Florêncio

British Library Cataloguing-in-Publication Data
A catalogue record for this book is available from the British Library

Library of Congress Cataloging-in-Publication Data
Names: Florêncio, João, author.
Title: Bareback porn, porous masculinities, queer futures : the ethics of becoming-pig /
João Florêncio. Description: 1 Edition. | new york : routledge, 2020. | Series: Sex,
masculinity and popular culture | Includes bibliographical references and index. |
Summary: "This book analyses contemporary gay "pig" masculinities, which have
emerged alongside antiretroviral therapies, online porn, and new sexualised patterns
of recreational drug use, examining how they trouble modern European
understandings of the male body, their ethics, and their political underpinnings. This
is the first book to reflect on an increasingly visible new form of sexualised gay
masculinity, and the first monograph to move debates on condomless sex amongst gay
men beyond discourses of HIV and/or AIDS. It contributes to existing critical histories
of sexuality, pornography and other sex media at a crucial juncture in the history of
gay male sex cultures and the HIV epidemic. The book draws from fieldwork,
interviews, archival research, visual analysis, philosophy, queer theory, and cultural
studies, using empirical, critical, and speculative methodologies to better think gay
"pig" masculinities across their material, affective, ethical and political dimensions, in
a future-oriented, politically-inflected, reflection on what queer bodies may become.
Spanning historical context to empirical and theoretical study, Bareback Porn, Porous
Masculinities, Queer Futures will be of key interest to academics and students in
sexuality studies, film, media, visual culture, cultural studies, and porn studies
concerned with masculinities, sex and sexualities and their circulation across an array
of media"– Provided by publisher. Identifiers: LCCN 2020011481 |
ISBN 9780815357902 (hardback) | ISBN 9780367530358 (paperback) |
ISBN 9781351123426 (ebook) | ISBN 9781351123419 (adobe pdf) |
ISBN 9781351123402 (epub) | ISBN 9781351123396 (mobi) Subjects: LCSH: Gay
men–Psychology. | Gay men–Social conditions. | Internet and gay men. | Gender
identity. | Masculinity. Classification: LCC HQ76 .F566 2020 | DDC 306.76/62–dc23
LC record available at https://lccn.loc.gov/2020011481

ISBN: 978-0-8153-5790-2 (hbk)
ISBN: 978-0-367-53035-8 (pbk)
ISBN: 978-1-351-12342-6 (ebk)

Typeset in Sabon
by Wearset Ltd, Boldon, Tyne & Wear

For Ben,
my lover, my comrade, my friend

Contents

Illustrations

Preface

The process of researching and writing this book has been a tour de force, a reckoning with a history that is also very much mine whilst at the same attempting to negotiate, in my head, the boundaries that are often still expected to separate "rigorous" scholarship from more personal registers of writing. Yet, both as a scholar from a working-class background, the first in my family to get any sort of university degree, and as a gay man, all my work in academia has, since my undergraduate years, been both grounded in my own life—the only possible standpoint from which I am able to write—and driven by my political commitments, which started developing as I was growing up in a small rural Portuguese village generally proud of the anti-fascist history of the Portuguese Left whilst being simultaneously suspicious—to say the least—of identity-based politics and social movements. In a place where "community" and traditional working-class politics still plays such an important and valuable role, where everybody appears to be there for one another, it is, nonetheless, interesting to note the limitations of such experiences of "community" and the violence—symbolic if not physical, quotidian, microscopic and yet deeply felt—that it enacts against those who for one reason or another do not fully fit in. Having said that, I do not think any individual is to blame for the shortcomings of the structures that organise their lives; individualising the failings or the faults of some only diverts our attention away from the ideologies that sustain them.

As a scholar now working in a country that is not mine, some of the anxieties of growing up gay in a socially conservative environment have to a certain extent gone away. Yet, as I made my path into academia leaving my village—or my "roots" as my parents often tell me—behind, I encountered a whole new set of challenges. In some way, I seem to have brought my own background with me into a place where people like me still seem increasingly rare and where marrying political investments, personal narratives, and scholarly work can sometimes be seen as anathema to the spirit of the neoliberal university. And all that gets harder when one chooses to write about gay sex and sexual cultures in a way that doesn't necessarily fall under the poetic umbrella of love or ideologies of coupledom. In ways,

that is, that can seem to go against the narratives of equality and responsibility of mainstream LGBTQ+ politics; in ways that refuse to ignore the
messiness of sex, of bodies, and of what happens when the latter open
themselves to one another, particularly at an historical juncture when
we—queer folk—are still recovering from the catastrophic impact that the
AIDS crisis had on our dreams, our visions of a future, the fashioning of
our own subjectivities and our experiments with different modes of
kinship. And it becomes particularly hard when, in deciding to pursue such
avenues of scholarly enquiry, we fear the consequences of becoming too
personal, of revealing too much about ourselves, and how that may hinder
the reception of our work, our position in the institution of academia, the
opinions colleagues and students will have about us.

As a gay man living with HIV, trying to juggle all those questions and
fears of disclosure as I researched and wrote this book has been a daily
source of anxiety. And I still do not know whether I've made the right
choices. I still fear the consequences. But I also felt, as I encountered the
various men—my brothers—that populate this book, that the only way in
which I could give them the respect they deserve, the only way in which I
could try to do justice not only to their histories of struggle, of survival,
uncertainty and death but also to their histories of activism, of solidarity,
of mutual care and of life, would be if I also had the strength to disclose
my subject position, my very much embodied standpoint as a man, a
writer, and a scholar, without fearing that it will damage my work, its academic value, my reputation, my future. I hope I have made the right
decision.

Acknowledgements

I started thinking about this book during my first years at the University of Exeter, having noticed how the existing scholarship on bareback sex no longer fully accounted for the ways in which I saw other gay men around me thinking about and engaging in it. I had also noticed the exponential increase in the numbers of gay men who—around me and online—were identifying themselves as "pigs", and to whom the narratives of risk and flirtations with the death drive that had been at the core of a great deal of scholarship on bareback sex seemed not to make sense. Yet, the seeds of this book were sowed in my mind much earlier, as I encountered queer theory and what's come to be commonly known as continental philosophy on my path through graduate school.

I have learnt a lot from many people since then, both before and after this book project became possible thanks to the Arts and Humanities Research Council and their Leadership Fellows scheme for early-career researchers. I am grateful to my graduate school mentors Johnny Golding, when I was at the University of Greenwich, and Gavin Butt and Simon O'Sullivan, from my time at Goldsmiths, University of London. Together, they have set me on the scholarly path that has led me here. I am also thankful for the help, support, and words of encouragement from students past and present, and from colleagues in the College of Humanities at Exeter, especially Jana Funke, Adam Watt, Fabrizio Nevola, Melissa Percival, David Houston Jones, Sabrina Rahman, Camille Mathieu, Fiona Allen, Luna Dolezal, Rebecca Langlands, Kate Fisher, and Laura Salisbury. I am also grateful for the support of all my incredible colleagues in research support services who have been fundamental in helping me write the AHRC bid that allowed me to complete this book and manage the funding; namely, Charlotte Tupman, Sanja Djerasimovic, Aki Iskander, Mandy Bedford, and Emma Clarke. Academia should not be reduced to academics.

I am also most grateful to the colleagues, mentors, and friends with whom I've spent the last couple of years bouncing ideas about gay men and sex in the age of online locative media and antiretrovirals. Their help and advice have kept me going, and words cannot describe how thankful I am to them: John Mercer, Clarissa Smith, Kane Race, Susanna Paasonen, and my "sisters" Jamie Hakim, and Charlie Sarson—they have shown me generosity and what academic "families" ought to be about.

This book would also not have been possible without the support of all those whom I've encountered as I conducted the research that has led me here. Whether as friends, hosts, or archive guides, they have made this process smooth and deeply enriching on a personal as well as professional ways: Stefan Dickers at the Bishopsgate Institute, London; Peter Rehberg and Ben Miller at the Schwules Museum, Berlin; Bud Thomas and Joseph Hawkins at the ONE National Gay & Lesbian Archives at the USC Libraries, Los Angeles; Durk Dehner, Daniel Szuhay, S.R. Sharp, Marc Bellenger, Allison Schulte and Connie at the Tom of Finland Foundation, Los Angeles; the staff at the James C. Hormel LGBTQIA Center at the San Francisco Public Library; Paul Morris at Treasure Island Media; and Ron Athey, Cesar Padilla, Viron El Vert, Mohammad Salemy, Florian Hetz, Cassils, Christy Michel, Darren Kinoshita, Marval A. Rex, Mike Hoffman, Rich Villani, Rita D'Albert, Zackary Drucker, Lydia Lunch, Aurélien Nobécourt-Arras, Gio Black Peter, Marc Adelman, Liz Rosenfeld, and "big brother" Elijah Burgher for having made me feel at home and looked after me during my travels. A special thank you, too, to all the men I interviewed in London, Berlin, Los Angeles, and San Francisco. This would not have been possible without every single one of them.

Finally, I would like to thank Ben, my lover, my comrade, my friend, whom I would never have met were it not for this research project, who has held my hand throughout, and who has made me a better person by allowing me to look at the world through his beautifully generous and caring eyes. This book is his as much as it is mine.

Introduction
Pig masculinities

Dark Alley Media's gay porn video *The Real Pump N Dumps of New York City* mixes together scenes of "raw" condomless sex with intimate black-and-white interviews of the bottoming models during which the latter open up about their desires, fantasies, and what generally floats their boat when it comes to sex. According to the blurb on the back of its DVD cover, the video promises to give its viewers "an uninhibited look into the dark minds of our cum-thirsty bottoms, waiting with their eager holes open wide and twitching for seed". Thanks to what that blurb describes as its "candid Cumwhore interviews", its aim is to offer "a glimpse into their sweat-soaked world of manjuice drenched pump-n-dump fantasies".

The video, directed by I. Que Grande and released in 2010, opens with an establishing shot of New York City, before cutting to the first interview with bottoming model Jayson Park, who sits naked in bed and stroking his dick whilst answering questions about what turns him on: from his requirement that he be the only bottom in the room and having an older and a younger man "getting me on both ends", to his gym sock fetish—a "real masculine look" that reminds him of locker rooms and locker room sex. When asked about how he used to meet people for sex in the past, Park reminisces about using cruising areas, noting, however, that, now, one of the things he likes about the internet is that it can "cut through a lot of bullshit". The tone of the interviews is indeed "candid" and relaxed, with the camera moving back and forth from full to more intimate close shots. The gentle and friendly nature of the interview contrasts with the intensity of the sex scene that follows, a sequence in which Park is fucked rough and bareback—that is, without a condom—by Wade Stone, the top who eventually ejaculates on the bottom's ass before penetrating him again to the reassuring and comforting words "there you go, boy".

The remaining scenes of the video share the same form and aesthetic, with heavily saturated colour images of New York City set to swinging instrumental music giving way to intimate confessional-style interviews filmed in black-and-white, followed by formulaic intense scenes of bareback sex again shot in colour. Whilst the establishing shots repeatedly confirm New York City as the location of each of the scenes, the interviews stick to a uniform register, with the bottoms reminiscing about their past adventures and talking about their yet- and about-to-be-fulfilled sexual fantasies. Those range from big dicks and anonymous sex to double penetration and condomless group sex scenarios involving the exchange of ejaculate—"loads", as the slang goes—from the bottom's ass to his mouth via the mediating mouths of the tops—what is known as "felching". The editing together of scenes of confessional speech and sex echoes the complex articulation of documentary reality and scripted fantasy that has been widely recognised in critical literature as a fundamental feature of the pornographic imagination (see Paasonen 2011), the "real" in "real pump n dumps" being metonymically signalled by the interviews and seamlessly unfolding into pornographic sequences in which sexual fantasies are staged and bodily thresholds explored and trespassed. Here, the border between reality and fantasy is as thin as a simple fading from black-and-white to colour.

Scene four is, however, the one that struck me the most. It begins with bottoming model Marco Cruise standing by a window overlooking the New York skyline. "Do you see this?" he asks the cameraman. "This is my fucking playground right here." As the conversation continues, the model is asked "are you gonna take it like a man?" to which he confirms:

> I'm gonna take it like a man ... I fucking love getting it in my fucking ass ... and—like—taking it like a pig. And I'm not gonna fucking say 'oh I'm versatile' to make it seem like I'm more fucking masculine. Either you are or you aren't. You could be a fucking top and be a big old fucking queen. You kiddin' me? [...] You fuck me like a man, I'm gonna take it like a man!

At one point, as Cruise smokes a cigarette by the window, the director asks him "How'd you describe yourself in the nastiest, dirtiest words?" The model replies:

> If I was gonna describe myself, I would say I'm a ... hungry bottom, cum-loving, pig-ass, hole-dripping ... fucking cum-loving bottom. Love it in the ass, love it knowing that I'm getting my fucking ass fucking bred by a fucking macho fucking guy that wants it teared up.

The director retorts: "And how does one become a cum-loving cum dripping ..." "Pig whore?" Cruise interrupts, "Loving fucking pig whore bottom? Like me? ... Just enjoy it."

When I first watched the interview I've just described, I was taken back by the unabashed openness and intensity of the words chosen by Marco Cruise to describe himself, as well as by the never-ending series of expletives he used to emphasise how strongly he feels about the kinds of sex he enjoys, and how the latter appear fundamental to his own self-narration as a masculine bottom who's going to "take it like a man". Confessional speech has been a fundamental tool for the production and regulation of modern forms of subjectivity (Foucault 1978). In that context, the interview fascinated me due to way in which it operates on a confessional register similar to the one Foucault associated with the birth of biopolitics and the emergence, in the nineteenth century, of institutions and modes of discourse responsible for enacting modern biopower as the positive administration and optimisation of the life of the subject. In confessional speech acts, Foucault (1978) wrote, "the speaking subject is also the subject of the statement" (61). In other words, in being incited to speak their truth—just like the bottoms in *Real Pump N Dumps of New York City*—subjects become who they announce themselves to be. Whilst Foucault's work on confessional speech required a subject's incorporation into the power-knowledge formations of institutional discourse, with homosexuals adopting for themselves a designation that had been originally advanced by medical literature and, in doing so, occupying a position of both subjection and resistance to power, "pig" as used in *The Real Pump N Dumps of New York City* emerged as part of a subcultural system of classification, one that uses terms borrowed from a different taxonomic system—animal taxonomy—that were re-signified through a process of behavioural analogy. "Pig" thus appears as one of several sexual scripts that are today available to be taken up, embodied, and explored by gay men.

Developed by John Gagnon and William Simon, scripts are "a metaphor for conceptualizing the production of behavior within social life" (Simon and Gagnon 1986, 98). As a framework for research into sexual behaviour, sexual script theory has offered scholars and social scientists a tool to understand how sex informs the production of the self through an articulation of cultural scenarios, interpersonal scripts, and intrapsychic scripts, all of which provide individuals with meaningful guides to make sense of themselves vis-à-vis their sexual behaviours (Escoffier 2007; Whittier and Melendez 2007; Graham 2017). In sexual scripting, narrative and plot—just like confessional modes of speech—are fundamental for the self-reflexive development of the modern sexual self. Therefore, just like the homosexual was born in 1870 with Carl Westphal's classification of "contrary sexual sensations" (Foucault 1978, 43), I am concerned here with the birth of the "pig" in the early twenty-first century as a sexual script shaped and taken-up by gay men who engage in what could be seen as "extreme" kinds of sexual behaviour that often involve multiple penetrations and exchanges of bodily fluids. Importantly—as I will demonstrate later—"pig" masculinities have grown exponentially in the antiretroviral age—what some have called the "post-AIDS" (Dowsett and McInnes 1996) or "post-crisis" moment (Kagan 2015; 2018)—a geo-temporality of HIV corporealities marked by the introduction of combination antiretroviral regimes for the successful management and prophylaxis of HIV, as well as by a growing sense of condom fatigue amongst increasing numbers of gay men in so-called "developed" economies (Adam, Husbands, Murray and Maxwell 2005). I am further interested in theorising gay "pig" masculinities in relation to what Raewyn Connell has named "hegemonic masculinity" (Connell 2005). Namely, how the former may simultaneously reassert and trouble different core attributes of the idealised form of masculinity that, according to Connell, grants men a share of the "patriarchal dividend" (107) that is higher the closer they come to embody that ideal. Such an undertaking also has important repercussions for thinking the age-old metonymic relationship between the male body and the body politic. If, as Moira Gatens (1996) argued "the modern body politic is based on an image of a *masculine* body which reflects fantasies about the value and capacities of that body" (25), what happens when certain male bodies actualise themselves in such a way that all the ideals and values grounding the Hobbesian modelling of the "artificial" body politic on the "natural" male body are brought to tatters? Of course, it would be easier—like Western culture has famously done for centuries—to simply mark those male bodies as "deviant" or "unnatural" on behalf of a standard of masculinity and embodiment that has rarely, if ever, existed outside of anatomy atlases and works of political theory. Still, the task I would like to undertake in this book is the opposite one. That is, rather than dismissing those queer bodies as exceptions to the rule—as negligible glitches—I want instead to make them in-form (or, more likely, deform) the standards of masculinity that have been used throughout modernity to shape our understandings of the body politic and the kinds of ethics and communities such polity has sustained. In doing so, however, my aim is not to contribute to—or to reinforce—the hegemony of masculinity in our patriarchal conjecture. Instead, my aim is to add to the body of scholarship that has, over the last few decades, tried to think masculinities as forms of gendered embodiment that are contingent on specific spatiotemporal coordinates and that are thus not only susceptible to change but always-already ever-changing. From there—rather than wishing to reassert the male body as the privileged model for the social body—I would like to speculate on how certain twenty-first-century queer forms of male embodiment may trouble still widely held views of what being a man entails and, through that, help us challenge common assumptions of what a polity looks like. From that standpoint, my project is not only indebted to the large body of feminist cultural criticism produced over the last three decades, but—I believe—it also shares with the latter a common set of political commitments.

Watching *Real Pump N Dumps of New York City*, I could not but think about my own experience of living through the transition from the event of AIDS as crisis to the expanded temporality of HIV as chronicity—a transition that has been bookended on one side by the public health campaigns that environed my teenage years in the early 1990s—deeply and brutally shaping the anxieties of an already difficult coming-out story set in a small Portuguese countryside village—and, on the other, my first contact with the term "bareback" and its pornographic representations in the early 2000s, thanks to the internet and my having taken the clichéd small-town boy decision to move to the "big city". When I think about it now, the gap between the posters that used to tell me about the pain of an AIDS diagnosis, and the seemingly unconcerned, adventurous, intense, and joyful sex depicted in the porn I watch today couldn't have been wider. I particularly remember a large campaign poster produced in 1993 for the Comissão Nacional de Luta Contra a SIDA (CNLCS), the government agency that, between 1990 and 2005, coordinated the response of the Portuguese state to HIV and AIDS. The message carried by the poster was fairly straightforward and yet deprived of the shock tactics that, in the English-speaking world, have become associated with the major public health campaigns of the late 1980s and early 1990s—I'm here thinking of the British "tombstone" or the Australian "Grim Reaper" TV advertisements. That poster by the CNLCS was rather different, demurer. It was a large photograph of a single figure, a back-lit young man sat on a window-sill looking down, his face indiscernible, with a clock on the wall to the right of the frame. At the bottom of the photograph the acronym "SIDA" (AIDS) made sure we knew who this man was and what the poster was

Figure 0.1 Comissão Nacional de Luta Contra a SIDA, "SIDA: Sabe que se pode porrer de solidão?", 1993. Colour lithograph by Publicis/Ciesa.

Credit: Comissão Nacional de Luta Contra a SIDA.

about, whilst, on the right-hand side, right next to the clock, a simple and yet effective question: "Do you know loneliness can kill?" (*"Sabe que se pode morrer de solidão?"*).

Of all the campaigns that were around at the time, of all the charity gala fundraisers and all the news headlines on World AIDS Day, it was this poster that got stuck in the mind of ten-year-old me. Not because it was shocking—it certainly wasn't—but, I'm guessing, in hindsight, because it painted a gut-wrenching articulation of sex, isolation, and death, one according to which every single gay man would likely die alone, without pathos, without cries, without the apocalyptic sound of cages, metal chains, or tombstones falling and crashing on the ground. It was that simple, silent, and yet oh-so-terrifying image that would keep on haunting me as a teenager growing up to become the adult gay man I am today: an image of loneliness; the fear of loneliness.

How different was that from the seemingly proud and empowered manner in which, two decades later, I saw Marco Cruise speaking of his sex life and of his being a "pig whore"? Put differently, I cannot help reminiscing about how the spectre of AIDS informed the development of my own subjectivity as a queer boy, how it made my sexual life as a young adult become a constant, hyper-conscious, and vertiginous negotiation of trust, safety, risk, pleasure, and belonging—how that often felt both life-consuming and yet still titillating—and how the new millennium seems to have brought with it a new hope in the shape of new drugs that allow me—and others like me—to finally lift the weight of AIDS off our shoulders and, in so doing, set ourselves onto new paths of sexual fulfilment and self-discovery. Better perhaps, onto new paths of sexual self-invention. What is funny about my indulging in all this reminiscing, is that I never expected *Real Pump N Dumps of New York City* to become the madeleine to my Proust.

Importantly, despite all the feeling and seeing backwards that the video elicited in me, despite its triggering of yet another possible narrative of identity and self-actualisation to add to so many and often conflicting narratives of identity and self-actualisation that I—and most of us—keep on telling ourselves in order to give this thing we call life a reassuring semblance of a stable ground, *Real Pump N Dumps of New York City* also made me think about the creative openness of becoming that the introduction of antiretroviral drugs has catalysed, about all potential yet to be actualised in new queer forms of sexual sociability and communion. Granted, in many ways antiretroviral drugs epitomise the biopolitics of self-care and self-administration that sustain the subjectivation of the autonomous neoliberal subject as a healthy standing reserve of labour- and consumer-power (Dean 2015; Race 2009, 2018). And yet—and to the surprise of many—those same drugs also seem to have afforded gay men the chance of engaging in new creative modes of unproductive expenditure, intimacy, and sexual sociability that appear to veer away from the capturing forces of the apparatuses of production, accumulation, and capitalisation of identity that have come to define neoliberalism as a highly coded economic programme predicated on a double-gesture of decoding and recoding of desire (Deleuze and Guattari 1987). Such a tension between control and invention, between management and risk, is the same kind of productive tension we find between, on the one hand, the psychoanalytical reduction of desire to lack—with its satisfaction being both mediated and deferred by the authority of the Phallus—and, on the other hand, the schizoanalytical position that views desire as a positive flow fuelling becomings and opening up new pathways to unforeseen futures (Hocquenghem 1993, 1995; Guattari 1996; Deleuze 2004; Beckman 2013).

Inhabiting the vertiginous collision of centripetal technologies of biopolitical control with the centrifugal micropolitics of dissident desire, sexuality actualises itself in forms of pleasure that can lead either to a crystallisation of identities or to their undoing—to what Tim Dean (2012) called "self-confirming" and "self-dismissing" pleasures (487). In other words, sexuality can, when captured and overcoded by language, images, and biomedical technologies (antiretrovirals, Viagra, the contraceptive pill and other chemical prostheses), serve to guarantee the social reproduction of neoliberal subjectivity understood as "face", that is, the embodied and hardened "refrain" that demarcates the self as a self-contained existential territory (Guattari 1995, 2011). Yet, it can also, whilst still remaining a highly coded arena of biopolitical control, create the conditions of possibility for the emergence of new forms of pleasure and intimacy that may undo identities and trouble the wholesomeness of the neoliberal subject. If, as Frida Beckman (2013) argued in her attempt to use Deleuze and Guattari's work against their own privileging of plateaus of desire to the detriment of the latter's consummation in orgasmic pleasure, the fact that flows of desire are set free by capitalism's schizophrenic traits only to be recoded as utilitarian and monetised pleasure by its paranoid function, that does not necessarily mean that pleasure will always-already be a reterritorialisation of desire (146). Instead, whilst Oedipal, state-sanctioned, and neoliberal forms of sexual pleasure are certainly a means to secure the reproduction of the existing social order through ensuring the eternal return of the same, pleasure may still harbour within itself—when freed from its Oedipal associations with lack and reproductive futurity—the seeds for new becomings, for new modes of *futuring* that may allow us "to see and feel beyond the quagmire of the present" (Muñoz 2009, 1).

In line with the above, I argue that *Real Pump N Dumps of New York City* presents us with a new kind of gay masculinity, one that is grounded on what could be seen as "extreme" or "uncivilised" sexual behaviours, the emergence of which has been catalysed by the introduction of combination antiretroviral therapies in the mid-1990s and mediated by pornography produced and disseminated after the advent of the internet. In what follows I will start to draw a sketch of those "pig" masculinities and their sexual imaginary through a triangulation of the biopolitics, sexual behaviours, and twenty-first-century sex media that have sustained their development.

* * *

Marco Cruise's choice of the phrase "pig whore" to describe himself in *Real Pump N Dumps of New York City* is likely to come with no surprise to most gay men who are familiar with contemporary gay media landscapes. From mobile hook-up apps such as Grindr, Recon, or Scruff to studio and homemade gay porn, the number of gay men defining themselves as "pigs" seems to have increased exponentially in the last couple of decades. The term, as well as its social media identifiers—the pig head or pig snout emojis—have become ubiquitous features of contemporary urban gay sex cultures in cities like London, Berlin, New York, Los Angeles, or San Francisco.

Yet, identifying with an animal is not a new phenomenon in gay male subcultures; gay men seem to have had a penchant for identifying themselves with animal metaphors for much longer than "pigs" have been around. Website Pride.com, for instance, lists no fewer than 12 instances of what it calls "wild gay slang"—from the more common "bear" (bigger, hairy men, often seen as more masculine), "cub" and "otter" (the former, a younger "bear"; the latter, a hairier man with a more athletic figure), to the less familiar "gym rat" (always going to or coming from the gym), "giraffe" (really tall), "chickenhawk" (an older man with an interest in "chickens", younger, skinny, often more "effeminate" men), or "bull" (hyper-muscular men). Amongst them, we can also find mention of the "pig", which the website defines as being "more focused on sex than anything else, often into kinkier and somewhat seedier sexual practices". Urbandictionary.com, that infamous online well of slang knowledge, also follows along the same lines when it comes to "pigs", defining them as "someone who gets off sexually by doing raunchy things like licking sweaty armpits or sniffing dirty underwear and socks". "Pigs" have become so visible as a gay "counterpublic" (Warner 2002) that, as we entered the Chinese Lunar Year of the Pig in 2019, hook-up website Squirt.org conducted a survey of its users entitled "Consider yourself a pig?" Comprising three multiple-choice and one open-ended questions, the survey asked:

1. In your sex life, do you ever identify as a Pig? [Yes/No/Unsure]
2. What does being a Pig mean to you? [Sexual freedom/Uninhibited sex/Anonymous sex/Group sex/Gang-fuck/Cum play/All of the above]
3. Do you attend parties or events where you get to explore the Pig side of your sexual life? [Yes/No—but I'd like to/No—not something I'm interested in]
4. What's your ultimate Pig sexual fantasy? [free-form answer].

According to the results of the survey published on Daily.Squirt.org, of the more than 2,000 Squirt.org users who responded to it, 65% answered affirmatively to the first question; that is, they identify as "pigs". In what the company acknowledged as the likely result of a poorly devised question, every respondent also chose the "All of the above" option when answering question two ("What does being a pig mean to you?"). With regards to the comments its users proceeded to leave on that question, Daily.Squirt.org went on to state that a

> [...] sense of no limits and no inhibitions is a theme that came through really strongly. Lots of guys told us that a Pig-like session involved multiple partners, lots of cum, and sometimes public sex. For the Pigs amongst us, it seems that we're really revelling in an opportunity to release our inner-slut—it's a hedonistic embrace of pleasure, surrendering yourself to the intensity of a man-on-man encounter.

Reassuringly, the results of the survey also resonate with Tim Dean's brief mention of "pigs" in *Unlimited Intimacy* (2009), his ethnography of bareback sex published over a decade ago:

> A term of approbation in bareback subculture, *pig* refers to a man who wants as much sex as he can get with as many different men as possible, often in the form of group sex that includes barebacking, water sports, fisting, and SM ("pig pile" is a long-established term for a gay orgy or gang bang). There is really no such thing as a vanilla pig or a safe-sex pig, since the erotic identity of *pig* defies normative constructions of sexual behaviour. Being a pig entails committing oneself to sexual excess, to pushing beyond boundaries of propriety and corporeal integrity; being a pig thus positions a man for membership in a sexual avant-garde, and, unsurprisingly, some men advertise their pig status with tattoos, T-shirts, and various forms of braggadocio.
>
> (49)

Both the results of the Squirt.org survey and Dean's definition of the term highlight what appears to be a core feature of gay "pig" masculinities, one that sets "pigs" apart from the other members of the menagerie of animals with which gay men identify. Namely, whilst most other categories are predicated on physical attributes—what bodies look like, the qualities of their physique—gay "pigs" are instead defined by their behaviour; that is, by the way in which they approach sex and what they get up to when it comes to it. Unlike "bears", "otters", "giraffes", or "bulls", for instance, a "pig" is what a "pig" does. "Pigs" do not so much come together based on their appearance but, rather, on their sexual preferences and the intensity with which they live their sexual lives and pursuit of sexual pleasures. Whether defining themselves through the more general "pig" or the more specific "piss pig", "fist pig", "cum pig", "scat pig", etc., "pigginess" to them always involves sexual excess and a relentless violation or transgression of the boundaries of the body proper and of its integrity, two aspects of "pigsex" that will be fundamental to the argument I will build in the chapters that follow.

A quick analysis of #gaypig on Twitter and Instagram offers some further insight into the similarities and differences amongst gay men who identify as "pigs". According to social media analytics website Hastagify. me, at the time of writing #gaypig has appeared mostly in tweets from the USA, Western Europe, and Brazil, primarily in the English language (51%), and with a series of other hashtags associated with it. With related hashtags like #gayporn, #gayfetish, #gaypiss, #gayXXX, #fisting, #jockstrap, #gaybeard, #gaymuscle, #BBBH (acronym for "bareback brotherhood"), #ass, #gayscat, #smegma, etc., #gaypig cuts across various kinds of fetish and kinky sexual practices that could and indeed have been, in and of themselves, the subject matter of many academic studies. Still, if "pigsex" intersects with other sexual practices worthy of attention on their own, the breadth of their constellation allows us to distil a high level of intensity and sexual omnivorousness that I want to associate with gay "pigginess". Gay "pigs", it seems, aren't choosy and they are keen to experiment, to push boundaries, and to venture into new unchartered territories of sexual activity and sexual pleasure. In the age of online porn and social media platforms, #gaypig brings together a wide variety of kinks and body types and, in so doing, it evokes a counterpublic that, regardless of its apparent internal differences, comes together thanks to a shared sexual ethos; namely, the commitment of its members to sexual exploration through transgression of the boundaries between inside and outside, and proper and improper, in an attempt to take sex and sexual pleasure into new registers of embodied intensity. The life of #gaypig on Instagram confirms the above. Bringing up over 20,000 posts at the time of writing, the hashtag mostly delivers the platform's paradigmatic genre—the selfie—and through that gives us a glimpse of the diversity of looks and body types of self-identified gay "pigs", with a few of the images also hinting at the variety of fetishes and kinks that fall under the "pig" umbrella albeit without breaking Instagram's rules of engagement when it comes to nudity and sexual explicit content.

Notwithstanding the above, the term "pig" has a longer history in the gay male scene, being traceable to at least the 1970s and to printed media such as gay fetish magazines. In Germany, for instance, there is a longer history of using the words "*Sau*" ("sow") and "*Schwein*" ("pig") to designate gay bottoms who are not only always "hungry" for sex but are also often uninhibited, engaging in "extreme" sexual activities such as fisting, piss play and scat play (coprophagy). *Kumpel*, the gay fetish magazine published in Sweden for the German market between the 1970s and the 1990s, for instance, included in its pages several instances of the terms used in relation to men defined by their attitudes to sex and the kinky sexual practices they favoured, often as part of erotic photo shoots or erotic fiction. Similarly, in the personal ads section of French gay fetish magazine *Projet X*, there were already several instances throughout the 1990s of men self-identifying as "*porc*" or looking for men who identified as "*porc*" ("pig"), with the same pattern being found in the personal ads section of US magazine *Drummer* as early as the 1970s. Whether documented in *Kumpel*, *Projet X*, or *Drummer*, the early history of gay "pigs" seems to have already been marked by an eroticisation of bodily fluids and excreta such as urine and faeces, the two substances that writers for *Drummer* considered the last two sexual taboos (Sagan 1981). Early "pigs" inhabited and pushed the edges of the sexually permissible—there, where both pleasure and disgust went hand in hand with a stretching of bodily orifices and an embrace and exchange of their internal fluids. When it comes to film and video porn, the term "pig" only started appearing in titles of productions during the late 1990s, with the earliest title listed on the Internet Adult Film Database (IAFD) being Thor Stephens's *Biker Pigs from Hell*, released in 1999.[1] Over the two decades since *Biker Pigs from Hell* was released, the word "pig" or its plural "pigs" have appeared in increasing numbers of gay porn titles, often paired with qualifying words such as "bareback", "cum", or "piss", thus contributing to the increase in visibility, mediation, and circulation of "pig" masculinities and imaginaries in twenty-first-century gay male sex cultures.

In order to understand the exponential increase in the visibility of gay "pig" masculinities and the sexual practices on which they're grounded, it is important to take into account the biomedical developments that have taken place in tandem with it; namely, the development and progressive implementation of combination antiretroviral therapies for the management and, later, prophylaxis of HIV infection. Officially announced at the XI International AIDS Conference in Vancouver in 1996, combination antiretroviral regimes and protocols for monitoring the viral load of HIV patients were hailed by the *British Medical Journal* as "impressive advances in the understanding of the virology and immunology of HIV infection" (Cohn 1997, 487), with *Science* talking of "excitement infusing the field" of HIV research (Pennisi and Cohen 1996, 1884). The reasons for such excitement had to do with the fact that the drugs and clinical protocols presented in Vancouver seemed able to target HIV loads and lower them to undetectable levels. However, whilst much of the scientific community was excited about the new findings, journals such as the *Economic and Political Weekly* still appeared unconvinced, writing of an "AIDS Extravaganza in Vancouver" that, according to the author of the article, could lead people to "drop their guard against unsafe sex" and, most importantly, "failed to highlight the more immediate need to expand the AIDS prevention programmes in developing countries", particularly given the prohibitive costs of the new drug regimens being hailed by the medical community at that year's Conference, which would make them inaccessible beyond the wealthiest nations (Nag 1996, 2989).

The fair criticisms and warnings concerning access to the new drugs in developing nations notwithstanding, the years that followed Vancouver saw antiretroviral combination therapy, alongside regular viral load testing, turn HIV infection into a long-term chronic condition, leading to a radical transformation of the lives, subjectivities, and sexual practices of gay men, the demographic that has historically been most associated with HIV and AIDS in popular culture, and one with fairly easy access to sexual health services in high-income countries. Adding to the promise of those clinical developments, it would later become known that an undetectable viral load does not only halt the progression of HIV infection to AIDS but it also makes HIV-undetectable individuals uninfectious to others, even when engaging in condomless sex (Rodgers *et al.* 2016). More recently, the confirmation of the effectiveness of those drugs when taken as Pre-Exposure Prophylaxis (PrEP) also meant that those who are HIV-negative and have sex without condoms can avoid HIV infection by taking a pill daily (McCormack *et al.* 2016). As a result, condomless sex has been decoupled from the spectre of AIDS and the number of gay men engaging in "barebacking" or "raw" sex—that is, in intentional anal sex without condoms—has also risen exponentially, leading the practice to become part of mainstream gay male sexual cultures and providing many gay men with a newly found sense of sexual freedom (Berg 2009; Dean 2009, 2015; Race 2009, 2010, 2015; Ashford 2015; Varghese 2019).

At the same time, bareback porn has become the fastest growing subgenre of gay pornography and, today, only a very small and shrinking number of porn studios still continues to make visible use of condoms (Escoffier 2009; Mercer 2017). As the uptake of PrEP amongst gay men increased, so too did bareback gay porn produced by twenty-first-century studios like Cazzo Film, Lucas Entertainment, Treasure Island Media, Raw Fuck Club, Dark Alley Media, Dick Wadd, Sketchy Sex, Hung Young Brit, EricVideos, Pig-Prod, and many others, some of which are still active, whilst others have eventually ceased trading. Simultaneously, new platforms such as XTube, Twitter, Grindr, Recon, NastyKinkPigs, AssPig, Only-Fans, etc., have facilitated an ever-increasing prosumer culture (Kotler 1986; Fuchs 2014) of production, circulation, and consumption of homemade amateur and semi-professional gay porn, dramatically changing gay male sex cultures and their visual mediation in the twenty-first century.

Yet, whilst seemingly catalysing new experiences of heightened sexual freedom, pleasure, kinship, and intimacy amongst increasing numbers of gay men in wealthy nations (Dean 2009), combination antiretroviral therapies have also become one of the paradigmatic examples of the contemporary molecularisation of biopolitical control, whereby neoliberal subjects are produced and maintained through self-administration and self-management, therefore guaranteeing the survival of their bodies as standing reserves of life and thus consumer- and labour-power. As Miguel de Beistegui (2018) has argued, whilst in liberal societies—or in what Michel Foucault (1995, 2009) called disciplinary societies—the government of the living involved the state directly managing its populations, in neoliberal societies—what Gilles Deleuze (1992) called control societies—individuals are quantified and coded, with populations having become mere samples or data banks allowing for neoliberal rationality to be implemented as the self-administration of a subject who knows itself as a set of quantifiable properties, a data set: e.g. DNA, BMI, IQ, sperm count, testosterone and oestrogen levels, body fat percentage, heart rate, basal metabolism, cholesterol levels, blood pressure, liver and kidney function, bone density, glycaemia levels, viral load count, etc. For each and many others of these, various biomedical and wellbeing technologies were developed and offered to medical subjects who are then able to know and manage themselves in order to achieve their full "potential": Viagra, the contraceptive pill, anti-hypertensives, high-intensity interval training, statins, self-help books, yoga and meditation, erythropoiesis-stimulating agents, gym equipment, calorie-counted diets, CBT, SSRIs, 12-step programmes, testosterone patches, oestrogen-blockers, "superfoods", Ritalin, diuretics, Adderall, antiretrovirals, etc. (Race 2009; Preciado 2013, 2015; Dean 2015). In de Beistegui's words:

> Liberalism presents itself as the system of freedom in which individuals are free to pursue their own interests and desires. But [...], under the neoliberal paradigm, [...] freedom is not the ultimate goal of government, but that through which a specific way of governing—the way that sees every subject as a *homo economicus*, in charge of his or her human capital and responsible for his or her own promotion and self-esteem—is implemented. [...] Furthermore, [...] far from leaving the question of government open, this governing less has defined and shaped it in a very specific way, implemented in fields as different as the government of the poor, the workforce, or the family, to say nothing, of course, of the individual as consumer and producer of his or her own life. [...] And [...] the role of the state, far from being minimal, is actually crucial in providing and expanding the conditions for this transformation of the individual. Its role is that of an enabling condition, rather than a coercive force, and thus one that cannot function without our own consent and power of agency. It requires that we be free in order to operate as economic agents, and thus as adopting the normative framework of the market. If anything, the system of freedom to which neoliberalism gives rise amounts to a precise and systematic normalisation of the subject of desire [...]. Through a strict and highly sophisticated government of desire, advanced, technological capitalism has managed to blur the boundary not only between

labor and leisure, the public and private, but also, and to turn to another example, between freedom and surveillance. To be sure, we have now overcome discipline in Foucault's sense [...]. But this free space of desire and pleasure comes at a price, inasmuch as all the formerly coercive surveillance technology has. Been woven into it [...].

Never have we been freer, and yet never more closely watched, monitored, scrutinized, or evaluated. Never have we had our intimate self so systemically exposed, plundered, and exploited.

(de Beistegui 2018, 210–212)

It is in that context that contemporary gay "pig" masculinities have emerged and gained momentum as contemporary forms of masculinity mediated by gay hook-up platforms and pornography, and predicated on specific sexual practices that, catalysed by the introduction of antiretroviral drugs, have picked up on and accelerated earlier forms of gay male sexual sociability and self-identification that had been hindered or driven underground by the onset of the AIDS crisis and its tying of the knot that connected sex with death. However, the newly found sexual freedom that antiretroviral drugs have facilitated should not be equated too quickly with a liberation from contemporary regimes of power and knowledge. After all, just like Foucault (1978) alerted us to the fact that the birth of the homosexual had been a consequence of—not a rebellion against—the modern *dispositifs* of sexual knowledge and confession that aimed to govern Victorian populations, so can the experience of sexual freedom mediated by antiretrovirals be understood as part of the wider conceptualisation of freedom that characterises neoliberal rationality, namely, the freedom to pursue our own individual satisfaction. Neoliberal ideology internalised control in the form of an "economic regime of desire", leading to a "normalization of subjectivity" not only via the "promotion of self-interest and the maximization of utility" characteristic of earlier liberal societies, but also by adding to self-interest and maximised utility the new norms of "competition, efficiency, and management (of one's life, one's human capital, and the risks one is willing or encouraged to take)" (de Beistegui 2018, 63–64). This complex articulation of freedom and control that converges in the development of gay "pig" masculinities is the central focus of this book in which I'll be asking what is at stake here for the intersecting histories of masculinity and biopolitics. How can gay pigs help us frame our understandings of contemporary subjectivity, produced as they are at the intersections of twenty-first-century media, sexual practices, biomedical technologies, community formations, affects, and experiences of identity and belonging?

With that in mind, gay pornography will become one of the central primary sources informing the argument I'll be making throughout the chapters that follow. As a source for cultural critique, porn has been receiving increasing scholarly attention over the last decades of the twentieth century. Thanks to the likes of Richard Dyer (1985), Lynn Hunt (1993), Linda Williams (1999, 2004), Laura Kipnis (1996), Tim Dean, Steven Ruszczycky, and David Squires (2014), Susanna Paasonen (2011, 2018), Feona Attwood (2002, 2007, 2018), Clarissa Smith (2007, 2010), John Mercer (2017), and others, pornography has become a legitimate object of cultural analysis and criticism, more so in the aftermath of its online availability and dissemination (Paasonen 2011; Grebowicz 2013; Preciado 2013; Attwood 2018; Paasonen, Jarrett and Light 2019). At the same time, porn remains a source of moral panics, be it through the reproduction of older radical feminist positions that argued for the inherently exploitative nature of pornography (e.g. Dworkin 1981, 2019; MacKinnon 1987; Mason-Grant 2004), or thanks to more recent controversies surrounding the relationship between gay porn and sexual risk-taking (Dean 2009; McNamara 2013; Ashford 2015) and concerns with the ways in which widespread online pornography may lead to misleading sexual expectations amongst teenagers and even "rewire" their brains (e.g. Paul 2005; Dines 2010; Wild 2013; Voon *et al.* 2014; Mechelmans *et al.* 2014; Love *et al.* 2015).

Still, porn studies scholarship has convincingly moved beyond the so-called feminist "sex wars" of the late twentieth-century and their debating of porn's ontology in rather reductive binary terms that sought either to protect it under free speech laws and as a sex-positive form of female empowerment, or to fight it as evidence of the actual sexual abuse and exploitation suffered by women under patriarchy. Rejecting the "either/or" of the feminist "sex wars", Susanna Paasonen (2011), for instance, has argued that porn uses the affordances of technology to create a reality-effect that "grabs" the bodies of viewers and makes them "resonate" with the bodies on screen, noting how it is both a fantasy and a hyperbolised depiction of actual sexual behaviours. Paul Preciado, on the other hand, claimed that pornography is part of a wider network of material and semiotic prostheses that in-form—that is, that give form to—bodies and subjectivities in what he calls the "pharmacopornographic era" (2008, 2013). Beyond the artifice-or-reality debate, most contemporary scholars who have written about gay bareback porn agree that the genre depicts a gay male utopia of unbridled sexual pleasure and *jouissance* (Bersani and Phillips 2008; Dean 2009; Halperin 2007; Morris and Paasonen 2014). Yet, regarding bareback simply through the Lacanian lens of *jouissance*—understood as the violent pleasure derived from the drive to self-obliteration—cannot fully exhaust my concerns here. Namely, what gay men get out of it that is experienced positively; the future-orientated and life-affirming dimensions of "pig" masculinities and sexual ethics; the ways in which—as I will show—they often involve practices of care and communion that are all-too-often also alluded to in their pornographic mediations.

Like pornography, gay masculinities have also been increasingly theorised since the late twentieth-century and in relation to changing societal and political responses to homosexuality. Crucial here is Martin Levine's *Gay Macho* (1998), the first ethnography of the "clone", the form of gay male gender performance that became prominent in cities like San Francisco and New York during the 1970s. The image of the clone, inspired by American "blue collar" masculinities and immortalised in the works of Tom of Finland, marked a shift towards a hypermasculine form of embodiment and subjectivity amongst gay men. That shift, a subcultural reaction that sought to overcome associations of homosexuality with femininity, would, throughout the 1990s, further develop into a new ideal embodied in the "Chelsea boy" look (Halkitis 2000) as a result of the AIDS crisis and of its cultural dimensions as an "epidemic of signification" (Treichler 1987, 1999). As Halkitis (2000) noted, the AIDS crisis led gay men to pursue increasingly muscular and "healthy" looks in an attempt to visually detach themselves from the bodily signs that had become associated with AIDS, most notably emaciated physiques. Further, the crisis also led to an increase in the demeaning of bottoms within the gay community. If indeed homosexuality had, for many years, been associated with effeminacy and receptive sexual roles—thus leading to the development of the macho "clone" as a reaction to those associations—the perceived higher risk of contracting HIV as a bottom contributed to a later demarcation of top and bottom roles, along with an increasing demeaning of the latter (Nguyen 2014, 6–18; Escoffier 2009, 185; Halperin 2012, 46–55). Still, such demeaning of bottoms was much older and associated with the renunciation of femininity—and, therefore, of penetrability—that had been one of the founding gestures of Western male psychosexual development (Frosh 1994; Brannon 1976; Levant *et al.* 1992; Grosz 1994; Anderson 2009). As a result of hegemonic forms of masculine socialisation, and strengthened by the AIDS crisis, gay men have, throughout the last decades of the twentieth century, increasingly pursued hypermasculine forms of gender performance and presentation. Accordingly, those who are muscular, demonstrate higher levels of physical and sexual endurance and athleticism, and take up the role of tops during sex have become perceived as being more "manly" than the effeminate "sissies" or those who bottom.

Given the above, gay "pig" masculinities like the one embodied by Marco Cruise in *The Real Pump N Dumps of New York City* appear to be not only a further development but a complication of that history of gay masculinities. Unlike their predecessors, gay "pig" masculinities seem to be predicated on a transgression of the boundaries of the male body, a blurring of inside and outside, of self and other, through the pursuit of relentless penetrations and exchanges of bodily fluids. As Lee (2014) and Tomso (2008) have argued in relation to the bareback bottoms depicted by porn studios like Dark Alley Media or Treasure Island Media, rather than coming across as emasculated, the masculine subjectivity of those bottoms is enhanced by their ability to endure consecutive penetrations by a large number of men and by taking in their bodily fluids. Thus, whilst continuing to manifest normative traits of masculinity such as physical endurance, athleticism, and heroism (Pronger 1990; Kimmel 1997; Lancaster 2002; Connell 2005), "pig" bottoms do, nonetheless, trouble hegemonic masculinity by foregrounding heroic penetrability as its most praised attribute. A similar logic can also be seen in scenes of fisting, when a bottom is penetrated by fists and/or arms. Produced by porn studios like Cazzo Film, Pig-Prod, or Studfist, fisting scenes often also depict fistees as trained hypermasculine sexual athletes that have developed superhuman—or *supermanly*—muscular skills that allow them to be penetrated by all kinds of large objects and bodily appendages. Furthermore, those skills are also something to brag about, with both professional and amateur fistees often taking to social media platforms like Twitter to show off their skills by posting videos of their latest achievements, or sporting a dark red hanky in the right back pocket of their jeans to display to others their ability to take in two fists simultaneously.

Such a context, one in which gay "pig" masculinities have emerged at the intersection of pornographic representations, sexual behaviours, changing societal responses to homosexuality, and the molecularisation of biopolitical control through the introduction of combination antiretroviral therapies, makes theorising those emerging masculinities a timely task. Not only can this theorisation contribute to ongoing histories of sexualities and their visual representations, but it also allows for a better grasp of the complex interplay of material, fleshy, technological, political, and semiotic agents that feed into contemporary subjectivities and modes of embodiments, in line with existing scholarship in the wider posthumanities (Haraway 1991; Latour 1993; Hayles 1999; Preciado 2013). Further, and considering the ways in which hegemonic masculine bodies have served as analogues for the formation and development of the modern body politic and the nation-state (Theweleit 1987; Rabinbach 1990; Grosz 1994; Gatens 1996; Mosse 1996; Hengehold 2007; Cooper 2008; Braun and Whatmore 2010; Rasmussen 2011), a focus on the ways in which gay "pigs" emerge as *both* masculine *and* porous can help us speculate on alternative formations of the body politic, predicated on an openness to displaced bodies and border crossings rather than on policed self-containment, thus welcoming rather than fearing the foreign and the strange at a time when discourses of national identity and security are, once again, becoming increasingly invested in immunising the body of the state against foreign bodies through a closure of its borders.

To carry out my aims here, in Chapter 1 I start by tracing the history of the term "pig" from its emergence in gay magazines of the 1970s published in Europe and the USA, all the way through to contemporary online pornography. In doing so, I reflect on the ways in which gay "pigs" have been thought in relation to the wider spectrum of gay masculinities, and how the AIDS crisis brought about a particular set of challenges that triggered a shift in the forms of embodiment and sexual sociability that had been associated with early iterations of the "pig" script, leading many men to abandon the earlier sexual politics of gay liberation and to start pursuing a rights-based agenda of inclusion in mainstream society. The crisis notwithstanding, a minority of gay men continued to engage in practices that were seen to put them at risk of acquiring HIV, the very same practices that would eventually return and be taken up by increasing numbers of men and porn studios in the aftermath of the introduction of combination antiretroviral therapies for the management and prophylaxis of HIV infection. Those practices, often centred on an eroticisation of both penetrability and porosity to bodily fluids, led to the emergence, in the age of antiretrovirals, of contemporary gay "pigs" as embodiments of a porous kind of masculinity, as men who script their senses of self through their sexual athleticism, ability to endure multiple penetrations, and a willingness to welcome inside their bodies the bodily fluids of others.

That embrace of bodily porosity brings with is some important challenges to the ways in which masculinity and the male body have been conceived throughout European modernity. In Chapter 2, I explore those challenges by drawing from the work of French writers Guillaume Dustan and Érik Rémès, the gay erotic art of Bastille and Marc Martin, pornography and interviews I conducted with gay men, as well as philosophy, political theory, anthropology, art history, and literary criticism. If the project of European bourgeois modernity was sustained through the construction of an idealised male body that—in being autonomous, able to reason, and hermetically closed to its outside—also functioned as a model for the body politic of the modern nation-state, the radical openness and porosity of gay "pig" masculinities offer us a form of embodied subjectivity that inhabits the thresholds of distinctions between mind and body, inside and outside, human and animal, cleanliness and dirt, male and female, life and death, and health and disease, all of which have sustained the development and hegemony of the bourgeois body, its thinking, subjectivity, and the sphere of the politically possible.

In opening themselves to foreign matter—to relentless penetrations and bodily fluids and excreta—gay "pigs" do not just present us with a form of masculinity that troubles the foundational distinctions of modern European thought, however. They also constitute themselves through a process of addition; that is, by augmenting themselves and their masculinities to superhuman levels. In Chapter 3, then, I continue to move through pornography and interview materials, as well as philosophy and psychoanalytical theory, to explore the ways in which bodily fluids function, in "pigsex", as media of both self-intoxication and self-augmentation that highlight the plasticity of masculinity itself, sending it on a path towards a posthuman becoming sustained by an economy of unproductive excess that rejects both the symbolic primacy of the Phallus in the constitution of masculinity and the capitalist reduction of the body to a standing reserve of consumer- and labour-power.

By rejecting the Oedipal structures and body schemas that have sustained the development of the modern autonomous subject and its sanctioned forms of kinship, gay "pigs" experiment with alternative experiences of communion that they enact through exchanging bodily fluids with strangers. In Chapter 4, therefore, I present and develop this idea by exploring the limitations of dominant conceptualisations of community and showing how forms of gay "pig" sexual sociability in the age of antiretrovirals can offer an alternative model for thinking experiences of kinship and belonging that no longer require that something is held in common amongst the members of a given community. Gay "pigs" are bought together less because of any pre-existing qualities or attributes they share with others but, instead, by the flows of bodily fluids that cut across their bodies and circulate between them. Their sexual practices symbolically call into question the paradigms of immunity that have sustained both the idealised autonomy of individual bodies and that of modern nation-states. Through that, they can help us think through what a polity could look like that is no longer dependent on the policing of borders between self and other, between the familiar and the foreign.

A polity thus conceived would resonate with recent scholarship in both ecocriticism and ethics, for it would ask from us that we rethink the ways in which we make ourselves hospitable to others by making ourselves radically open to alterity, even if that requires a sacrifice of that which we currently are. In Chapter 5, I explore the relationship between sacrifice and hospitality as it plays out in gay "pigsex" and as it has been theorised in contemporary philosophy. Highlighting how hospitality always requires a degree of self-obliteration, in that final chapter I grapple with the extent to which self-sacrifice may, nonetheless, still be a pathway to forge subjectivities and collectivities anew. Yet, there is always a risk that practices of radical openness such as the ones sustaining gay "pig" subjectivities may be taken too far to the point of radical self-annihilation. After all, relentless penetrations and exchanges of bodily fluids, recreational drug use, and some of the more toxic aspects of masculinity itself can carry with them a threat not only for the survival of the men who embrace them but also for the survival of those around them. Thus, in order for the self to be undone on behalf of what could become more capacious embodied subjectivities and liveable communal formations, structures of care and comradeship ought to be forged, nurtured, and made available, so that no sacrifice is definitive and sex can cease to be reduced to a mere pursuit of self-annihilation, coming instead to be embodied and lived as a legitimate world-making practice that may set us all on a path towards new unknown islands of queer pleasure, solidarity, and possibility.

Note

1 The Gay Erotic Video Index lists an earlier title from 1995, Atlas Productions' *3 Pigs and a Wolf*. However, as the title hints at, the name is likely to have started as a play with the children's fable *The Three Little Pigs* rather than implying an understanding of "pigs" as gay men who engage in the kinds of sexual practices I've been describing.

References

Adam, Barry, Winston Husbands, James Murray, and John Maxwell. 2005. "AIDS optimism, condom fatigue, or self-esteem? Explaining unsafe sex among gay and bisexual men". *The Journal of Sex Research* 42 (3): 238–248.

Anderson, Eric. 2009. *Inclusive Masculinity: The Changing Nature of Masculinities.* Abingdon: Routledge.

Ashford, Chris. 2015. "Bareback sex, queer legal theory, and evolving socio-legal contexts". *Sexualities* 18 (1/2): 195–209.

Attwood, Feona. 2002. "Reading porn: The paradigm shift in pornographic research". *Sexualities* 5 (1): 91–105.

Attwood, Feona. 2007. "No money shot? Commerce, pornography and new sex taste cultures". *Sexualities* 10 (4): 441–456.

Attwood, Feona. 2018. *Sex Media.* Cambridge: Polity.

Beckman, Frida. 2013. *Between Desire and Pleasure: A Deleuzian Theory of Sexuality.* Edinburgh: Edinburgh University Press.

Beistegui, Miguel de. 2018. *The Government of Desire: A Genealogy of the Liberal Subject.* Chicago: The University of Chicago Press.

Berg, Rigmor. 2009. "Barebacking: A review of the literature". *Archives of Sexual Behavior* 38 (5): 754–764.

Bersani, Leo, and Adam Phillips. 2008. *Intimacies.* Chicago: The University of Chicago Press.

Brannon, Robert. 1976. "The male sex role—And what it's done for us lately". In *The Forty-Nine Percent Majority: The Male Sex Role*, edited by Deborah David and Robert Brannon, 1–40. Reading, MA: Addison-Wesley.

Braun, Bruce, and Sarah Whatmore. 2010. "The stuff of politics: An introduction". In *Political Matter: Technoscience, Democracy, and Public Life*, edited by Bruce Braun and Sarah Whatmore, ix–xl. Minneapolis: University of Minnesota Press.

Cohn, Jonathan Allen. 1997. "Recent advances: HIV infection–I". *BMJ: British Medical Journal* 314 (7079): 487–491.

Connell, Raewyn. 2005. *Masculinities.* Cambridge: Polity.

Cooper, Melinda. 2008. *Life as Surplus: Biotechnology and Capitalism in the Neoliberal Era.* Seattle: University of Washington Press.

Dean, Tim. 2009. *Unlimited Intimacy: Reflections on the Subculture of Barebacking.* Chicago: The University of Chicago Press.

Dean, Tim. 2012. "The biopolitics of pleasure". *The South Atlantic Quarterly* 111(3): 477–496.

Dean, Tim. 2015. "Mediated intimacies: Raw sex, Truvada, and the biopolitics of chemoprophylaxis". *Sexualities* 18 (1/2): 224–246.

Dean, Tim, Steven Ruszczycky, and David Squires, eds. 2014. *Porn Archives*. Durham: Duke University Press.

Deleuze, Gilles. 1992. "Postscript on the societies of control". *October* 59: 3–7.

Deleuze, Gilles. 2004. "Preface to Hocqhenguem's *L'Apres-Mai des Faunes*". In *Desert Islands and Other Texts, 1953–1974*, edited by David Lapoujade, 284–288. Los Angeles: Semiotext(e).

Deleuze, Gilles, and Félix Guattari. 1987. *A Thousand Plateaus: Capitalism and Schizophrenia*. Minneapolis: University of Minnesota Press.

Dines, Gail. 2010. *Pornland: How Porn has Hijacked our Sexuality*. Boston: Beacon Press.

Dowsett, Gary, and David McInnes. 1996. "Gay community, AIDS agencies and the HIV epidemic in Adelaide: Theorising 'post AIDS'". *Social Alternatives* 15 (4): 29–32.

Dworkin, Andrea. 1981. *Pornography: Men Possessing Women*. New York: G. P. Putnam's Sons.

Dworkin, Andrea. 2019. *Last Days at Hot Slit: The Radical Feminism of Andrea Dworkin*, edited by Johanna Fateman and Amy Scholder. South Pasadena: Semiotext(e).

Dyer, Richard. 1985. "Male gay porn: Coming to terms." *Jump Cut* 30: 27–29.

Escoffier, Jeffrey. 2007. "Scripting the sex: Fantasy, narrative, and sexual scripts in pornographic films". In *The Sexual Self: The Construction of Sexual Scripts*, edited by Michael Kimmel, 61–79. Nashville: Vanderbilt University Press.

Escoffier, Jeffrey. 2009. *Bigger than Life: The History of Gay Porn Cinema from Beefcake to Hardcore*. Philadelphia: Running Press.

Foucault, Michel. 1978. *The History of Sexuality, Volume I: An Introduction*. New York: Pantheon Books.

Foucault, Michel. 1995. *Discipline and Punish: The Birth of the Prison*. New York: Vintage Books.

Foucault, Michel. 2009. *Security, Territory, Population: Lectures at the Collège de France, 1977–1978*. Basingstoke: Palgrave Macmillan.

Frosh, Stephen. 1994. *Sexual Difference: Masculinity & Psychoanalysis*. London: Routledge.

Fuchs, Christian. 2014. *Social Media: A Critical Introduction*. London: Sage.

Gatens, Moira. 1996. *Imaginary Bodies: Ethics, Power and Corporeality*. London: Routledge.

Graham, Philip. 2017. *Men and Sex: A Sexual Script Approach*. Cambridge: Cambridge University Press.

Grebowicz, Margret. 2013. *Why Internet Porn Matters*. Stanford: Stanford University Press.

Greenblatt, Stephen. 1982. "Filthy rites". *Daedalus* 11 (3): 1–16.

Grosz, Elizabeth. 1994. *Volatile Bodies: Toward a Corporeal Feminism*. Bloomington: Indiana University Press.

Guattari, Félix. 1995. *Chaosmosis: An Ethico-aesthetic Paradigm*. Bloomington: Indiana University Press.

Guattari, Félix. 1996. "A liberation of desire: An interview by George Stambolian". In *The Guattari Reader*, edited by Gary Genosko, 204–214. Oxford: Blackwell Publishers.

Guattari, Félix. 2011. *The Machinic Unconscious: Essays in Schizoanalysis*. South Pasadena: Semiotext(e).

Halkitis, Perry. 2000. "Masculinity in the age of AIDS: HIV-seropositive gay men and the 'buff agenda'". In *Gay Masculinities*, edited by Peter Nardi, 130–151. Thousand Oaks, CA: Sage.

Halperin, David. 2007. *What Do Gay Men Want? An Essay on Sex, Risk, and Subjectivity*. Ann Arbor: The University of Michigan Press.

Halperin, David. 2012. *How to be Gay*. Cambridge, MA: The Belknap Press of Harvard University Press.

Haraway, Donna. 1991. *Simians, Cyborgs, and Women: The Reinvention of Nature*. New York: Routledge.

Hayles, N. Katherine. 1999. *How We Became Posthuman: Virtual Bodies in Cybernetics, Literature, and Informatics*. Chicago: The University of Chicago Press.

Hengehold, Laura. 2007. *The Body. Problematic: Political Imagination in Kant and Foucault*. University Park, PA: The Pennsylvania State University Press.

Hocquenghem, Guy. 1993. *Homosexual Desire*. Durham: Duke University Press.

Hocquenghem, Guy. 1995. "To destroy sexuality". In *Polysexuality*, edited by François Peraldi, 260–264. New York: Semiotext(e).

Hunt, Lynn. 1993. *The Invention of Pornography: Obscenity and the Origins of Modernity, 1500–1800*. New York: Zone Books.

Kagan, Dion. 2015. "Re-crisis: Barebacking, sex panic and the logic of epidemic". *Sexualities* 18 (7): 817–837.

Kagan, Dion. 2018. *Positive Images: Gay Men and HIV/AIDS in the Popular Culture of 'Post Crisis'*. London: I.B. Tauris.

Kimmel, Michael. 1997. *Manhood in America: A Cultural History*. New York: The Free Press.

Kipnis, Laura. 1996. *Bound and Gagged: Pornography and the Politics of Fantasy in America*. Durham: Duke University Press.

Kotler, Philip. 1986. "Prosumers: A new type of consumer". *The Futurist* 20: 24–28.

Lancaster, Roger. 2002. "Subject honor, object shame". In *The Masculinity Studies Reader*, edited by Rachel Adams and David Savran, 41–68. Oxford: Blackwell Publishing.

Latour, Bruno. 1993. *We Have Never Been Modern*. Cambridge, MA: Harvard University Press.

Lee, Byron. 2014. "It's a question of breeding: Visualizing queer masculinity in bareback pornography". *Sexualities* 17 (1/2): 100–120.

Levant, Ronald *et al.* 1992. "The male role: An investigation of contemporary forms". *Journal of Mental Health Counseling* 14: 325–337.

Levine, Martin. 1998. *Gay Macho: The Life and Death of the Homosexual Clone*, edited by Michael Kimmel. New York: New York University Press.

Love, Todd *et al.* 2015. "Neuroscience of internet porn addiction: A review and update". *Behavioral Sciences* 5 (3): 388–433.

MacKinnon, Catharine. 1987. *Feminism Unmodified: Discourses on Life and Law*. Cambridge, MA: Harvard University Press.

Mason-Grant, Joan. 2004. *Pornography Embodied: From Speech to Sexual Practice*. Lanham: Rowman & Littlefield.

McNamara, Michael. 2013. "Cumming to terms: Bareback pornography, homonormativity, and queer survival in the time of HIV/AIDS". In *The Moral Panics of Sexuality*, edited by Breanne Fahs, Mary Dudy, and Sarah Stage, 226–244. Basingstoke: Palgrave Macmillan.

McCormack, Sheena *et al.* 2016. "Pre-exposure prophylaxis to prevent the acquisition of HIV-1 infection (PROUD): Effectiveness results from the pilot phase of a pragmatic open-label randomised trial". *The Lancet* 387 (10013): 53–60.

Mechelmans, Daisy *et al.* 2014. "Enhanced attentional bias towards sexually explicit cues in individuals with and without compulsive sexual behaviours". *PLoS ONE* 9 (8): e.105476. http://doi.org/10.1371/jpournal.pone.0105476.

Mercer, John. 2017. *Gay Pornography: Representations of Sexuality and Masculinity.* London: I.B. Tauris.

Morris, Paul, and Susanna Paasonen. 2014. "Risk and utopia: A dialogue on pornography". *GLQ* 20 (3): 215–239.

Mosse, George. 1996. *The Image of Man: The Creation of Modern Masculinity.* New York: Oxford University Press.

Muñoz, José Esteban. 2009. *Cruising Utopia: The Then and There of Queer Futurity.* New York: New York University Press.

Nag, Moni. 1996. "AIDS extravaganza in Vancouver". *Economic and Political Weekly* 31 (45/46): 2989–2990.

Nguyen, Hoang Tan. 2014. *A View from the Bottom: Asian American Masculinity and Sexual Representation.* Durham: Duke University Press.

Paasonen, Susanna. 2011. *Carnal Resonance: Affect and Online Pornography.* Cambridge, MA: The MIT Press.

Paasonen, Susanna. 2018. *Many Splendored Things: Thinking Sex and Play.* London: Goldsmiths Press.

Paasonen, Susanna, Kylie Jarrett, and Ben Light. 2019. *NSFW: Sex, Humor, and Risk in Social Media.* Cambridge, MA: The MIT Press.

Paul, Pamela. 2005. *Pornified: How Pornography is Damaging our Lives, Our Relationships, and Our Families.* New York: Henry Holt and Company.

Pennisi, Elizabeth and Jon Cohen. 1996. "Eradicating HIV from a patient: Not just a dream?" *Science* 272 (5270): 1884.

Preciado, Paul. 2008. "Pharmaco-pornographic politics: Towards a new gender ecology". *Parallax* 14 (1): 105–117.

Preciado, Paul. 2013. *Testo Junkie: Sex, Drugs, and Biopolitics in the Pharmaco-pornographic Era.* New York: The Feminist Press.

Preciado, Paul. 2015. "Condoms chimiques". *Libération*, 11 June 2015.

Pronger, Brian. 1990. *The Arena of Masculinity: Sports, Homosexuality, and the Meaning of Sex.* New York: St. Martin's Press.

Rabinbach, Anson. 1990. *The Human Motor: Energy, Fatigue, and the Origins of Modernity.* New York: Basic Books.

Race, Kane. 2009. *Pleasure Consuming Medicine: The Queer Politics of Drugs.* Durham: Duke University Press.

Race, Kane. 2010. "Engaging in a culture of barebacking: Gay men and the risk of HIV prevention". In *HIV Treatment and Prevention Technologies in International Perspectives*, edited by Mark Davis and Corinne Squire, 144–166. Basingstoke: Palgrave Macmillan.

Race, Kane. 2015. "Reluctant objects: Sexual pleasure as a problem for HIV biomedical prevention". *GLQ* 22 (1): 1–31.

Race, Kane. 2018. *The Gay Science: Intimate Experiments with the Problem of HIV.* London: Routledge.

Rasmussen, Claire. 2011. *The Autonomous Animal: Self-Governance and the Modern Subject.* Minneapolis: University of Minnesota Press.

Rodgers, A. J. *et al.* 2016. "Sexual activity without condoms and risk of HIV transmission in serodifferent couples when the HIV-positive partner is using suppressive antiretroviral therapy". *JAMA: Journal of the American Medical Association* 316 (2): 171–181.

Sagan, Terrance. 1981. "Though golden showers may come your way: The next-to-last taboo makes its case". *Drummer* 5 (48): 18–21.

Simon, William and John Gagnon. 1986. "Sexual scripts: Permanence and change". *Archives of Sexual Behavior* 15 (2): 97–120.

Smith, Clarissa. 2007. *One of the Girls! The Pleasures and Practices of Reading Women's Porn*. Bristol: Intellect.

Smith, Clarissa. 2010. "British sexual cultures". In *The Cambridge Companion to Modern British Culture*, edited by Michael Higgins, Clarissa Smith, and John Storey, 244–261. Cambridge: Cambridge University Press.

Theweleit, Klaus. 1987. *Male Fantasies: Women, Floods, Bodies, History*. Minneapolis: University of Minnesota Press.

Tomso, Gregory. 2008. "Viral sex and the politics of life". *South Atlantic Quarterly* 107 (2): 265–285.

Treichler, Paula. 1987. "AIDS, homophobia, and biomedical discourse: An epidemic of signification". *October* 43: 31–70.

Treichler, Paula. 1999. *How to Have Theory in an Epidemic: Cultural Chronicles of AIDS*. Durham: Duke University Press.

Varghese, Ricky. 2019. "The mourning after: Barebacking and belatedness". In *Raw: PrEP, Pedagogy, and the Politics of Barebacking*, edited by Ricky Varghese, xv–xxxii. Regina: University of Regina Press.

Voon, Valerie *et al.* 2014. "Neural correlates of sexual cue reactivity in individuals with and without compulsive sexual behaviours". *PLoS ONE* 9 (7): e102419. https://doi.org/10.1371/journal.pone.0102419.

Warner, Michael. 2002. *Publics and Counterpublics*. New York: Zone Books.

Whittier, David and Rita Melendez. 2007. "Sexual scripting and self-process: Intersubjectivity among gay men". In *The Sexual Self: The Construction of Sexual Scripts*, edited by Michael Kimmel, 191–208. Nashville: Vanderbilt University Press.

Wild, Jim, ed. 2013. *Exploiting Childhood: How Fast Food, Material Obsession and Porn Culture are Creating New Forms of Child Abuse*. London: Jessica Kingsley Publishers.

Williams, Linda. 1999. *Hard Core: Power, Pleasure, and the "Frenzy of the Visible"*. Berkeley: University of California Press.

Williams, Linda. ed. 2004. *Porn Studies*. Durham: Duke University Press.

1 A pig is what a pig does

Released by 3rd World Video in 2003 and directed by Frank Ross, *Pig Sty* stars Brad McGuire, Frank Toscano, and Brian-Mark in intense uninhibited sex scenes that include fisting, dildo play, bareback sex, exchanges of all kinds of bodily fluids and—in its more scatological version release that same year, *Pig Sty Brown*—coprophagy. Capitalising on the shock-value of the scenes it depicts, the promotional text for *Pig Sty* on the studio's website[1] describes it as follows:

> One of the most over-the-edge, pissing, bareback fucking, barehanded fisting, butt stretching videos ever made. Foreskin gnawing, jizz crazed, ass sucking bottoms Brian-Mark and Frank Toscano surrender totally to uncut 9 inch top Brad McGuire. Frank's hungry, throbbing hole get [*sic*] fucked and double fucked by two big cocks at the same time followed by intense, deep fisting. Then Brad fists both bottoms at the same time. Open mouths guzzle piss and stretched holes are filled to the brim with it and hot creamy loads are greedily lapped up with insatiable lust.

The tone and language of the promotional text sells the frisson of transgression that has become associated with "pig" porn over the last two decades, alluding to the qualities of endurance, insatiability, limitlessness and boundary-pushing that are, today, part of the set of affects, practices, and pleasures that constellate as "pigsex". Throughout the video's various scenes, verbal play and grunting also punctuate and emphasise the intensity of the physical sexual practices seen on screen, with the models who take the bottoming roles being regularly addressed as "pigs" and told to "take it".

The central role played by uninhibited sexual behaviour and insatiable sexual desire in the formation of "pig" masculinities—which *Pig Sty* strongly depicts—is also echoed in a feature profile of model Brian-Mark, published in the *Chicago Reader* the same year the video was released. Titled "This Little Piggy", the feature is a candid profile of a performer whom, according to the story, porn producer Dick Wadd called the "biggest pig in the business". When confronted with such a title by the journalist, Brian-Mark retorted "That's quite an honor, you know. People ask, 'Are you a top or a bottom?' I say, 'I'm a pig' " (Knight Jr. 2003).

Yet, despite the ways in which Brian-Mark comes across on screen, the *Chicago Reader* painted him as a rather banal guy with an average upbringing and quite tame interests in music, literature, ornithology, and food. Ron, the photographer who shot him during the interview, highlighted that tension between people's perception of Brian-Mark, informed by his porn persona, and his life off-camera:

> People think he's like that 100 percent of the time [...]. When they see the videos and the magazines people think he's really mean, really satanic. They think he's gotta be a baby killer because of the way he looks. They really buy into it. It's so funny because it's so far from the truth.
>
> (Ron quoted in Knight Jr. 2003)

As the feature tells us, Brian-Mark was raised on a farm in Holstein, Iowa, became interested in theatre and music whilst in school, graduated in theatre and education, and worked as a high school teacher for a short period before moving to Omaha and—later—Chicago. In Chicago, he eventually started getting parts in theatre shows and, at the same time, exploring the kink gay scene at his local leather bar, The Eagle, now defunct. There, in the Chicago leather scene, Brian-Mark met Ron who took his first professional pornographic photos in 1993. From there, his professional career in fetish and sex gained momentum and he starred in his first porn video—Dick Wadd's *N.Y.P.D.: New York Piss Daze*, from 1997. As his career moved from teaching and theatre to pornography, "his appearance began to reflect the changes" (Knight Jr. 2003). He started going to the gym to develop muscle, pierced his penis, got several tattoos—including a pentagram above his shaft and an "enormously endowed Satan on both his arms" (Knight Jr. 2003)—and had the words "sex pig" scarified on his back. The ways in which his developing tastes in uninhibited kinky sex with little to no personal taboos started marking not only his own identity but also his own body were described by Brian-Mark as follows:

> I had a man cut that ["sex pig"] into my skin. This was more of me releasing and trying things in a healthy way. Deciding to get all the tattoos has sort of been like marking myself, identifying who I am to the world. That's also what I like about all the pornographic choices. I'm not an 18-year-old boy who's been told he's pretty and he didn't go to college and he thinks this is the only thing he has. This is me coming out of a big shell.
>
> (Brian-Mark quoted in Knight Jr. 2003)

From his words, we understand how Brian-Mark makes sense of the changes he sought for himself and his body. To him, undergoing body modification procedures was a way of signalling whom he *was* to the world. The sexual practices and pleasures he discovered as he started engaging with the gay leather scene triggered such a radical process of self-fashioning that he found himself having to mark his own body, to transform it to communicate to others the kind of gay man he was, the kind of sexual subjectivity he had developed. This, of course, was also catalysed by his entering the porn industry and subsequent cultivation of a particular form of marketable pornographic image:

> At 46, he might seem old for an industry that thrives on twinks [younger-looking, hairless gay men] and surfer boys. But "older men are now a hot item," he says. "I came around at the right time." The secret to his success, he says, is that "my look is mean. Guys love that arrogant, threatening male stuff from me."
>
> (Knight Jr. 2003)

Browsing through PornHub, I came across a video that does claim to be a mantra for gay pigs and which capitalises on that same architecture of sexual fantasy that Brian-Mark described. Uploaded in August 2019 by user Biker_BB under the title "My Mantra: Pig Sleazy Raw Pervert Filthy Life", the video is a homemade fast-paced edit of several scenes of hardcore condomless sex featuring clips of watersports (urophagia), double penetration, felching (eating ejaculate out of someone's rectum), etc.[2] Beyond the phototextual manner in which the images work with the title to build a claim of what being a gay "pig" is about, what is also interesting about this video mashup is the writing that its original creator laid over the sex clips, which seems to refer at once to the contemporary understanding of what "pigsex" is, as well as to the ways in which it informs the subjectivity of those engaged in it, so much so that they embrace it as a core part of their sense of self. Accompanied by the electro track "All the Sex" by Mazer, a gay music producer hailing from Portland, the titles laid throughout the video read:

YOU ARE A CUMDUMPSTER

POPPER PIG

Use drugs to turn yourself into a total pig

BAREBACK ONLY

Take anon cock bareback

PISS SLUT

BECOME A FILTHY PISS PIG

SURRENDER TO LUST

Find men to rape and breed you

You are controlled by lust

TAKE RAW COCK AT GLORYHOLES

BE NASTY

REVEL IN FILTH

Be a disgusting filthy pervert

Crave the taste and smell of cum

OBSESS OVER FILTH AND PERVERSION

Have the nastiest sex imaginable

Fall in love with the taste and smell of sweaty, hairy assholes

Enjoy the scent of bareback sex

All sex should be bareback

Live out your kinkiest fantasies

Go out and be a total pig bottom

take drugs and cock all night

Put your cock in every hole

Take every cock inside you

Don't think anymore

Only worship cock

Get bred

Drink piss

Sniff armpits

Eat cum out of assholes

Be like a pig in mud. Love filth!

Relinquish all control

Surrender and give in to lust

Take his condom off

You want to feel him pump seed into you

Being filled with seed gives you a high like no other drug

You are driven crazy with lust for cum

You crave it. You need it.

Surrender to lust. Be free.

This is your nature

There's no use fighting it

You're a cum-obsessed pig

You'll let any man cum in you

You want to be filled up with seed

And you'll do anything to get it

The more cocks in you, the better you feel about yourself

Nothing feels better than being a nasty filthy cumdump

Use drugs and become a total cockwhore for anon men

Door unlocked, blindfolded, ass up, let strangers breed you

How many loads have you taken today?

Be a proud cumdump

Show off your load count to the world

Become obsessed with taking as many loads as possible

Put up ads online advertising yourself as a bareback cumdump

Find men to rape and breed you and keep you drugged

Let them piss in your ass

Let them fuck you until the sun comes up

Never refuse a man's precious seed

Take every load inside you

Let strangers breed you

Bathe in filth and perversion

You are a proud pervert

You are a proud cumdump

Take videos of yourself being a pig

Show the world who you truly are

Surrender and be free

With uncommonly high user ratings of 93% for the oldest upload and 87% for the earliest at the time of writing, both uploads are also accompanied by viewers' comments, with user tsy67 responding to the earliest upload with praise for "the perverted mind in this vid", and claiming that "it explains everything i am. and what i was born for as a bottom. serve men be a slut when they need you to be! and train my hole to perversion and lust for real men". What also strikes me in the video or, better, in the titles laid over it, is how the latter hint at the ways in which scenes of unhinged, no-limits sex—framed as a surrender to animalistic instinct and desire ("Don't think anymore/Only worship cock") and going as far as using the difficult term "rape"—do, nonetheless, offer a view of those scenes as arranged or staged in such a way that submitting to other men, for instance, is described not as something that is forced or lacks consent but is, instead, something that is sought out ("Find men to rape and breed you and keep your drugged [...]. Let them fuck you until the sun comes up"). The practices depicted in the images and alluded to in the titles are—paradoxically perhaps—seen both as a form of submission and as a path to self-determination ("Surrender and be free").

Such a description of sexual fantasies, whether actualised or not, and their role in shaping the architecture of gay "pigsex" and "pig" masculinities, places them firmly within the realm of sexual play, as recently theorised by Susanna Paasonen (2018), according to whom "sex involves experimentation and quest for intensity of sensation and experience where the possibilities of what bodies want and do are never quite set, knowable or stable" (2). "Sexual play", Paasonen continues, "presents one means of testing out bodily capacities, and of pushing their perceived limits" (38), opening bodies to new "horizons of possibility" (132). Crucially, this "emphasis on bodily potentialities, changing sexual palates and fickle desires sets in motion, and rubs against, the logic of categorisation central to the politics of identity" (134), showing "the sexual self as a work in progress" (137). Paasonen's focus on sexual play as a creative practice that opens the body to affective and material becomings that can cause "ripples across identities" (131) helps us understand how, in the examples I've been describing, being a "pig" is seen as something one does, as the enactment of the subject's own sexual subjectivity—a work in progress through a pushing or even undoing of boundaries, a commitment to radically opening one's body to the bodies and bodily fluids of known and unknown others. Being a "pig" is thus always a *becoming*-pig, a task to which one dedicates oneself, one that can always be pushed further as if it were an athletic practice or a competitive sport and, therefore, also one in which achievements ought to displayed with pride ("show the world who you truly are").

Yet, despite the manner in which online media have increased the subcultural visibility of "pigs", at the same time helping define and disseminate "pig" as a sexual script (Simon and Gagnon 1986) that is up for grabs by gay men who are into pushing sexual and bodily boundaries, condomless sex, exchanges of bodily fluids, and so on, according to the Internet Adult Film Database (IAFD) the term can be traced, in porn, at least as far back as 1998, when *Biker Pigs from Hell*, directed by Thor Stephens, was released by Wildcat Productions. *Biker Pigs from Hell* is, in many ways, a standard late-1990s production that stars tattooed, muscular performers Bo Garrett, Steve Cannon, and others. Garrett plays a member of a biker gang who gets his wallet and Harley-Davidson motorbike stolen by a guy (played by Cannon) with whom he had sex the night before. What follows is a sexual fantasy of a biker's pursuit of a thief, punctuated along the way by scenes of chaps-wearing men having greased-up "macho" sex. Interestingly, however—because all the penile penetrations featured in the video make use of condoms—the video hints at an earlier framing of the term "pig" taking place before the age of antiretrovirals and the mainstreaming of condomless sex turned "pigs" into the uninhibited bodily-fluid fiends of today. Reviewing the video for the online forum AdultDVDTalk.com in 2003, user BillyJizz wrote:

> I've been getting a little bored with the body beautiful and vanilla fuck and suck porn I've been watching lately. So I went in search of something a little more raunchy, filthy, and piggy—the kind of stuff that would, maybe, make both my hair and my dick stand on end. First up I thought that any porn with the outrageous term "Biker Pigs" in the title might be a possibility. And with inky bad boys Bo Garrett and Steve Cannon starring in this one, I figured it held some promise of what I was looking for.

Despite the promise of its title, *Biker Pigs from Hell* appears to not have fully matched the high expectations BillyJizz had for it. Towards the end of his review, after describing the kind of sex featured in each of the video's four scenes, he writes:

> On my raunch scale of 1 to 10, I'm giving this a 7—very good, but it just doesn't quite hit the high notes of sleaze. Overall, this DVD is clearly above average, with more than enough hot muscle man sex (no boys allowed, thank God) to get you humming and going. And if you find bikes and tattoos, and grease and rough stuff and bad boys and low life exciting, that's even more reason to check out what is a pretty good DVD.

Yet, the video, as well as BillyJizz's review, hint at some—though, crucially, not all—of the features of what we understand "pigsex" and gay "pigs" to be today. Unlike mere "boys", gay "pigs" appear to fall under the umbrella of "bad boys" and "low life", with the term "pig" promising—even if not always delivering—sex that is "raunchy", "rough", and "sleazy". Further, just like the video's association of "pigs" with the "raunchy", "sleazy" "man sex" did not depend on bareback sex, other videos similarly produced during the 1990s did not even seem to require anal penetrative sex to warrant the adoption of the term "pig". A case in point is Rick Bolton's *Muddy Pig Sex*. Released in 1994 by Bob Jones Productions!, the video opens with a notice that reads:

> The producer of this video wishes to educate the viewer about safer sex practices. The models in this video have been given carefully scripted instructions as to how they will interpret this adult material on the screen.
> Every effort has been made to incorporate safer sex activities into the video. In view of the AIDS crisis. The producer wishes to educate the viewer while at the same time providing a safer sex fantasy.

Considering that *Muddy Pig Sex* was released at the height of the AIDS crisis, the disclaimer falls in line with what had become common practice amongst producers of gay sex media, whether in video or in print, from the late 1980s onwards. Driven by both a sense of responsibility towards their viewers and political pressures on the gay porn industry, producers were forced to clearly lay out the space of fantasy to which their videos and magazines contributed, adopting a certain didactic or pastoral role towards both their models and viewers or readers (Burger 1995). In such a context of high levels of anxiety and social panic surrounding gay sex in the early 1990s, *Muddy Pig Sex* delivered a single-scene domination fantasy in which two tops in military uniform wrestled a bottom in the mud, hosed him down, grabbed him by the dog collar and leach he was wearing, slapped his buttocks, pushed him against a wall, forced him to suck them off, and penetrated him with a long dildo, eventually ejaculating on the bottom's chest. Interestingly, a review of the video signed by "E-Tron" in issue 13 of French magazine *Projet X* (1996), noted how the scene was nonetheless too "clean" and "without surprises". "Unfortunately", the reviewer continued, "there's nothing very good to say about this video" (49).

From 1996, directed by Steve Johnson and released by Close Up Productions, *Russo's Sex Pig* followed a similar script of domination and humiliation amongst men who—pardon the pun—wore their masculinity on their jockstrap. Jack Russo, the top, met another muscled man outside an apartment in what could be New York City before both going in. Inside, the bottom, on his knees, performed oral sex on the top who responded with words of encouragement: "You're a good pig!" The scene proceeded to flogging, domination, dildo penetrations on a sling aided by Crisco (a cooking fat historically used by gay men as lubricant), beer spitting, etc. And just like *Muddy Pig Bottoms*, no penile anal penetration ever took place in the fantasy. The following scene continued along the same lines, this time with the bottom on a St Andrew's cross being flogged by the top, performing oral sex, having hot wax dripped on his bare skin, and eventually being penetrated by the condom-wearing top, who eventually pulled out to masturbate and ejaculate onto the bottom's chest.

What *Biker Pigs from Hell*, *Muddy Pig Sex*, and *Russo's Sex Pig* show us, then, is that the earlier iterations of gay "pig" masculinities were associated in porn videos with performers who not only read as "manly" due to their body types, body language, or clothing, but also did so through both their willingness to get dirty—with oil, grease, mud, beer, etc.—and their investment in "rough" sexual scenarios in which endurance, self-reliance, emotional unavailability, and other features associated with hegemonic masculinity (Kimmel 1996; Connell 2005) were enacted in the context of sexual roleplay. Added to that, "pigs" also appear to have been associated in early video pornography with submissive and eager bottoms who were willing to surrender to the pleasure of their tops. Yet, the earlier subcultural uses of the term "pig" amongst gay men were not restricted to porn videos but had a parallel and slightly longer history in printed gay media that predated the invention of VHS in the 1970s and the subsequent boom in the gay video porn industry (Burger 1995).

Traceable in printed matter to at least a decade prior, "pig(s)" appeared in publications such as US gay fetish magazines *Drummer* and *Honcho* as early as the 1970s, and in Sweden-published and German-written *Kumpel* around the same time, albeit predominantly as "*Sau*" ("sow") rather than "*Schwein*" ("pig"). Its printed occurrences continued throughout the 1990s in titles like *Projet X*, the French gay fetish zine published during the last decade of the twentieth century, where the term appeared as either "*porc*" or "*couchon*" ("pig" and "piglet", respectively). Attending to those earlier uses of the term gives us a better and more complex grasp of the early history of "pig" masculinities and how they would eventually become mediated and signified in VHS porn produced during the AIDS crisis and—later—in DVD and online porn videos. That process of signification and mediation took place in ways that were informed by the material conditions, narratives, and anxieties brought to bear on gay sexual subcultures by the onset of the AIDS crisis and the eventual development and introduction of antiretroviral regimes for the successful management and prophylaxis of HIV infection.

One of the earlier usages of the term I could find was in *Kumpel*, published in Sweden for the German market between the 1970s and the 1990s, likely in order to circumvent various German legal limitations on the production of hardcore materials.[3] Printed in a black-and-white A5 format, *Kumpel* included written sex stories and photographs of hardcore sex including piss play, fist-fucking, scat (coprophagy), mud play, bondage, domination, master/slave role play, sadism and masochism, leather and rubber fetishes, illustrations by erotic artists, and a scene guide of fetish bars, clubs, and parties across Europe. Not unexpectedly given the decades of its production, *Kumpel* never featured condoms in either its photographs or drawings of penile penetration—AIDS wouldn't be known until the 1980s and condom promotion wouldn't be taken up by the gay porn industry until the very late 1980s, early 1990s (Burger 1995).

Initially accompanied by the tagline *"das Magazin fuer Männer die Männer mögen"* ("the magazine for men who like men"), *Kumpel* had, by issue 11, replaced it with the line *"das Magazin für Lederkerle"* ("the magazine for Leatherguys") and, by issue 17, simply with *"für Lederkerle"* ("for Leatherguys"). It was in its pages that I found some of the earliest references to *"Sau"* ("sow"), a term that, according to two of my German informants, has a longer history in the German gay fetish scene than *"Schwein"*, and which has been used for several decades to describe "hungry", eager bottoms who rarely feel satiated. *"Schwein"*, according to the same two informants, started being used later in relation to men with few sexual limits and to whom everything goes. The contents of *Kumpel* resonated with my informants' views: whilst references to both *"Schwein"* and *"Sau"* appeared regularly throughout its various issues,[4] *"Sau"* was normally used as a qualifier of gay men due to their sexual insatiability, and *"Schwein"* was more often used to describe men into "extreme" sex (as in the term "pigsex"). For instance, whilst issue 18 had a cover story entitled *"Latrinen Sau"* ("Toilet Sow"), issue 21 included a piece called *"Schweine Hund"* (literally "Pig-Dog", used in the German gay context to mean something akin to "megapig", i.e., someone into total sexual degradation); and whilst issue 22 had an erotic coprophagy story illustrated with photographs under the title *"Supersau & Supersau"* ("Supersow & Supersow"), issue 35 included a piece on—and interview with—gay fetish visual artist Bastille with the subtitle *"schweinische Fantasien"* ("Piggish Fantasies").

On the other side of the Atlantic, in California, *Drummer*, the internationally renowned magazine for leathermen, featured written and visual references to some of the sexual practices that have today become associated with "pigsex"—piss play, scat play, fisting, cum play and other forms of "sleazy" sex—very much from the first issue of that scene-defining US publication. Whilst straightforward references to "pigs" or "pigsex" were rarer than in *Kumpel*, they still appeared sporadically and mostly in the personal ads section of the magazine. In issue 41 (1980), for instance, the following two personal ads were published amongst a plethora of others advertising masters, slaves, uninhibited players, strict doms, cigar smokers, wrestlers, sadists, etc:

VENICE. Intelligent pigs wanted for dirty sex. Your scat/w.s. fantasies are mine. Box 820.

And, a couple of pages on:

PIGGY RAUNCH
Versatile NYC Chelsea w/m, Scorpion, 33, 5'7", 130 lbs., 7" cut, for uninhibited scenes. Heave ass play (FF), L/L, W/S, scat, jocks, sweat, oil, shaving, tits, c/b torture, boots, and socks with REAL creative men into role switching. Willing to explore new realms. No overweights or fats. Beards a plus. Include photo and scene. Box 703.

Later, in issue 48 (1981):

PORTLAND PIG
Hairy, M, 22, 5'10", 170 lbs., wants aggressive top to help expand my limits into W/S, FF, Toys and want to learn more. Box 1336.

The fewer references to "pigs" notwithstanding, *Drummer* still championed the most "extreme" or uninhibited forms of gay sexual behaviour with think pieces, advice columns, and visual as well as written stories featuring all kinds of bodily fluids, BDSM, fetish gear (mostly leather gear and blue collar attire), and—more rarely but yet still present—stories involving substances like mud and faeces. Interestingly, whilst *Kumpel* seemed, just like the early porn videos of the 1990s discussed above, to associate being a "pig" with taking on the role of an insatiably filthy and submissive bottom, some of the personal ads in *Drummer* also extend the designation to versatile men, implying that one can be a "pig" regardless of whether one tops or bottoms. Its defining feature appeared to be one's commitment to uninhibited sexual play.

The association of "uninhibited" sex with masculinity was also very present throughout the run of *Drummer*, often taking the form of heated debates in "Male Call", the magazine's letters section. In its first anniversary issue (issue 7, of July 1976), for instance, a reader named Don, from Tucson, Arizona, sent in the following letter:

HATES CRAP, LOVES SCAT
The review of the stage musical, "Boy Meets Boy", in DRUMMER No. 5 is exactly the kind of faggotry I had hoped to avoid in The Leather Fraternity. The two illustrations are revolting, and even the tenor of the article is faggy. Please don't louse up future issues of what is otherwise a good Macho magazine with this kind of crap.
But thanks for the "Scat" article in the same issue.
It is high time someone brought this "taboo" subject out into the open. I can think of more appealing and exciting ways to enjoy the scat scene than those in the Frank Edwards article, but ... to each his own.

The excellent sketch accompanying the article hints at some real excitement. Who did it? It is unsigned, unless that tattoo on the stud's shoulder is the signature....
"The Poundcaker"? Whozat?

Outrage such as that of Don from Tucson at what he perceived to be a betrayal of the gay "macho" sexual culture that he saw as *Drummer*'s remit was also echoed in another letter, published in issue 11 (1977, the year the magazine relocated to San Francisco from Los Angeles and started being edited by Jack Fritscher). Responding to a cover feature about drag queen troupe The Cycle Sluts, which had been published two issues earlier, Bruce from Seattle, wrote the following:

> THINKS SLUTS SMUT
> The cover picture and the associated article you used in your latest issue (No. 9) disgusted me beyond words. I thought, when you started out, that this was to be a unique magazine—for men—not for the campy bar queens. I was wrong. The Cycle Sluts have no place in my lifestyle or that of my friends. If I want to read that kind of trash I will subscribe to *After Dark* or *The Advocate*. Such junk should get you all sorts of subscribers off the street. You shouldn't miss mine when it comes time for renewal. So have fun with your new format ... and don't forget heels and purses.

French gay fetish magazine *Projet X*, which ran more or less uninterrupt-edly over two series between November 1993 and April 2000, followed a similar editorial path to both *Kumpel* and *Drummer*. It too, featured por-nographic stories, illustrations and photoshoots, sex advice columns (eve-rything from douching to stretching anal sphincters, bondage, etc.), travel guides, bar and club reviews, porn reviews, news stories (such as reports on the UK's infamous Operation Spanner which saw a group of gay men prosecuted for consensual BDSM sex), op-eds, and the ever-present per-sonal ads section. It is in the latter that references to "*porc*" ("pig") also appeared, even if not that frequently. For example, in a few consecutive issues starting with issue 3 (1996), the same personal ad was listed, written in both French and German, which translates as:

> PURE PIG
> Pig, 36 y.o., 1.65 m, 55 Kg, dark-haired, moustachioed, looking for farmer, breeder, butcher for cattle wrangling, mastering, rearing, insemination. Similar trips okay. Also seeking position as stableman. Age, looks, and location indifferent if serious and like-minded. Réf: X2097.
>
> (56, my translation)[5]

Whilst references to "hard" and "perverse" sex including fist-fucking, watersports/pissing, cum play, rubber, etc. featured in many other personal ads in the magazine, men self-identifying as "pigs" were less common in *Projet X* than in *Kumpel* or even *Drummer*. Yet, another example appeared in issue 20 (1997), the first bilingual (French and English) edition of the magazine, where the following personal ad can be read:

E ENGLISH SKINHEAD PIG
Living in Belgium, 40, tattooed, shaved, seeks skin, army, rubber, leather guys, less than 50 yrs, into long piss and filth scenes. Brown ok. Unwashed body and underwear a must. Also penpals for wank letters and packages. Write in English or French with photo. Benelux, France, Germany. Can travel, sometimes accommodate.

(75)

A trilingual add, which appeared in issue 42 (1999), highlighted the equivalent ways in which terms like "pig", "*porc*", and "*Sau*" were being used by gay men, in subcultural sex media of the late 1990s, to self-define themselves in relation to the sexual practices they were into:

PORC CRAD ALLEMAND
Porc allemand 23 ans cherche trips pisse, merde, gerbe, sperme, etc. Faut que tu sois réel porc experimenté! Photo intégrale souhaitée pour réponse assurée. Recherche aussi vidéos et vêtements crad.

E GERMAN FILTH PIG
23yo, German pig, is looking for hot piss, shit, puke, shot [of cum], etc. You need to be a real pig and experienced! Send your picture with face and body. All replies will be answered. Also looking for videos and filthy clothes.

D DEUTSCHE SIFFSAU
23, deutsche Sau, sucht heiße Pissse, Scheiße, Kotz, Spermasaft, usw. Du mußt eine richtige Sau sein und Erfahrung haben! Bildzuschrift mit Foto von gesicht [sic] und Body. Alle Zuschriften werden beantwortet. Suche auch Videos und vergifte Klamotten.

(74)

The international reach of subcultural fetish magazines like *Kumpel*, *Drummer* or *Projet X*, and the subsequent boom in video pornography thanks to the invention of VHS, DVD and online streaming technologies, seem to have accelerated the dissemination of the word "pig" amongst Western gay male populations, where it started being used as a term of proud self-identification by men invested in pushing the boundaries of sex and sexual pleasure beyond hegemonic and socially-sanctioned sexual practices. Yet, even amongst gay men, divides had started forming between those into "extreme" forms of sex and those who would abide by more demure or "vanilla" kinds of sexual scripts. According to the editorial of issue 22 of *Projet X* (1997) signed by "Dick", such a divide between "good" and "bad" gays was a betrayal of the political project of homosexual emancipation:

> Here and there in the "community" press that pretends to represent "ideal" gay life, politically correct, cultivated, elegant, humorous (often bitchy) and where the only eccentricity allowed is a certain non-vulgar campuses (except on Saturday nights), there have recently been some statements that are astonishing considering the clichés of tolerance that abound as far as so called "gay solidarity" is concerned.
>
> Hard queers have been represented as freaks by the comparison of fist fucking with emptying out a chicken (Têtu), by the opinion that most of us have dangerous sexual activities (Têtu again), and by the idea that we all read controversial literature like Projet X ... (Ex-Aequo).
>
> May we remind all these people who have embraced the idea that homosexuality is acquiring a certain social acceptance that the ideals that they once defended (with us) are still valid for all of us.
>
> There is no division to be made between "uncontrollable SM queers" (even though I find such a tag appealing) and "clean, nice homosexuals". The number of people that drift somewhere in the middle between these two categories with more or less hard, extreme and fetishist practices is so vast that any idea of two opposing groups is ridiculous.
>
> As if inserting one, two or three fingers in a guy's arse is correct, the fourth signals the danger line of debauchery and with the fifth you become politically incorrect?
>
> A piercing is cool if it's to wear out to a club, but not if it's used within sexual activity?
>
> Is this social dynamics expressing itself? Is this a group of once outcasts integrating society and in doing so relegating some of their brothers to the role of scapegoats to strengthen their feeling of belonging to society?
>
> Perhaps it is logical and useful to some gay media to try to portray us as the black sheep of the affair....

(3)

Given the date of the editorial, one can suspect that the schism the editor of the magazine was referring to is the same that has been documented in scholarship as having been a partial outcome of the onset of the AIDS crisis in the early 1980s. Whilst the 1960s and 1970s had been a period of increasing sexual licence and experimentation, the discovery of HIV and

AIDS in the 1980s caused many gay men to reconsider their lifestyles and thus to eventually split in two broad groups: on the one side, those who started fighting for civil rights through a narrative of equality and a politics of respectability; on the other, those—a minority within a minority—who continued to push for liberation with a politics of difference in which the embrace of sexual exploration and transgression was one of the primary means to perform, nurture, and signal their difference vis-à-vis the heteropatriarchal norm from which they wished to liberate themselves (Levine 1998; Shepard 2001; Halperin 2012). To this latter group, whilst the AIDS crisis presented a serious challenge, it did not necessarily have to lead to a surrender to hegemonic straight morality and institutions. As Martin Levine (1998) wrote in 1984, three years after the CDC's *Morbidity and Mortality Weekly Report* (MMWR) noted the unexplainable deaths from pneumocystis pneumonia of previously "healthy" gay men in Los Angeles:

> The AID [*sic*] outbreak—some call it the gay cancer or the gay plague, which is no help at all—undoubtedly is our community's main concern now. Wherever we gather—at our gyms, in bars, at parties—clone banter is switching from the four D's (disco, drugs, dick, and dish) to who is the latest victim of Kaposi's sarcoma. Hospital visits and funerals are becoming as commonplace as Levi's 501 jeans. Friends who never before showed the slightest interest in gay causes are now besieging us for donations to Gay Men's Health Crisis. [...]
>
> We are overcome by hysteria, afraid of the consequences to our health of the way we have been living.
>
> The panic originates in the widespread belief that clonedom—that is drugs and fast sex—causes the disease.
>
> [...]
>
> After watching friends and lovers die, certain that tricking and drugs killed them, many of us now regard our once-glamorous and exciting lifestyle as toxic. [...]
>
> To cope with this panic, many of us are radically rearranging our lifestyles. The gay man of the 1980s is temperate, dates or has a lover, all because he believes the clone theory. If drugs and quick sex kill, then shunning both will keep him healthy. Convinced that this switch is self-protective, some of the city's hottest men are forsaking clonedom. In droves, they are abandoning legendary pleasure spots. The fashion now is not to go out, to stay away from the tubs, discos, and sex clubs. It is becoming terribly *déclassé* to be ripped to the tits.
>
> (138–140)

The changes in behaviour Levine saw taking place amongst "clones"—the hypermasculine gay male subculture that had developed throughout the 1970s—was a consequence of AIDS having originally been approached from an epidemiological standpoint, one that is radically different from the virological paradigm that would, in the 1990s, start to inform research and public health education on HIV. That is, AIDS—or, as it was first known, "GRID" or "Gay-Related Immune Deficiency"—was thought to concern specific populations and, it would then be inferred, their sexual behaviours and "lifestyles" (Treichler 1999). As that infamous MMWR report of June 1981 had already noted, all the five diseased men were homosexuals, two of them had a history of sex with multiple partners, and all of them reported having taken inhalant drugs (likely amyl nitrate, also known as "poppers"). In the words of the editor: "The fact that these patients were all homosexuals suggests an association between some aspects of a homosexual lifestyle or disease acquired through sexual contact and *Pneumocystis* pneumonia in this population" (CDC 1981). It is therefore no surprise that the hyper-sexual masculinity of the clones, which had become so prevalent in large cities across the USA a decade prior, would end up being seen to have been at least partially responsible for the epidemic. As Michael Kimmel and Levine wrote a few years later, the risk-taking, fearlessness, emotional detachment, aggressiveness, and promiscuity associated with traditional Western masculine scripts and which had been taken up by clones had eventually led gay men to become a population at risk. The solution, according to the authors, had to involve not only safer sex education but also "to transform the meaning of masculinity, to enlarge our definition of what it means to be a man, so that sexuality will embrace a wider range of behaviors and experiences" (Levine 1998, 154). That process would eventually lead to what Kimmel called the "the death of the gay clone" (Levine 1998, 125) and the emergence of a new form of gay masculinity, the prototype of which became New York City's "Chelsea boys" ((Halkitis 2000) and London's Soho gays of the 1990s (Andersson 2018), the epitome of the late twentieth-century "A-gays". That new gay masculinity which would replace, in the eyes of the mainstream at least, the "macho man" of the 1970s, was triggered by a raising interest in health and "clean" looks as a response to the AIDS crisis: gay men started cultivating bodily signifiers of "health" by hitting the gym, grooming their body hair, and by developing "sexy", "perfect" and carefully-trimmed "buff" looks that would differentiate them from those who were "sick" (Halkitis 2000). Such changes, Andersson (2018) noted, went as far as catalysing the appearance of "clean", "sophisticated", sanitised and "minimalist" gay bars and culture in London's Soho, which replaced the previous "dirty" image of homosexual culture and paved the way for the inclusion of male homosexuals in heteropatriarchal institutions and kinship structures, winning that demographic a series of legal rights in the decades that followed. However, such a process of normalisation happened alongside what Sarah Schulman (2012) called a "gentrification of the mind", leading to a "queer/gay assimilationist split" (Shepard 2001) that was further facilitated by an increase in collaboration between gay men and neoliberal governmental institutions in an attempt to tackle the AIDS crisis (Richardson 2005; Haus 2016; Freeman 1992), making the 1990s the beginning of "a period which has become associated with the deradicalisation and commodification of gay culture in the West" (Andersson 2018, 14).

Simultaneously, a significant shift was also occurring in gay porno-graphic representations due, in part, to the boom in the porn video indus-try and the subsequent development of a thriving home video market for gay porn. Because the industry had begun turning substantial profits, straight-identifying men started taking jobs in it, though primarily in top sexual roles, for being penetrated would be seen as a betrayal of their het-erosexuality (Burger 1995; Escoffier 2009). That, alongside the perception that bottoming would increase one's chances of acquiring HIV, led to a polarisation of top and bottom roles in the gay imaginary, made "bottom-shaming" a lot more common, and eventually brought back the perception—common before the advent of the clone—that bottoming was an emasculating practice due to it involving being penetrated and it being perceived as a form of "abdication of power" to tops (Nguyen 2014, 12; see also Halperin 2012, 51 and Wittman 1992, 333–335). Another visible outcome of the gay male responses to the AIDS crisis I've been discussing was the development of what John Mercer (2017) identified as the homo-geneous vernacular of an "international style" of sexualised gay masculin-ity, which the author associated with gay porn of the early 2000s released by studios like Bel Ami, Kristen Bjorn or Men At Play (161–168).[6]

When I interviewed him in Los Angeles, Durk Dehner—president and co-founder, along with the artist himself, of the Tom of Finland Foundation—reflected not only on the changes that the AIDS crisis had brought to the gay leather and fetish scenes but also reminisced about how activist groups would, during the crisis, call the Foundation "com-plaining about how Tom was such a rip-off and that he … that his work was just glamourising this heterosexual role model [of the hypermasculine male]". Following on from Kimmel and Levine's claims above, it is easy to understand how the kinds of masculinity and sex depicted by Tom of Finland could—if one considers the immense subcultural reach and impact his illustrations had, to the point that they became inseparable from leathermen's identities themselves (Snaith 2003, 2009)—have been seen to catalyse or condone certain types of behaviour that offered a perfect environment for HIV to replicate itself. Yet, blaming visual media for behaviours and the latter, in turn, for the life cycle of a virus requires a giant leap of faith. The first causal relation attributes full agency to the visual medium—to the omnipotent "text"—and ignores the agency of viewers and the dynamic and creative negotiations that take place in one's encounter with all kinds of media, not to mention the various degree of media literacy that different viewers will have. The second, in turn—and as I've already alluded to above—establishes a causal relation between behaviours and illness, one that favours an epidemiological reading of infection—that it happens to certain demographics—rather than a micro-biological or virological one—that infection is caused by an infectious *agent*. Whilst earlier epidemiological approaches to HIV and AIDS tended to tackle the infection by calling for changes in sexual behaviour, later virological approaches tackled it by targeting the virus itself and its mech-anisms of replication through antiretrovirals used as either treatment-as-prevention (TasP) or pre- and post-exposure prophylaxis (PrEP and PEP). And yet, the thought of that possibility—that his work had played a role in catalysing the epidemic—had also occurred to Tom of Finland himself, leaving him with a certain sense of guilt. As Dehner told me:

> And, you know, it was extremely painful when we were having such an amazing time and AIDS came. And he [Tom of Finland] was just so heavy with what his participation had actually been part of ... not the cause, because he didn't cause AIDS ... but that, that he encouraged us to be vulnerable and to be free. And then this horrible disease came upon us and just took so many of us. And, and he and us and me, I mean, we came about with the best strategy we could and that was to try to save as many assets as we could. And we did that through just trying to promote safer sex until there was some other solution, you know, and ... but it was not easy for him. But he rose, you know, just like every other ... he rose to that occasion and did drawings that reflected that. And we did PR campaigns and things like that. But [...], when ACT UP would call, I would say ... if I was the one who answered I'd say, "You know what? If he was alive today, he would draw you with a skirt on. And he would do whatever it ... he would want you to, to just follow your path. And if you want it, to be liber-ated by it, by wearing a skirt, he would absolutely promote and condone that." Because what he was about was freedom for us, you know?

Yet, whilst the cultivation of the highly sexually uninhibited gay "macho" of the 1970s was definitely shaken by the onset of the AIDS epidemic in the early 1980s, it was certainly not erased. Instead, his scripts, fantasies, and visual mediations were simply adjusted and reconfigured to suit the time, anxieties, realities, and rituals of the epidemic. When it comes to the work of Tom of Finland, for instance, the artist eventually started produc-ing illustrations that promoted and eroticised condom use, whilst his com-position style also underwent visible changes, with the large group sex scenes set in identifiable locations (often forests or parks) that had become ubiquitous to his illustrations giving way to a privileging of single figures or couples drawn on blank backgrounds. Such a renegotiation—rather than full-on abdication—of a subcultural form of sexually-experimental gay masculinity that had been developing since the 1970s also unfolded on the pages of the same gay fetish periodicals that had played a central role in narrating and establishing the early gay "macho" scene: *Drummer* and *Honcho* in the USA, *Kumpel* in Germany or, throughout the 1990s, *Projet X* in France.

When it comes to *Kumpel*, and as an example, issue 40 included the erotic story "*Safer Sau*" ("Safer Sow") printed alongside a safer sex column titled "*AIDS Zwei Drei ...*". Sometimes, the magazine's references to AIDS would take the form of sexual health advice pieces published in collaboration with the Deutsche AIDS-Hilfe (German AIDS-Relief). One of those, published in issue 26, also included a safer sex cartoon created by the US Gay Men's Health Crisis—evidence of the dialogue and syner-gies developing amongst gay AIDS organisations and activist groups based in the USA and Europe, despite the financial and political relations between each of those organisations and their national governments being rather different and presenting very specific sets of localised challenges.[7] Around the early 1990s, references to safer sex also started appearing reg-ularly in the magazine's personal ads section albeit never at the expense of the fetishistic practices that had united its readers. Rather than having to surrender their subcultural masculinity to the AIDS crisis, the readership of *Kumpel* seemed to have chosen instead to manage the potential risk of the sexual practices that had become so fundamental to their sense of identity, making them "safer" rather than abandoning them *tout court*.

Drummer, in turn, first mentioned AIDS in its issue 65, of 1983, only two years after the MMWR marked the mythic beginning of the epidemic. In a "special report" entitled "Some of Us are Dying", which deserved a prominent highlight on its front cover, writer John Preston took over three pages of the magazine not to, in his words, "deal with the medical aspects of AIDS" but, instead, "to talk about the victims and how we treat them" (Preston 1983, 20). The piece was, amongst other things, a rebuttal of the narratives that sought to blame gay men for having developed AIDS. "We", he wrote, "have every right and every obligation to examine every opportunity to combat this disease. We have no right to desert the men who have already contracted it" (21). Preston's piece was also the topic of the editorial for that issue, with John Rowberry, the magazine's associate publisher at the time, drawing attention to it as well as to the safer sex advice piece that immediately followed it, noting that, whilst he expected many readers to be annoyed by the magazine's "case for printing *anything* that could infringe on the intense sexual communication that *Drummer* strives to bring", Preston's "perspective on the holocaust that threatens us all is one that needs to be in this magazine at this time". Rowberry then proceeded to build a very strong takedown of president Reagan's decision to allocate $12 million to AIDS research and spread over one and a half years, calling it "less than a crumb" when a lot more money was being invested in the military "to puppet dictatorships in other countries" (Rowberry 1983). Rowberry's words would inaugurate a shift in the editorial line of *Drummer*—which had theretofore shied away from overt engagements with politics—with the numbers of political editorials on various matters of concern to gay men starting to have not only a presence but a rather regular one in the issues published during the 1980s and 1990s.

From issue 99 (1986) onwards, *Drummer* started including a notice on the contents page of all its issues, stating that, in "other than fictional pieces", the magazine would "emphasize safe sex with respect to contagious diseases and safe and sane behaviour with respect to all activities", whilst nonetheless highlighting that "each competent adult must set for themselves the level of risk he or she is willing to accept". The reason for such clarification, the notice continued, was that "While *Drummer* hopes to educate its readers on a wide variety of topics, its main purpose is to entertain!" Considering the contents of the magazine throughout the AIDS crisis, it is easy to see why the editors of *Drummer* felt like taking a position to avoid being blamed for the continued spread of HIV, particularly at a time when knowledge of the virus was still rather limited. All through the 1980s and 1990s, the magazine continued to include written and illustrated sexual fantasies following their original brand of leather, SM, and fetish sex that would at times include behaviours seen to be "riskier", whilst simultaneously continuing to periodically publish educational pieces on safety and risk in BDSM and other sexual scenarios. At the same time, references to bodily fluids, "limitless" sex, and "pigginess" became increasingly rare in its personal ads section, with mentions of "healthy" and "safe sex" increasing. A similar trend could also be seen in *Honcho*, with the editors starting to include, in the late 1980s, a note claiming the contents of the magazine were "in no way meant to encourage unsafe forms of sexual behaviour", and references to condoms and "safe" and "disease free" sex also starting to appear in their personal classifieds around the same time. That trend—one that maintained fantasies of "free" sex, promiscuity, experimentation, and boundary-pushing, whilst simultaneously accompanying them with didactic pieces on HIV and safer sexual practices—resonates with Douglas Crimp argument, in "How to Have Promiscuity in an Epidemic", that it was exactly gay promiscuity—the same promiscuity that was now being blamed for the AIDS crisis—that had given gay men the knowledge about bodies, sex, and its myriad of pleasures that they needed in order to adjust to the new realities of the epidemic, ultimately arguing that it was that "lack of promiscuity and its lessons that suggests that many straight people will have a much harder time learning 'how to have sex in an epidemic' than we did" (Crimp 1987, 253).

Born already during the AIDS crisis— its first issue only being published in 1994—and thus being much younger than *Kumpel*, *Drummer* or *Honcho*, French gay magazine *Projet X* offered a much more complex set of visual and written outputs. Whilst it often included illustrated safer-sex guides, its written and visual content was a lot more daring, considering the scale of the epidemic in the 1990s: fantasies of condom sex appeared next to fantasies of condomless sex; fist-fucking could be seen depicted both with and without gloves; and references to "no limits" or "all perv" continued to populate its personal classifieds, sometimes with self-declared HIV+ men looking for "animal sex" and stating "all filthy suggestions considered", alongside others clearly making reference to condoms or "SSR" ("*sex sans risque*", that is, "sex without risk"). For instance, one of the personal ads, written in both French and German and published in issue 23 (1997) read:

SPUNK
Active-passive guy looking for a group of guys for a maximum of loads in my mouth and ass. Also seeking guy to suck his hole after receiving multiple dumps and pinning him thoroughly. I travel to all regions. Photo means response guaranteed.

(79, my translation)

Another, written in French, English and German and published in issue 33 (1998), stated the following:

CUM RESERVOIR – PARIS
35 years, 1m 85, 78kg, brown hair, shaven, muscley, pierced, offers beautiful hole to cram and fill, no condoms, uro, dildo, fist, group sex, orgy, exhibition. Looking for guy or group of guys, who cum a lot, who like stuffing a real whore's arse and mouth. Possible to switch roles, reply guaranteed, voyages throughout Europe, can accommodate.

(76)

The variety of more-or-less conflicting messages being published in those magazines throughout the AIDS crisis, give a more nuanced understanding of how gay men responded to the epidemic and the extent to which their sexual behaviours may or may not have changed as a result. Whilst it is often accepted knowledge that gay men were quick to take on safer sex practices, that seems not to have been the full story. As Michael Warner had already highlighted in an infamous piece that he wrote for the *Village Voice* on 31 January 1995—right in the middle of the epidemic—and which was later republished in David Halperin's *What Do Gay Men Want?* (2007), many gay men, including Warner himself, had continued to forego condoms in all or some of their sexual encounters. Noting how "[most] efforts to encourage us to take care of ourselves through safer sex also invite us to pretend that our only desire is to be proper and good", Warner suggested that "[the] queerness that is repressed in this view may be finding expression in risk. Sex has long been associated with death, in part because of its sublimity", adding that "[in] this context, the pursuit of dangerous sex is not as simple as mere thrill seeking, or self-destructiveness. It may represent deep and mostly unconscious thinking about desire and the conditions that make life worthwhile" (Warner 2007, 163). Already pointing to the tight relationship between modern sexual behaviours and the meanings we create for our own lives and subjectivities—of which being a "pig" is only one—Warner finished his piece with a quote from Walt Odets, the famous San Francisco-based gay psychologist, writer, and AIDS activist:

> "The safest way to not get HIV," says Odets, "is never to touch another human being. So if someone is anxious, start there. But then you have to ask: what do you want to do? How important is it to you? Who are you? What do you want your life to be about?"
>
> (Warner 2007, 167)

Yet, despite the ways which some gay men continued to engage in "bareback" or intentional condomless anal sex throughout the AIDS crisis, and despite the history of gay "pig" self-identifications tracing the term and its association with uninhibited "no-limits" sex at least as far back as the 1970s, it would take a few more years for the first video bringing the terms "bareback" and "pigs" together in its title to be released. Whilst the appearance of bareback porn in the late 1990s is often associated with studios like Hot Desert Knights or Treasure Island Media, the latter having been founded in 1998 as the first commercial studio exclusively dedicated to bareback porn (Dean 2009; Escoffier 2009; Florêncio 2018), it wasn't until 2002 that *Barebackin' Cum Pigs*, directed by Justin Thomas for his eponymous studio, was released as the earliest gay porn video listed on the IAFD to include both terms in its title. Quite a lot has changed ever since. Marked by bareback videos being released at such increasingly high rates that the practice has become normalised and now dominates gay porn production (Mercer 2017, 139), the changes I'm referring to happened in tandem with the progressive uptake, by gay men, of combination antiretroviral therapies, first for the successful management of HIV after 1996, and later—since 2012 in the USA—as a successful protocol for pre-exposure prophylaxis (PrEP). Thus, since the late 1990s and especially after the turn of the twenty-first century, the number of porn videos with "pig(s)" on their titles has also grown exponentially, with studio titles such as *Fist Pigs* (Hot Desert Knights, 2000), *Pig Pen* (3rd World Video, 2002), *A Pig's Adventure* (Oink Video, 2003), *Pig Sty* (3rd World Video 2003), *Bareback Pigs at Play* (Marina Pacific, 2004), *Bay of Pigs* (Dick Wadd, 2005), *Bareback Cum Swapping Pigs* (Sebastian Sloane Productions, 2007), *Ass Pigs* (Hothouse Entertainment, 2009), *Berlin Pigs Unleashed* (Dick Wadd, 2011), *Buddies and Pigs* (Next Door Entertainment, 2013) or *Sexpigs in a Man-tramp Promised Land* (Treasure Island Media, 2019) accounting for only a selected few.

Recently, and to accompany the release of his *Sexpigs in a Man-tramp Promised Land*, pornographer Paul Morris (2019) wrote a text he titled

"A Sexpig Manifesto". According to it, "[for] the first time in human history, there's no reason why all men shouldn't be fucking all the goddamn time". The reasons for that are, following Morris, that overpopulation and automation have been doing away with the need for reproduction and work. As such, the answer to all the free time men apparently now have is to "TAKE YER BLOATED DRIPPIN' DICK IN HAND AND LET IT LEAD YOU TO A MANSLUT PROMISED LAND!" Calling on gay men to pursue—not sublimate—their sexual desires, Morris's "Sexpig Manifesto" thus invites us to embrace our "drives and needs and hungers".

Interestingly, a lot of what is argued in his "Sexpig Manifesto" and riding the rhetoric frisson of a polemic call to arms, resonates deeply with his earlier text "No Limits: Necessary Danger in Male Porn" (Morris 2011), the infamous speech he delivered at the World Pornography Conference in Los Angeles in 1998. Together, both texts help us situate gay "pig" masculinities not just as a reaction to the "clean" masculinities that had started developing in the later years of the AIDS crisis, but also as a revisiting and re-visioning of pre-AIDS masculinities, modulated by the biopolitical affordances of the pharmacological and medical infrastructures of HIV care and prophylaxis in the twenty-first-century. Let us consider the following two quotes, each taken from one of the texts:

> In the 80s, porn culture turned to straight men and bisexual scenes in order to move away from this vertiginous point—the ejaculatory consummation—while still maintaining the rote and perfunctory porn genre mechanics. We watched beautiful straight men, shaved to look more innocent and healthy (i.e. too young and too straight to have been infected) engaging in the mechanics of sex with none of the damning heat of passion that might lead one to slip up and either ingest semen or take it up the ass. These men didn't like semen, didn't live for it. [...]
>
> In the 90s, maverick video producers reintroduced semen worship and the lust for ingestion as an element in their sex scenes. [...] For the most part, however, the style of the late 80's [*sic*] had become too successfully commodified for most companies to risk change.
>
> (Morris [1998] 2011)

> For men, sex is the key. We're lied to; a lot of male-male porn lies and tells us that the best sex is reserved for men who look a certain way, dress a certain way, live in a great house, a beautiful place, and so on.
>
> These fuckin' liars tell us that our dick has to be a certain size, our body needs a lotta muscle and on and on and on. With the complicity of even our own gay pornographers, great sex and plenty of it is the carrot on a stick that keeps all us poor suckers locked in slavery.
>
> Fuck that shit.
>
> (Morris 2019)

Both passages, written just over two decades apart, make an argument for the rejection of the kinds of gay masculinity that had emerged in the aftermath of the public onset of the AIDS. Considering them an affront of the "real" nature of gay men, of their desires and actual sexual practices—advanced by both texts as gay men's inherent truth—Morris pointed the finger at the likes of the "Chelsea Boys" (Halkitis 2000), the "Soho gays" (Andersson 2018), and the "international style" of gay masculinities that dominated pornography at the turn of the twenty-first century (Mercer 2017), blaming them for betraying the "danger, death and communion" (Morris 2011) that was the defining feature of gay male sexual cultures, one that had to continue being fostered if one were to ensure the survival of one's subculture. If, as he noted in 1998, "the subculture and the virus require the same processes for transmission", the men who confronted death in the name of remaining faithful to their desires—the men who continued to bareback throughout the AIDS crisis—served the "heroic purpose" of guaranteeing the survival of the collective subcultural body even if, in doing so, they may have had to jeopardise the survival of their own. "What is at stake", he wrote, "isn't the survival of the individual, but the survival of the practices and patterns which are the discoveries and properties of the subculture". As a result, and against the "slick porn" of mainstream studios like Titan or Falcon, Morris called for a new kind of "documentary" gay porn that offered a "detailed and truthful depiction of this creative world, a world of men who are risking life itself in the pursuit of the possibility of cultural survival and personal happiness" (Morris 2011).

Now if, still according to Morris, the sex that had already been taking place at the time of his 1998 speech—the sex that, according to him, ought to therefore be "documented" by porn—involved a high degree of risk, by the time his 2019 "Sexpig Manifesto" was released things couldn't have been more different. Today, thanks to developments in HIV research, exchanges of sexual fluids no longer have to mean a potential threat to gay men's lives. Thanks to the antiretroviral drug protocols that have progressively been introduced since the late 1990s—Treatment-as-Prevention (TasP), Post-Exposure Prophylaxis (PEP) and, more recently, Pre-Exposure Prophylaxis (PrEP)—the life cycle of HIV can be successfully interrupted. A telling sign of such success story is that, whilst data shows that barebacking amongst gay men has been increasing exponentially and become mainstream practice within and without porn (Vasconcelos da Silva 2009; Rojas Castro *et al.* 2012; Garcia 2013; Davis 2015; Mercer 2017), the rate of new HIV diagnoses in men who have sex with men (MSM) in London, for instance, has been steadily dropping despite falling rates in condom use amongst the same demographic (Public Health England 2018), leading the London HIV Prevention Programme—a partnership of 32 local authorities led by Lambeth Council—to declare London a "world leader in reducing HIV" (Graves 2019). Considering the significant changes in HIV research and healthcare that have taken place between Morris's 1998 speech and his 2019 "manifesto", I would like to contend that the shift in tone and message from "necessary danger" (Morris 2011) to "the time for a sexpig promised land is now!" (Morris 2019) can be understood in a new materialist fashion by taking into account the unfolding of the temporality of HIV from having been a sentence to an AIDS-related death to having become a chronic infection that is manageable by those who have it and avoidable by the ones who don't. To follow along Morris's line of reasoning, it appears that the tempestuous, life-threatening seas of the AIDS crisis have ended up delivering those of us who survived to a "sexpig promised land" of exquisite pharmaceutically-mediated beaches. And, to still follow Morris's rhetoric, that has only happened thanks to all the gay men who were willing to risk their own lives in the name of the survival of their subculture.

We certainly do not need to endorse Paul Morris's statements, particularly those concerning the "heroism" of the men who continued to put their lives at risk throughout the crisis. And we should also not ignore how his ramping up of the rhetoric millieu surrounding his videos functions as a marketing strategy to ensure continuing sales of Treasure Island Media's brand of transgressive porn, at a time when barebacking has become the porn industry's standard and been taken up by most of the very same studios his company had set itself against back in the late 1990s. Further, and despite what he claimed in the 2019 text quoted above, the body types we see in Treasure Island Media today are no longer *that* significantly different from those we see working in other studios, even if their sexual performances tend to present them as "rougher" and "scruffier"—more "unhinged" even. A reason for that may actually be that the introduction of antiretrovirals has taken away the "risk" that had been associated with bareback sex, thus opening up the industry—including Treasure Island Media—to men with more mainstream porn looks. Casting will have been much different during the late 1990s, when the "risk" of contracting HIV was still very much present and the body types seen in Treasure Island Media productions consequently seemed radically different from those of other studios, often including both bellied and skinny bodies, and hyper-tattooed men with "bad boy" attitudes. Today, even marked "bad boy" attitudes have, just like bareback, reached the mainstream of porn, albeit often coating pornographically safer "buff" looks.

Yet, all of those caveats should still support—rather than deter—what should be our acknowledgement of the radical changes that have been taking place in both gay porn and gay sex cultures at large over the last two decades. For what we are able to identify today, after the introduction of successful drug regimens managed to cut the viral knot that used to tie gay sex with death, is—to appropriate Morris's own words—a "sexual Renaissance" (Morris 2011) of the subcultures and masculinities that characterised the pre-AIDS years and which did not so much disappear as they went underground, becoming rather niche throughout the crisis (as my discussion of print and video porn in this chapter has shown) only to re-emerge in force in the age of antiretrovirals. It is within that framework of pharmaceutically mediated historical continuity that—I argue—the newly found hyper-visibility of gay "pigs" in twenty-first-century gay male sex and porn cultures should be understood.

Taken as a development of the gay masculinities and sexual practices that were cut short by the AIDS crisis, "pig" has today become a form of self-identification that is taken up by gay men who like to "wallow in filth" as it were, who are willing to test and push the boundaries of their bodies, and experiment with horizons of bodily pleasures, opening themselves to exchanges of all kinds of bodily fluids whilst no longer having to be haunted either by the spectre of HIV and AIDS, or by fears of emasculation through penetration. I would thus like to close this chapter by narrowing down on the work of French photographer and pornographer Marc Martin, whose porn studio he launched in 2008, aptly named Pig-Prod, as well as body of fetish photography, offer a consolidated picture of the more European strand of the "pig" subcultures this book is about.

Martin's work feeds off and builds on the homosexual and masculine imaginaries that, as I've been arguing, were threatened by the onset of the AIDS crisis. Whether in his photographs—which he has exhibited in museums and galleries in the USA and Europe—or in the productions of his porn studio, Martin's work is marked by a certain dark romanticism—a longing for a pre-AIDS era of gay cruising and experimentation in often derelict public spaces, as well as an attempt to re-enact them in the space of fantasy by chasing, filming and photographing locations and men that have not succumbed to the clean-up of gay culture that happened during the 1990s. Deeply invested in his vision of masculinity, Martin's work often depicts models in derelict abandoned buildings, industrial wastelands, farms, factories, public toilets, sewers, and other spaces often associated, in mainstream bourgeois culture, with dirt. Further, and just like the locations of his shoots, so do his men, who are often photographed and filmed in dirty outfits associated with the working classes and manual labour—skinheads, mechanics, farmers, construction workers, etc.

It is this pursuit of derelict or dirty environments with unpolished "dirty" kinds of masculinity—the kinds that fall outside the parameters of bourgeois demeanour, looks and behaviours—that drives Marc Martin's eye. As he wrote at the start of his photobook *Dur Labeur* [*Hard Labour*]:

> To my eye, real virility is not found in images of genitalia. Proudly displaying a hard penis does not define a man. Nor does the image of a resting cock free it from a pornographic context. For me, the eroticism of the male body is always looming in its contours and its confrontations.
>
> [...]

Figure 1.1 Marc Martin, "Brothers in Farm". *Dur Labeur*, 2009.
Courtesy of the artist.

Figure 1.2 Mar Martin, "Brothers in Farm". *Dur Labeur*, 2009.
Courtesy of the artist.

My images are inspired by a bygone era, a time before the fixation on performance became the driving force of everything; before the obsession with hygiene destroyed any appreciation of its absence; before cruising by numbers had begun to dehumanise all eroticism. So much for nostalgia!

[...]

I love shades and contrasts, in photography and in life. Troubles and joys. Rust speaks to me, in its colours, its texture, its symbolism. Faded photos too, with those blurred images that say so much. And sometimes I prefer my own pictures to be blurred; to leave others to find in those shadowy images the cruel beauty of truth when the make-up is stripped away.

I love the playful gaze of brutal men. I love their rough hands but also their gentle gestures. I love poets and punks; coyness in porn. I love pigs and I love flowers. And so I try very hard to marry all that together. Hard labour indeed!

(Martin 2015, 8)

A few thoughts arise from this passage, which illuminates my understanding of the twenty-first-century gay masculinities with which I'm trying to grapple. For Martin, masculinity—or "real virility" as he put it—does not require the phallic, erect penis to affirm it, confirm it, and protect it from symbolic emasculation. Refusing the dominance of the role of the phallus as *the* visual synecdoche—or, better, the part *sine qua non*—of masculinity in Western culture (Potts 2000), the French photographer and pornographer proposes instead fantasies of homoerotic masculinities founded on a rejection of the hygiene and sanitation practices that, as several authors have argued, have been fundamental for the development of bourgeois consciousness and its class-defining pursuit of the "proper" body through an ethics of cleanliness and self-control (Kristeva 1982; Bauman 1992; Elias 2000; Douglas 2002; Menninghaus 2003). In a move that echoes the "primitivist homopoetics" of the early Gay Liberation Movement (Miller 2019), Martin eschews bourgeois so-called "good taste" and propriety and replaces it with a "pig" homoerotics that references a "bygone era" in which gentleness coexisted with roughness, beauty with filth. "So much for nostalgia!" as he wrote.

One of the instances in which his dark nostalgic romanticism is most successfully composed and conveyed is his 2008 photograph "Partage". With a French title that means at once "sharing" and "division", "parting" and "participation", the photograph appropriates the classical Christian iconography of the *pietà*—the Virgin Mary's Lamentation of Christ after his death by crucifixion—and turns it into a striking image of one man carrying another out of what looks like an access to an underground sewage system.

Figure 1.3 Marc Martin, "Partage", 2008.
Courtesy of the artist.

The two men look appear caught in the middle of a poignant, almost solemn act, one in which their bodies have become photographically suspended together in what would otherwise be their parting away. Were they parting away from one another? Away from the underground from which they had emerged? Both, perhaps. Our uncertainty with regards to the narrative of which the image is only a snapshot of frozen time adds affective intensity to the photograph, making it all the more piercing because it is all the more ineffable. The combination of the rough looks of the men with their tattoos, piercings, dirty skin and stained clothing, the darkness and filth of their surroundings, and their gentle and caring embrace, produces an aesthetics of contrasts that invites a consideration of the psychic depths and affective richness of the two male figures, as well as of the intensity of the bond that connects them as kin, conveying a sense of sublimity through negative transcendence. By that I mean that the sublimity of the photograph's dark romanticism is achieved not through alluding to the high philosophical domains of sun-like figures such as God, Reason, Nature, or Morality, but through a downward investment in the subterranean dimensions of existence and of the psyche. In so doing, the image brings to mind both the spirit of the *sous*-realist thought of Georges Bataille (2017), who saw "destruction and decomposition […] as an achievement, not as a negation of being" (137), and the sacred aesthetics of other homoerotic works such as Robert Mapplethorpe's "Jim and Tom, Sausalito" from 1977, which Dave Hickey (2009) said depicts "the intersection of mortal suffering and spiritual ecstasy, where the rule of law meets the grace of trust" (33), a description that also resonates with the affective charge of Martin's "Partage".

It is their investment in transgression of bodily boundaries, pleasures, and desires, as well as their eroticisation of "low" matter—that is, matter such as bodily fluids that has been judged as dirty and thus abjected by bourgeois culture—that define gay "pig" masculinities and their dark queer aesthetics of existence. Heirs to the sexual experimentation and rituals that helped define, before the onset of the AIDS crisis, gay masculinities in opposition to the middle-class heteropatriarchal privileging of reason over the body and its messy interiors (Levine 1998, 53; Mains 2002, 2004; Rubin 2004), twenty-first-century gay "pigs" seem to have picked up where their forefathers had left, putting promiscuity and uninhibited sexual practices back at the centre of their processes of subjectivisation. As such, and aided by the pharmaceutical developments that have finally provided effective means to manage and prevent HIV infection, today's gay "pigs" can be seen to constitute a new chapter in a longer history of sexual emancipation and gay masculine self-fashioning that was not so much brought to an end as it was suspended by the epidemic. Unlike kinds of gay male self-identifications such as "bears" or "twinks", dependent as they are on body shape and physical appearance, "pigs" are "pigs" because of what they do, not because of what they are; and what they do is to wallow in filth.

Notes

1 At some point as I was writing this book, the website for the studio (http://3rd worldvideo.com/) went offline for reasons unknown to me. However, a capture of its page for *Pig Sty*, archived on 7 February 2019, is still available on the Internet Archive here: https://web.archive.org/web/20190207010102/http://3rdworldvideo. com/PIG%20STY.html.

2 I should note that the video had been previously uploaded to PornHub at least once, six months prior, by user poppershaven, with the title "Filthy Bareback Lust". As it is quite common, videos in porn tube platforms tend to be replicated and re-uploaded by different users. The one attributed to user poppershaven was the earliest upload I could find of this particular video.

3 I'm thankful to Mario, archive volunteer at the Schwules Museum in Berlin, for the information about the approximate run of *Kumpel*, given that the issues of the magazine did not include publication date.

4 I was able to consult, in the archives of the Schwules Museum in Berlin, issues 5 to 78.

5

> PUR PORC
> *Porc 36 a., 1m65, 55kg, brun, moustachu, cherche fermier, éleveur, boucher por prise en main de la bête, mise en conditionnement, élevage, saillies. Ok pour tous trips similaires. Cherche aussi place valet de ferme. Âge, physique, region indifférents si sérieux et conforme.*
>
> D 100 PROZENT SCHWEIN
> *Schwein, 36/165/55, dunkelhaarig, Schnauzer, sucht Bauer, Landwirt, Viehzüchter, Metzger, un das Vieh anzupacken, zu beherrschen, zur Aufzucht und Besamung. OK für ähnliche Trips. Suche auch Stelle als Stallknecht. Alter, Aussehen, Gegend gleichgültig bei Sërosistät und Überseinstummung. Réf: X2097."*

(56)

6 I would note here that Mercer (2017) does not connect this "international style" to the advent of the AIDS crisis as much as I do here, associating it instead with the blurring of national and regional gay masculinities caused by the online circulation of porn, the increasing mobility of middle-class gay men, and the popularisation of international "circuit parties" during the 1990s. Yet, I would contend that, even if not having been the sole trigger for the "international style", gay men's responses to the AIDS crisis and the latter's association, in the dominant culture, with certain kinds of gay masculinity were also a significant factor in the development of the visual porn vernacular Mercer identified.

7 The Deutsche AIDS-Hilfe (German AIDS-Relief) was founded in Berlin in 1985 as an umbrella organisation for the various gay-led regional AIDS-Hilfen that started emerging independently throughout the then FDR two years prior. Not only was the creation of the DAH facilitated by informal meetings set up by the Federal Centre for Health Education, but the national organisation would also be financed by the Federal Government, which saw the DAH as a mediator between Germany's gay population and the state, which would allow for increased collaboration and dialogue between health and policy-making authorities on the one hand and one of the demographics most affected by the epidemic

on the other (see Freeman 1992; Haus 2016). Interestingly, an year earlier in 1984, Jürgen Roland, who would become a board member of the DAH, had travelled to New York to witness first-hand the impact of the AIDS crisis on the gay scene and to accompany members of the Gay Men's Health Crisis (GMHC) on visits to patients in hospitals (Haus 2016). Whilst German activists' early contact with the GMHC did certainly inform the work of the DAH in West Germany, evidenced by their inclusion of a GMHC cartoon alongside their own piece in *Kumpel* 26, the relationship between the GMHC and the US Federal Government couldn't have been more different than the one between the DAH and the German Federal Government. Whilst the FDR funded the DAH from its very infancy as an NGO, in the USA senator for North Carolina Jesse Helms would, in 1987, introduce and amendment to a Labor, Health and Human Services, and Education bill allocating money to AIDS research and education. That amendment, which would be passed in a slightly reworded version, would prohibit, *de jure* if never really de facto, the use of public money to fund sexual health campaigns that could be seen to promote or condone homosexual acts, i.e. any campaigns directly addressing homosexuals and the kinds of sex they were having. Curiously, it was a comic book produced by the GMHC to promote safe sex amongst gay men that Helms referred to, in his opening remarks in Senate that day, as a book that "promotes sodomy and the homosexual lifestyle as an acceptable alternative in American society" (Helms quoted in Crimp 1987). It is entertaining to think that, at the height of the AIDS crisis and during the later years of the Cold War, two of the most significant allied states this side of the Iron Curtain could have dealt in such different ways with the lobbying, support, and activist grassroots AIDS organisations that were being set up by gay men and women and their allies.

References

Andersson, Johan. 2018. "Homonormative aesthetics: AIDS and 'de-generational unremembering' in 1990s London". *Urban Studies* 56 (14): 2993–3010.

Bataille, Georges. 2017. "Programme". In *The Sacred Conspiracy: The Internal Papers of the Secret Society of Acéphale and Lectures to the College of Sociology*, edited by Marina Galletti and Alastair Brotchie, 137–138. London: Atlas Press.

Bauman, Zygmunt. 1992. *Mortality, Immortality and Other Life Strategies*. Cambridge: Polity.

Burger, John. 1995. *One-Handed Histories: The Eroto-Politics of Gay Male Video Pornography*. New York: Routledge.

Davis, Oliver. 2015. "Introduction: A special issue of *Sexualities*: Bareback sex and queer theory across three national contexts (France, UK, USA)". *Sexualities* 18 (1/2): 120–126.

CDC. 1981. "Epidemiologic notes and reports: *Pneumocystis* pneumonia—Los Angeles". *Morbidity and Mortality Weekly Report* 30 (21): 1–3.

Connell, Raewyn. 2005. *Masculinities*. Cambridge: Polity.

Crimp. 1987. "How to have promiscuity in an epidemic". *October* 43: 237–271.

Dean, Tim. 2009. *Unlimited Intimacy: Reflections on the Subculture of Barebacking*. Chicago: The University of Chicago Press.

Douglas, Mary. 2002. *Purity and Danger: An Analysis of Concept of Pollution and Taboo*. London: Routledge.

58 *A pig is what a pig does*

58 *A pig is what a pig does*

58 *A pig is what a pig does*

Elias, Norbert. 2000. *The Civilizing Process: Sociogenetic and Psychogenetic Investigations*. Oxford: Blackwell.

Escoffier, Jeffrey. 2009. *Bigger than Life: The History of Gay Porn Cinema from Beefcake to Hardcore*. Philadelphia: Running Press.

Florêncio, João. 2018. "Breeding futures: Masculinity and the ethics of CUMmunion in Treasure Island Media's *Viral Loads*". *Porn Studies* 5 (3): 271–285.

Freeman, Richard. 1992. "Governing the voluntary sector response to AIDS: A comparative study of the UK and Germany". *Voluntas* 3 (1): 29–47.

Garcia, Christien. 2013. "Limited intimacy: Barebacking and the imaginary". *Textual Practices* 27 (6): 1031–1051.

Graves, Jack. 2019. "We can achieve zero new HIV infections—if Londoners keep making safer choices". *London Councils* newsletter, 1 July 2019. www.london councils.gov.uk/press-release/01-july-2019/'we-can-achieve-zero-new-hiv-infections-if-londoners-keep-making-safer [accessed 9 November 2019].

Halkitis, Perry. 2000. "Masculinity in the Age of AIDS: HIV-Seropositive Gay Men and the 'Buff Agenda'". In *Gay Masculinities*, edited by Peter Nardi, 130–151. Thousand Oaks, CA: Sage Publications.

Halperin, David. 2007. *What Do Gay Men Want? An Essay on Sex, Risk, and Subjectivity*. Ann Arbor: The University of Michigan Press.

Halperin, David. 2012. *How to be Gay*. Cambridge, MA: The Belknap Press of Harvard University Press.

Haus, Sebastian. 2016. "Risky sex—risky language. HIV/AIDS and the West German gay scene in the 1980s". *Historical Social Research/Historische Sozialforschung* 41 (1): 111–134.

Hickey, Dave. 2009. *The Invisible Dragon: Essays on Beauty, Revised and Expanded*. Chicago: The University of Chicago Press.

Kimmel, Michael. 1996. *Manhood in America: A Cultural History*. New York: The Free Press.

Knight Jr., Richard. 2003. "This little piggy". *Chicago Reader*, 28 August 2003. www.chicagoreader.com/chicago/this-little-piggy/Content?oid=913015 [accessed 14 November 2019].

Kristeva, Julia. 1982. *Powers of Horror: An Essay on Abjection*. New York: Columbia University Press.

Levine, Martin. 1998. *Gay Macho: The Life and Death of the Homosexual Clone*, edited by Michael Kimmel. New York: New York University Press.

Mains, Geoff. 2002. *Urban Aboriginals: A Celebration of Leathersexuality*. Los Angeles: Daedalus Publishing Company.

Mains, Geoff. 2004. "The view from a sling". In *Leatherfolk: Radical Sex, People, Politics, and Practice*, edited by Mark Thompson, 233–242. Los Angeles: Daedalus Publishing Company.

Martin, Marc. 2015. *Dur Labeur*. Paris: Agua.

Menninghaus, Winfried. 2003. *Disgust: The Theory and History of a Strong Sensation*. Albany: State University of New York Press.

Mercer, John. 2017. *Gay Pornography: Representations of Sexuality and Masculinity*. London: I.B. Tauris.

Miller, Ben. 2019. "This thing of darkness I acknowledge mine: Notes on primitivist homopoetics". Paper presented at *Queer Modernisms*, University of Oxford, 25 April 2019.

Morris, Paul. 2011. "No limits: Necessary danger in male porn". *Treasure Island Media Blog*, 15 November 2011. https://blog.treasureislandmedia.com/2011/11/no-limits-necessary-danger-in-male-porn/.

Morris, Paul. 2019. "A Sexpig Manifesto". *Sexpigs in a Man-Tramp Promised Land*. https://store.treasureislandmedia.com/wigs-in-a-man-tramp-promised-land.html [accessed 14 November 2019].

Nguyen, Hoang Tan. 2014. *A View from the Bottom: Asian American Masculinity and Sexual Representation*. Durham: Duke University Press.

Paasonen, Susanna. 2018. *Many Splendored Things: Thinking Sex and Play*. London: Goldsmiths Press.

Potts, Annie. 2000. "'The essence of the hard on': Hegemonic masculinity and the cultural construction of 'erectile dysfunction'". *Men and Masculinities* 3 (1): 85–103.

Preston, John. 1983. "Some of us are dying". *Drummer* 7 (65): 19–21.

Public Health England. 2018. *Annual Epidemiological Spotlight on HIV in London: 2017 Data*. London: PHE Publications. https://assets.publishing.service.gov.uk/government/uploads/system/uploads/attachment_data/file/767460/LondonHIVSpotlight2017.pdf [accessed 8 November 2019].

Richardson, Diane. 2005. "Desiring sameness? The rise of a neoliberal politics of normalisation". *Antipode* 37 (3): 515–535.

Rojas Castro, Daniela *et al*. 2012. "Barebacking and sexual health in the French setting: 'NoKondom Zone' workshops". *AIDS Care* 24 (8): 1046–1051.

Rowberry, John. 1983. "Getting off". *Drummer* 7 (65): 5.

Rubin, Gayle. 2004. "The catacombs: A temple of the butthole". In *Leatherfolk: Radical Sex, People, Politics, and Practice*, edited by Mark Thompson, 119–141. Los Angeles: Daedalus Publishing Company.

Schulman, Sarah. 2012. *The Gentrification of the Mind: Witness to a Lost Imagination*. Berkeley: University of California Press.

Shepard, Benjamin. 2001. "The queer/gay assimilationist split: The suits vs. the sluts". *Monthly Review* 53 (1): 49–62.

Simon, William and John Gagnon. 1986. "Sexual scripts: Permanence and change". *Archives of Sexual Behavior* 15 (2): 97–120.

Snaith, Guy. 2003. "Tom's men: The masculinization of homosexuality and the homosexualization of masculinity at the end of the twentieth century". *Paragraph* 26 (1/2): 77–88.

Snaith, Guy. 2009. "Corps dessines, corps crees, signes 'Tom of Finland'". *Itinéraires* 2009–1. DOI: 10.4000/itineraires.364.

Treichler, Paula. 1999. *How to Have Theory in an Epidemic: Cultural Chronicles of AIDS*. Durham: Duke University Press.

Vasconcelos da Silva, Luís Augusto. 2009. "Masculinidades transgressivas em práticas de barebacking". *Estudos Feministas* 17 (3): 675–699.

Warner, Michael. 2007. "Unsafe: Why gay men are having risky sex". In David Halperin, *What Do Gay Men Want? An Essay on Sex, Risk, and Subjectivity*, 155–167. Ann Arbor: The University of Michigan Press.

Wittman, Carl. 1992. "A gay manifesto". In *Out of the Closets: Voices of Gay Liberation*, edited by Karla Jay and Allen Young, 330–342.

2 Porous man w/holes

In order to explore the ways in which "pigsex" is reframing masculinity, I would like to start this chapter by looking at the two "bad boys" of French gay literature at the turn of the antiretroviral age: Guillaume Dustan and Érik Rémès. Highly controversial figures in the French literary and LGBTQ+ scenes, Dustan and Rémès moved AIDS narratives away from their more established literary tropes of illness, death and mourning, towards what Lawrence Schehr (2009) called a "post-gay" register, one in which their HIV-positive status was embraced as a vantage point from where to "explore the possibilities of an *Aufhebung* of received knowledge through a violation of taboos and a positing of sexual and textual imaginaries that far outstrip a received notion of homosexuality, gayness, or even queerness" (74–75). Both in their autofictional novels and in their lives, the two authors have undertaken that enterprise through a positive engagement with bareback sex during the years that immediately followed the introduction of combination antiretroviral therapies for the management of HIV. Such an unashamed "bad-boy" attitude made the two writers infamous figures in French literary and queer circles, leading to public feuds with members of activist group ACT UP Paris, who, at the time, had become known for their continued—and some could argue, unproductive and anachronistic—condemnation of condomless sex (Rees-Roberts 2008; Davis 2015; Evans 2015; Rojas Castro and Girard 2015; Girard 2016). A paradigmatic episode of that feud took place in 2004 on the French TV show *Tout le Monde en Parle*, where Rémès and Didier Lestrade, one of the founders of ACT UP Paris, became involved in a heated confrontation that included the latter blaming the former for giving young people the impression that it would be acceptable to fight AIDS by intentionally seroconverting through bareback sex. To that accusation, Rémès responded with an equally intransigent defence of sexual freedom and free speech, calling Lestrade "the Marine Le Pen of darkrooms" (France 2, 2004).

Whilst it is not my aim here to go over that infamous feud in the early-twenty-first-century French cultural response to HIV, I believe the confrontation between ACT UP activists on one side and Dustan and Rémès on the other, highlights the tension between health anxieties and the new senses of freedom and possibility that antiretroviral drugs brought into the lives of gay men able to access to them. HIV was, and still is, deeply weaved into our subjectivities, whether we lived through and survived AIDS or whether—if younger—we have had to, nonetheless, still grow up with the heavy spectre of the virus constantly haunting us, our pathways to pleasure, and our sexual decision-making. Younger or older, and despite antiretrovirals having allowed us to put AIDS to rest (at least those of us lucky enough to have access to the drugs), the fact is that, as "they" say, "we are all (still) living with HIV", in that our own identities and sexual behaviours are still shaped by the ways in which we think and approach the virus and its impact on our subcultural histories, regardless of our own serostatus. With that in mind, the feud involving ACT UP Paris, Dustan, and Rémès did not only encapsulate the ever-present coexistence of conflicting views on gay sex, pleasure and risk but it also—for that same reason—seems to me to have been underlined by two very different conceptualisations of the material substrate of gay sex—that is, male bodies. As a result, two equally different positions on the kinds of sexual subjectivities afforded to gay men have also been foregrounded by that confrontation taking place in the first decade of antiretrovirals. In this chapter I explore how the debates on gay male bodies, subjectivity, and sexual behaviour that have spiked in the aftermath of the introduction of antiretroviral therapies relate to wider histories of "the body", that universalised abstraction of an equally abstract *male* body that has been a defining concern of modern European thought, the roots of which can be traced at least as far back as the development of early modern medicine and the synchronous attempts to grasp the dynamics of order and chaos, of morality and nature, during the late Renaissance. In so doing, I will reflect on the ways in which "pig" play scenarios and forms of embodiment may offer an alternative to the principles of wholeness and autonomy that have guided Western thought about the body and turned it into a model for the theorisation and eventual development of the modern nation-state.

There are two passages, one in Erik Rémès 2003 novel *Serial Fucker: Journal d'un Barebacker* and another in Guillaume Dustan's *Plus Fort Que Moi*, that are as intense as they are enlightening of the dynamics of self/other and part/whole that I want to explore in this chapter, particularly as they are played out in "pig" sex play:

> We are the fetishists of the juice. Sperm makes us hard. We are the ones to whom condoms never or hardly ever existed. Our fantasies and our desire go beyond potential health problems! For us, exchange of fluids is essential. Fertilisation. It is no longer a question of HIV or STDs. It is a matter of complete sharing.
>
> Sexuality is immediate. Condoms kill the very essence of sexuality, which is immediacy. True sex cannot be done by having condoms at

hand. Sex is mucus, secretions, raw membranes. Sexuality is sperm, mucus, piss, shit. Safer sex is something else; it is a sexuality that prevents. But sexuality itself cannot be prevented. It cannot create distance. It is fusion. Nothing is stronger in merging you with your partner than receiving or giving your sperm. The givers feel a sense of total possession. A part of themselves, no less, is in the other like a part of their soul. The receivers keep the hot cum as a souvenir of their lover and of the sexual act. They want to feel it in them to complete the union. Sperm is the most powerful physical expression of intimacy.

(Rémès 2003, 41–42, my translation)[1]

I stopped sucking but stayed bent in two, fascinated by what I saw, the cock that I sucked, the hands, the crotches, all those increasingly indistinct bodies that surrounded me. I could drown in this magma of hands, cocks, mouths. I couldn't care less about who owned what, who was fat, old, ugly, contagious. I pretty much could get off, go crazy, eat each cock that passed by, become a beast, leave hours later, clothes torn, stained, naked, covered in sweat, saliva, sperm. I imagined how the bourgeois at the Trap [Parisian gay bar] would see me as a slut, a tramp. I got up abruptly with tears in my eyes. I stumbled to the exit holding my jeans in my hands. I got dressed on the doorstep, my heart beating, without daring to face ahead.

(Dustan 1998, 22–23, my translation)[2]

The differences between their works notwithstanding (see Schehr 2009), Rémès's and Dustan's framing of gay male sex, written soon after antiretrovirals were introduced for the successful management of HIV infection but before their introduction as PrEP or the confirmation that U = U ("undetectable = untransmittable"), offers important insights into the ways bodily fluids have been conceptualised in gay male subcultures, informing the constellation of meanings that has coalesced around gay "pig" masculinities. Both Rémès and Dustan—just like the gay men, pornographers, and artists already discussed in the previous chapter—see sex as a transgression of bodily boundaries between inside and outside, as an opening of bodies to one another and to the stuff of which they are made, to such an extent that the wholeness of the body breaks down into a machinic arrangement of de-individualised parts connected to one another by means of a hydraulic circuitry. It is through such openness—such embrace of bodily porosity and of fucking as a practice of fluid mechanics—that desire fulfils in both authors its aim of fusing bodies by plugging together body parts in various creative permutations. Rather than having to be kept private and inside the male body defined as an impermeable container, bodily fluids appear here as mediators or catalysts of intimacy that fragment bodies and rearrange their parts, producing a form that, in being multiple and its ephemerality notwithstanding, is also irreducible to any pre-existing unifying gestalt. No longer accepted as an instance of whole-some bodies allowed to connect to one another as long as they don't end up losing their cohesion, sex is embraced as a creative dissolution of the boundaries of the unitary body and, by extension, of the autonomous subject. Rémès: "Sex is mucus, secretions, raw membranes." Dustan: "I could drown in this magma of hands, cocks, mouths." The outcome of such sexual ethics, of such an investment in a promiscuous fluid mechanics, is a radical overturning—or, at least, a radical questioning—of some of the fundamental principles that have guided modern Western thought in its thinking of the relation between the body and the subject. For, as Rémès put it in a passage in *Serial Fucker*—one that flies in the face of all the ways in which the hegemonic Oedipal subject of Western modernity has been conceptualised at least since the Enlightenment:

> Body-phallus, object of desire, necessarily. Body of others, of my lovers: caressed, massaged, loved. Free in my body and my sexuality. Active and passive: penetrating and penetrated. And this desire of others, always present, that traverses me, that scans me. These bodies, which follow and resemble one other, encircle, assemble, slot and fit together. And tire. To continue tirelessly. To run from body to scream since it is through them that I rise. Gobbling the other, sucking souls and their envelope to revel in them.
>
> What if the body and the act came before the mind and thought? I have a body, therefore I am. A desire in perpetual fall that quashes and kills itself at every encounter. That is then reborn and gets hard.
>
> (Rémès 2003, 22, my translation)[3]

In what is clearly an inversion of both the Cartesian dualism that became a foundational stone of the European "Age of Enlightenment", and of the "somatophobia" (Grosz 1994, 5) of Western philosophical history that equated masculinity with reason, activity and political autonomy, and femininity with the body, passivity and political immaturity (Grosz 1994; Rasmussen 2011), the masculinity put forward in Rémès's novel is enacted through an embrace of bodily transgressions and an openness to the bodies of others and their fluids. Unlike Descartes, who thought and therefore *was*, it is only in his surrender to bodies—his own and those of others—that the narrator of Érik Rémès's *Serial Fucker* gets to *become*. And what he becomes when doing so is a man, a particular kind of gay man. As Lawrence Schehr (2009) wrote of the two authors:

> In their work, both Guillaume Dustan and Érik Rémès conceive of a world of gay masculinity that is in no way limited by the received knowledge of the past and one that takes into account, in one way or another, the derailing of a straightforward process of liberation over time because of the AIDS crisis. [...] Both Dustan and Rémès internalize

and reinscribe their seropositivity in their writing, and each uses the writing as a vehicle, not for some sort of self-pity, but rather for an exploration of what it means to be in their position, to write from their position, and to go on from their position in the age of AIDS.

(75)

Whilst over 20 years have passed since the introduction of combination antiretroviral therapies and almost a decade since they were first approved as PrEP by the FDA in the USA, both developments having hopefully kick-started the end of what Schehr called the "age of AIDS", Rémès's and Dustan's approaches to sex and promiscuity, as well as their eroticisation of bodily fluids (whether carrying HIV or not), is still helpful for framing the processes of sexual self-fashioning that, as we've already seen in the previous chapter, have been taking place at last since the 1970s, shaping gay masculinities and sexual politics on the way. Whilst those processes of sexual self-invention—inseparable as they had been from Gay Liberation politics—were indeed "derailed" by the AIDS crisis and receded, as a result, into less visible subcultural niches such as the ones narrated in Dustan's and Rémès's novels—where they often evolved into queer forms of masculinity, biosociality, and kinship mediated by HIV itself (Dean 2009)—today, and thanks to antiretrovirals, they are re-emerging again, this time decoupled from the virus and the spectre of AIDS, in what Evangelos Tziallas (2019) called "the return of the repressed". In our geo-corporeal context, one in which HIV infection can be both chemically managed and chemically prevented, the sexual experiments with bodily integrity and subjectivity that had sustained queer lives and queer utopias in the 1970s only to then become associated with queer deaths and queer nostalgia in the two decades that followed, seem to have come back into the gay subcultural mainstream, where they have started to facilitate, amongst others, the popularisation of "pig" masculinities and their continued troubling—as we've seen in Rémès and Dustan—of the idealised conditions of male embodiment that have secured the survival of the autonomous liberal subject of Western philosophy. In so doing, they invite us to reconsider the continued dominance of the latter as a paradigm, and the role played by fields such as anatomy, medicine, and visual culture in its construction, mediation, reproduction, and undoing. Whilst critical projects of this kind already have an established, valued, and important tradition in feminist theory, I would like to approach them from within the space of gay masculinities. If masculinities themselves have been privileged by Western heteropatriarcal thought, and if the body has been relegated to the realm of the abject by bourgeois hegemony, my aim is to consider the extent to which gay "pig" sexual play and masculinities can—to paraphrase Schehr's writing on Rémès and Dustan—become a vehicle for an exploration of what it means to be a man today, to attempt to rewrite masculinity as a man, and, on the way, to consider where masculinities can go on from here, as well as the allegiances those sexual practices and forms of self-identification may foster across the gender and sexuality spectra.

One of the main features of gay "pig" masculinities is, as I've been arguing, their refashioning of the male body as a porous, penetrable body. One of the artists who has become known for exploring that porosity and penetrability as a medium both for the becoming-homosexual of the body and for the invention of homosexual forms of relating and kinship that went beyond the intrapsychic and interpersonal scripts (Simon and Gagnon 1986) offered by heteropatriarchal Western culture was Frank Webber. Born in New Jersey on 14 July 1929, the artists who would rename himself as Bastille left the USA for France, where he settled and where, in his 50s, he started producing a body of illustration works that, despite being produced throughout the AIDS crisis, helped define—or, at least, explore, investigate, and disseminate—the masculinities and sexual practices that would inform the late twentieth-century development of gay "pigs" and their contemporary subcultural popularity. Despite having never received the levels of critical validation and attention from main-stream art institutions that some of his own peers such as Tom of Finland have, Webber a.k.a. Bastille, remains an artist with a dedicated subcultural following. His work is characterised by what Ralf Marsault (2019) described as an "imagining of the body as being not so much a discrimi-nated anatomy but more like an on-going *technology* or interconnected agency" that "shows a critical re-appropriation of the body and its fluids, if not a metaphorical representation of the body as a fleeting self, a vecto-rial fluidity". Bastille's illustrations are populated by male figures often covered in various kinds of dirt or ripped and soiled clothes, sometimes wearing latex, sometimes donning helmets or various other metallic acces-sories that give the works a certain futuristic flair. Whatever they're wearing, Bastille's men are commonly connected to one another either through their own bodily appendages or via a series of technical contrap-tions such as metal chains and bars or rubber tubes, which plug together their bodily orifices in a myriad of permutations of mouths, dicks, and asses. Even in those instances in which his figures are not depicted in such connected ways, their bodies plugged into a collective hydraulic circuit of internal bodily matter—sperm, urine, faeces, saliva—bodily fluids are still often seen dripping down their bodies onto dirty, filthy floors on which they mix.[4]

Deeply influenced by Bastille, French photographer and pornographer Marc Martin released, in 2017, a book of some of his and Bastille's works, accompanied by a variety of written pieces—some more personal, others more critical—authored by artists and academics. In the book, aptly enti-tled *Schwein: Bastille Traces*, Martin claimed that "Instead of seeing the decline of humanity in his [Bastille's] most explicitly scatological works, what I unearthed was the notion of sharing, of letting go, of indulging into

Figure 2.1 Marc Martin, "Cul de Sac", 2007.
Courtesy of the artist.

the most beautiful enjoyment with, and of, another" (Martin 2017, n.p.).
One of Martin's works included in the book—*Cul de Sac* (2007)—
exemplifies the influence that Bastille has had in the aesthetic and iconography of the French photographer.

In it, just like in the works of the earlier American artist, a space associated with dirty underground places and low excretory bodily functions serves as the set where the insides of faceless male bodies are plugged into other bodies, assembled to create a closed circuitry of matter usually deemed to be excessive and private, here presented as that which transgresses the bodily boundaries of individuals to sustain an erotics that violates their individual autonomy. Writing about how despotic formations discipline bodies through an overcoding of the face, Deleuze and Guattari claimed that "if human beings have a destiny, it is rather to escape the face, to dismantle the face and facializations, to become imperceptible, to become clandestine" (Deleuze and Guattari 1987, 171). Deprived of a face, that surface on which modern subjectivisation and significance play themselves out to produce and regulate all relations of identity and alterity (Deleuze and Guattari 1987), Martin's figure in *Cul de Sac* renounces the centre of gravity of the hegemonic apparatus of capture of the modern autonomous subject. Without a face to at once anchor and stand in for their subjecthood, the facelessness of the figure is depersonalising. Depersonalised, its existence becomes actualised in and through the de-individualised excreta that circulate in and out of its fragmented body-cum-machine, in a smooth circuitry of matter and productive desire with no predefined end.

Commenting on Bastille in Marc Martin's book, Rudi Bleys noted the ways in which the erotic imaginary of the US artist was not only concerned with sexual practices and pleasures but also with the nature of the body and, by extension, the nature of subjectivity itself:

> The prominence of tubes, catheters, and, inseparable from these, bodily fluids (sweat, saliva, sperm, urine, faeces) reveal an eroticism also, that is distinct from penetrative genital sex [...] and converges around circuitry and mutual exchange instead. The human body's singularity is lifted in a play towards fusion and depersonalisation, alternating between the realm of the animalistic on the one hand, the realm of the machine-line on the other. The radical validation of bodily creases and orifices as well as of its products is pushed as a via regia towards male-to-male intimacy [...].
>
> (Bleys 2017, n.p.)

Bleys's argument is useful here, for it also resonates with the conception of bodily fluids that emerged out of Dustan's and Rémès's autofictional novels. Just like Jean-François Lyotard's concept of the "Great Ephemeral Skin", which the French philosopher infamously introduced in *Libidinal Economy* (1993), these are plastic, polysemic, polyvalent, unframed, unsedimented bodies, sets of parts and labyrinthine pathways, flows, folds, crevices, tubes, roads, valleys, and apertures through which matter flows to implode the theatricality of inside and outside, of interior and exterior, of self and other. They are arrangements of unstratified desire, of thirst or hunger without lack, of circulation as libidinal hydraulics. In them, in those bodies such as they are disassembled in their individual unity for as long as they are connected in such a multiplicity of ways, "there is no hole, no interior, no sanctuary to respect" (Lyotard 1993, 22).

The sexual arrangements of bodies seen in the examples I've given thus far—I argue—pose a threat to the hegemony of bourgeois conceptions of the body, a threat that is not only material (in that it may be seen to, *in extremis*, lead to the actual annihilation of particular bodies) but is also political (in that it forces us to reconceptualise the very male body that has served as the model for the liberal autonomous subject by framing the scope and limits of political agency, that helped create and sustain the public/private divide, and that thus ultimately grounded modern European notions of citizenship). It is on the progressive historical development of that idealised autonomous body and on the ways in which gay "pig" sex and masculinities may threaten it that I would like to focus for the remainder of this chapter.

In her book *Embodying the Monster*, Margrit Shildrick (2002) noted that "In terms of modernist ontology, epistemology and ethics, the ideal parameters of thought and action in the social world point to an inviolable self/body that is secure, distinct, closed and autonomous" (51). The autonomous subject Shildrick makes reference to emerged in modern European thought as both the privileged agent of politics and the basic—self-contained and indivisible—unit of "civilised" society. Compelled to constitute itself by emerging out of *"his* self-incurred immaturity" (Kant 1991, 54, my emphasis), the modern autonomous subject was thus defined as the outcome of a process of teleological unfolding that saw *man* differentiating *him*self from pre-modern "savages", children and women—all embodiments of the uncivilised and primitive "state of nature" (Elias 2000; Federici 2004; Rasmussen 2011)—by virtue of *his* ability to reason. This process was understood to be necessary both for the emancipation of *man*kind and *men*'s participation in political life (Kant 1991), and for the development and protection of the social contract between the sovereign and *his* subjects, which would grant the latter access to civil and political rights (Hobbes 1996). As Claire Rasmussen (2011) wrote:

> If autonomy is both the condition of boundaries and the process by which boundaries are drawn between the self and the world, it also implies the necessary boundaries of the political sphere. Autonomy becomes the precondition for participation in the democratic polity since the right to self-governance is dependent on the judged capacity of that individual to govern herself.
>
> (xii)

That co-dependence of a modern autonomous polity and a modern autonomous subject required the development of a whole set of disciplinary discourses, institutions and techniques of the body (Maus 1973) aimed at both governing the autonomy of individual men and at surveilling and managing those—"savages", children and women—who were seen to exist in a state of nature due to the ways in which they were thought to lack the ability to exercise reason and self-control and, thus, be unable to control the urges and bodily rhythms that men were, in turn, supposedly able to manage through an ethics of the self *qua* an ethics of the "proper body" (Kristeva 1982; Theweleit 1987; Creed 1993; Shildrick 2002). For that reason, the body became one of the main targets of those disciplinary apparatuses—from talk therapies to psychiatric asylums, schools and prisons to settler missions and hospitals—that aimed to produce "proper" subjects, "proper" citizens, and efficient workers (Rabinbach 1992; Foucault 1995, 2003; Federici 2004;

Rasmussen 2011). As a site of uncivilised urges, appetites, and desires, one's animal and inhuman tendencies had to be tamed by an ethos of mind over body, a form of civilised self-production through self-control and self-differentiation from the external world, which Freud thought to be essential for the development of the ego and for one's inclusion as an active participant in society (Freud 1962; see also Marcuse 1966). Yet, of course, that was a process only truly and fully available to white European men, separate as they were thought to be, both materially and psychologically, from both the "savagery" of pre-modern and colonised societies and the overwhelming "natural" cycles that marked women's bodies (Gatens 1996; Federici 2004; Ahuja 2017; Beistegui 2018). As Robyn Longhurst (2001) put it:

> Of course, in "reality", both men and women "have" (or rather, "are") bodies. The difference is that men are widely considered to be able to seek and speak universal knowledge, unencumbered by the limitations of a material body placed in a particular material context whereas women are thought to be bound to the desires of their fleshy, "natural" bodies placed in time and space. In western culture, while white men may have presumed that they could transcend their embodiment (or at least have their bodily needs met by others) by seeing the body as little more than a container for the pure consciousness it held inside, this was not allowed for women, blacks, homosexuals, people with disabilities, the elderly and children. This masculinist separation of minds from bodies, and the privileging of minds over bodies, remains a dominant conception in western culture although it has been challenged.
>
> (13)

Longhurst's quote is a stark reminder not only of how the Western civilising process that delivered us the modern body was a deeply phallogocentric epistemic and political project with very material consequences and roots in the first European colonial projects (McClintock 1995; Federici 2004; Ahuja 2017), but also of how its ideology still permeates twenty-first-century societies, despite decades of being challenged from within academia as well as feminist, Black, and queer liberation movements. Such challenges notwithstanding, the white bourgeois male body is still today commonly taken as the model for wholesomeness, for a body that is whole, self-contained, uncorrupted, unpolluted, clean. It is also a kind of body—or, better, a kind of ideological body schema—that has been and continues to be produced, maintained, and guided by moral and political systems that, in depending on autonomous subjects grounded in autonomous and self-contained bodies, polices, controls, and regulates all kinds of matter that are seen to be displaced or out of place—that is, everything that could be seen to threaten the integrity of the body and, by extent, the autonomy of the subject. As Nick Land put it in his book on Georges Bataille:

> Knowing that its community with nature sucks it into psychosis and death mankind valorizes its autonomy, whilst cursing the tidal desires that tug it towards fusional dissolution. Morality is thus the distilled imperative to autonomous integrity, which brands as evil the impulse to skinless contact and the merging of bodies.
>
> (Land 1992, 124)

The ways in which autonomy and wholeness have been *conditio sine qua non* for the development of the modern subject and *his* active participation in both the polity and the workforce through the recognition of *his* rights as a citizen of the state was deeply influential in the changes that, as already discussed in the previous chapter, have taken place in mainstream LGBTQ+ politics in the aftermath of the AIDS crisis. That is particularly evident in what concerns gay men and their shift away from a liberation agenda towards a rights-based political project devised under the conditions of the social contract, whereby rights ought to only ever be granted to bodies who fully meet the criteria for citizenship, including criteria for biological and sexual citizenship (see Croce 2018). A recent example of that appeal to autonomy and bodily integrity can be seen in the rhetoric deployed by Pete Buttigieg, mayor of South Bend, Indiana, and candidate to the Democratic Party nomination in the 2020 US presidential elections, in his proposed LGBTQ+ policy white paper aptly titled "Becoming Whole" (Buttigieg2020 2019). Whilst a discussion of the usefulness or political value of the specific policies proposed by Buttigieg is beyond the scope of this book, attending to the rhetorical register through which they were articulated as campaign promises is enlightening in the context of what I've been arguing. In that 18-page document released with the subtitle "A New Era for LGBTQ+ Americans", one that includes the word "country" no fewer than 20 times, the Democratic presidential candidate hopeful, himself an out gay man and military veteran, exemplifies the ways in which mainstream LGBTQ+ politics, in the USA at least, have succumbed, in their imagining of the politically possible, to the oedipalised and oedipalising structures that created and still sustain the modern masculinist and phallogocentric nation-state. If "[the] creation and maintenance of metaphors is [...] an inherently political project with material effects and consequences" (Cresswell 1997, 334), in the context of the history of modern European political thought, one in which the idealised image of a unified and coherent male body has served as metaphor for an equally unified body politic (Gatens 1996), Buttigieg's framing of his vision for LGBTQ+ politics under the image of wholeness was not accidental. It is, after all, only through such becoming-whole that, to him, gay men will no longer have to "choose between the person they [love] and the country they [love]" (Buttigieg2020 2019, 1). Being whole—that is, being one indivisible autonomous body—is a prerequisite for full citizenship and a condition for one to enjoy the political and civil rights that come with being granted membership of the state. It is only by being "whole" that gay men will be able not only to love their country but—most importantly, as Buttigieg's rhetoric highlights—to be loved in return. Through that, they will be able to "push [their] country to be what it has promised to be all along" (1), and thus tie the knot that makes their own survival dependent on the survival of the oedipal institutions of the state, its laws, and its morals. If the pursuit of unity, wholeness, and self-restraint have sustained the formation of the modern subject through a disciplining of the body (Foucault 1978, 1995; Freeman 2019), it has also guided its later development into the self-administering, self-entrepreneurial subject of neoliberalism, the very subject invoked in Buttigieg's "Becoming Whole" (Hengehold 2007; Cornwall 2016; Lindisfarne and Neale 2016; Beistegui 2018). As noted in his proposal to launch what he named the "We Belong National Mentorship Program" for LGBTQ+ youths, a Buttigieg presidency would "call on leaders in the public and private sectors to mentor LGBTQ+ youth and strengthen the resources, self-love, and sense of belonging they need to thrive" (Buttigieg2020 2019, 12).

Always-already oedipalised, the thriving subject of modern and contemporary history has to reject everything that could be seen to threaten the divide between *him*self and the world outside *him*. The way to do so is through hygiene: by—in a very literal sense—keeping *his* shit to *him*self (or at least to dispose of it in private). As Gay Hawkins put it in her book *The Ethics of Waste*, the relationship we establish with our waste is central to the development of our own subjectivity:

> Waste doesn't just threaten the self in the horror of abjection, it also *constitutes* the self in the habits and embodied practices through which we decide what is connected to us and what isn't. [...] This is why styles of waste disposal are also styles of self and why waste management, in all its cultural mutations, is fundamental to the practice of subjectivity. It is part of the way in which we cultivate sensibilities and sensual relations with the world; part of the way we move things out of our life and impose ethical and aesthetic order.
>
> (Hawkins 2006, 4)

The production of the modern bourgeois subject thus relies on what Tim Cresswell (1997) called a "geography of normality", a production of normative subjectivities "constructed through various acts of territoriality, in which there is a place for everything"—a right place—and where "nonconformity to spatial order results in dirt" (340). Just like the modern male body—idealised as whole, indivisible and autonomous—has served as the metaphoric model for the formation of the modern nation-state, the territorial claims that are made with regards to what belongs to an individual body and to what belongs to the body of the state—that is, to their "geography of normality"—are also defined negatively against "metaphors of displacement" (334): weeds, disease, plague, dirt, or excrement, all of which need to be managed or controlled so that the body is guaranteed its propriety and right of place (342; see also Kristeva 1982; Douglas 2002). In Georges Bataille's words, "[the] place for filth is in the dark, where looks cannot reach it. Secrecy is the condition for sexual activity, just as it is the condition for the performance of the natural functions" (1991, 62).

In pursuing wholeness via an enforcement of the boundaries between the body and its outside, Western modernity idealised the autonomous subject as a body that abides by the principles of the classical aesthetic order, harmony, and proportion that were popularised in art by the likes of Giorgio Vasari and his *Lives of the Most Eminent Painters, Sculptors & Architects* (1912–1914), and turned, more or less explicitly, into universalising metaphors or analogues for "manly" morality and temper in the works of Enlightenment critics and philosophers such as Johannes Winckelmann ([1755–1756] 2013), Immanuel Kant ([1790] 2007), or Friedrich Schiller ([1795] 2004), whose works informed the parallel development of modern masculinities, aesthetics, and liberal governmentality (Mosse 1996; Hengehold 2007). As Peter Stallybrass and Allon White (1986) noted:

> [The] classical body was far more than an aesthetic standard or model. It structured, from the inside as it were, the characteristically 'high' discourses of philosophy, statecraft, theology and law, as well as literature, as they emerged from the Renaissance. In the classical discursive body were ended those regulated systems which were closed, homogenous, monumental, centred and symmetrical.
>
> (22)

It is, then, no surprise that such a paradigm of wholeness also dominated, as ideal, not only European art but also medicine, as far as their conceptualisations of the body were concerned. As Anthea Callen (2018) has shown, the parallel development of art academies and anatomy theatres in early modern Europe was marked by a privileging of classical ideals of order whereby it was the harmonious relationship of parts and whole that granted the perfect body—always-already male—not just beauty but also health. And yet, Callen (2018) contended, even if "the canon of ideal human proportion represented universal man: man as the image in microcosm of the order of the universe" (14), the pursuit of that ideal was always somewhat doomed to fail, producing images of masculinity that tended to be—if anything—deeply unstable. Whereas the idealised body was always ideologically whole, the nature of anatomy classes, whether in art academies or in anatomy theatres, required the breaking of the body into various constituent parts and, because of that, threatened the ideal-ised stability and wholeness of the standard body. Equally, even if the idealised body was always white, bourgeois, educated, European, and male, the dead bodies being dissected on anatomy tables and the living nude models being drawn in academies were always, due to moral and religious imperatives, bodies of the lower classes—labourers, criminals, migrants, etc. "What, then", Callen asked, "is the status of an ideal or paradigmatic white Western masculinity if its physical and aesthetic per-fection were embodied in the physique of a classed and racialised male 'other' [...]?" (20).

That tight enmeshment of the idealised body of the modern European autonomous subject and its others was also famously highlighted by Mikhail Bakhtin. In *Rabelais and his World*, his landmark study of gro-tesque realism, Bakhtin (1984) has shown how early modern European thought had to define the ideal classical body against the grotesque body which, in embodying everything the former was not—the low, debased, popular, chaotic, earthly, extreme, monstrous, material, fecund, formless, ambivalent, unfinished, transgressive, abusive, open, disproportionate, filthy, and so on—helped define the ideal negatively, that is, by exclusion (see also Jeanneret 2001; Morgan 2016). The two, in having to always be thought together and against one another, became a regular feature in European thought, aesthetics, ritual, and culture at large, one being reas-suringly moral and aspirational, the other—its other—triggering feelings of awe, fascination and life-threatening horror. Inseparable as Dr Jekyll and Mr Hyde, the classical and grotesque body represent the two sides of the dialectics of the modern body as it has unfolded, surely even if at an uneven pace, since the Renaissance.

In the modern dialectical push and pull between ideal-and-whole and failed-and-broken body, two figures would eventually emerge and main-tain a continuous presence in our thought and culture, warning modern subjects against the dangers of surrendering to the filthy, debased, formless realms of existence. Those figures are the monster and the pig. As creatures that helped define the inhuman territory of all that which falls outside the idealised universal male subject of European history and politics, monsters and pigs are also—simultaneously and for that very same reason—figures to which the body of the ideal man is deeply indebted through a process of co-constitutive negation. Derived from the Latin etymons for both "to show" (*monstrare*) and "to warn" (*monere*),

> [...] the monster shows the unpredictability of categories, bodies, nar-ratives and lives. It does not simply disrupt, undermine and shift, but also reveals its own constitutive role in embodiment, where bodily integrity means living with others in the self, as well as with other in what we might call outside the self.
>
> (Hellstrand *et al.* 2018, 145)

Just like the monster—multiple, obscene, leaky, and constitutive of the modern subject as its other (Shildrick 2002)—so too did the pig become a matter of increasing concern in the long historical unfolding of that which we've come to know as "modernity". Both celebrated as sources of material sustenance and reviled for their wallowing in their own filth, pigs have always been—just like monsters—ambivalent creatures, what Stallybrass and White (1986) described, following Edmund Leach (1989), as "creatures of the threshold" (47):

> Mixing faeces and food, human and animal, human skin and animal hide, the household and the farmyard and the field, the pig also lived to die—unlike sheep, cows and chickens, the pig was useful only to each and, proverbially, only became valuable when dead.
>
> (Stallybrass and White 1986, 47)

If the body of the autonomous subject had been idealised as a body with clearly defined and impermeable boundaries, pigs would eventually become metaphorical anchors for modern contagion anxieties, not only because of their intimate closeness with excrement and all manner of filth, but also due to the ways in which, despite all of that, they did still resemble humans—their skin being human-like, for instance—and had been traditionally kept on our own doorstep as food sources. Neither pets nor wild animals, pigs were an ambivalent something-in-between, creatures that had historically inhabited the thresholds of the grids we developed to classify the world in its relationship to us (Leach 1989). Thus, and as part of wider processes of sanitation and hygiene that were implemented in tandem with the development of bourgeois hegemony, the presence of pigs in the fast expanding cities of industrial modernity would come to be seen as dangerous and associated with unclean slums—horrifying threats to the emerging bourgeois forms of "proper" embodiment and subjectivity. As Stallybrass and White (1986) asked, "To have nothing in common with pigs—was not that the aim of every educated bourgeois subject—to get as far away from the smell of the pigsty as possible?" (52).

Bringing filth and excrement to the threshold of the human, confusing the boundaries between inside and outside, between human and animal, the pig forced the developing bourgeois subject to confront his own antithesis up close—always dangerously too close. In so doing, it became a popular metaphor to characterise the others of the autonomous subject—the poor, the criminal, the nomads, the diseased, the colonised—and to guide the bourgeois organisation of urban life through quintessentially modern institutions and practices of education, policing, hygiene, and sanitation aimed at keeping pigs and what they stood for at bay—the danger they posed to the maintenance and containment of the "proper" body and of its clearly demarcated boundaries (Stallybrass and White 1986). Those practices would include the formulation and promotion of "codes elaborated for the management of the body's products: urine, feces, mucus, saliva, and wind" (Greenblatt 1982, 2), human excreta that would remind us of the porosity of our own bodies and of the functional limits of the skin understood as boundary in such body schema. From this discussion, it becomes clear how the production and maintenance of the bourgeois autonomous subject in its spatial embodied dimensions as a "geography of normality" depended on a clear distinction and policing of the boundaries between inside and outside, between the body as a sacred temple and the world as the realm of filth, profanity, and disease. If, as Bernhard Siegert (2012) noted, "[every] culture starts with the introduction of distinctions" (8), bourgeois culture started with a distinction between cleanliness and uncleanliness, which sustained, in the bourgeois imaginary, the difference between health and disease and, thus, the difference between life and death. In the words of Zygmunt Bauman:

> Hygiene is [...] the product of the deconstruction of mortality into an infinite series of individual causes of death, and of the struggle against death into an infinitely extendable series of battles against specific diseases. This deconstruction being an attempt to exhaust the inexhaustible, an attempt doomed from the start and thus bound to suppress the knowledge of its own impossibility merely to be able to continue [...]. Hence the obsession, the tension, the hysteria that surrounds hygienic concerns and activities. The dirt [...], bacteria, viruses, putrefying and thus surely toxic substances, all arouse intense fear and *disgust* (that emotional corollary of desire to create and maintain distance between oneself and offending object), themselves surrogate outlets for the great metaphysical horror of mortality. Such irrational emotions, and the irrational practices they trigger are, again, the other side of the modern rationalization of death.
>
> (Bauman 1992, 155, emphasis in original)

In functioning as gates or thresholds to the insides of the human body, bodily orifices are—to once again quote Siegert (2012)—"operators of symbolic, epistemic, and social processes that, with help from the difference between inside and outside, generate spheres of law, secrecy, and privacy" (9; see also Siegert 2015). As such, they have had to be monitored and regulated in the name of bodily integrity and autonomy. It is there, on that threshold, and as a disruptor of the clear demarcation and enforcement of boundaries between self and other, that gay "pigsex" operates its experiments with the body and subjectivity through a monstrous embrace of bodily fluids. To paraphrase Stallybrass and White's discussion of the symbolic apparatus that developed around nonhuman pigs throughout modernity, gay "pigs" offer us a contemporary example of what I'd like to call *masculinities of the threshold*.

Given what I've been discussing, it is unsurprising that the relationship between masculinity and bodily fluids has always been a difficult one, a source of anxiety concerning manliness and the threats posed to it by the circulation of matter in and out of the body. In her study of pissing figures in art and literature, for instance, Patricia Simons (2009) noted how early modern constructions of masculinity were as much based on the mechanics of penile penetration as they were on the liquidity of the fluids emitted by the penis, often leading to "visual metaphors [that] presented manliness in ways that were often humorous, usually public, and always assertive" (Simons 2009, 331). Being a regular presence in early modern art and visual culture (Lebensztejn 2017), pissing figures provided the upper classes with a morally sanctioned form of iconography that publicly alluded to ejaculation—that is, to the sexual climax of male masculinity—albeit vicariously through images of urinating children, young gods, and even animals. "Because the upper classes relieved themselves outside the realm of visual representation", Simons (2009) writes, "instead either charmingly idyllic babes or marginal people and dogs [...] perform quintessential acts of their sex captured in unremitting detail" (335). What is interesting about Simons's argument is that the act of urination was understood as a quintessentially masculine act because women "'don't piss,' that is, they cannot do it properly, in the manly way, because they do not stand up" (333). Often standing for semen itself via what Simons called a "semen-otic system of fluids", pissing and, by that analogy, ejaculation both signalled masculinity because they were understood as "bold, assertive acts that cast fluid far from the male body" (340). Yet, and as further evidence of how the monstrously ambivalent and obscene has always accompanied the modern pursuit of the classical ideal as its constitutive other, the metaphorical metamorphosis of water or wine into urine, of urine into semen, and of urine-as-semen back into drinking water, commonly found in humorous literature and dramatised in public fountains composed of pissing figures, was often read as risqué sexual wit by early modern Europeans:

> While some jokes relied on wordplay, actual fountains literalized the aqueous transformation. Pissing putti appear on ancient reliefs, while a phallic fountain survives from Pompeii's house of the Vetti in which water flowed from the tip of an ephebe's large, erect penis. Anyone drinking the cool water gushing through the marble phallus was put in the literal position of ingesting from a compliant ephebe, thereby enjoying the thrill of nearly overcoming the ancient taboo against oral sex.

> (351)

In considering a figure such as Guido Reni's *Drinking Bacchus* (c.1622), the recycling or transubstantiation of wine into urine and—more

Figure 2.2 Guido Reni, "Drinking Bacchus", *c.*1622. Oil on canvas, 72 × 56 cm. Courtesy of the Gemäldegalerie Alte Meister, Staatliche Kunstsammlungen Dresden.

Photo: Hans-Peter Klut.

troublingly—the possibility of its reversal, i.e. of urine transubstantiating back into wine, was kept under control first by being associated with the not-yet-adult, not-yet-matured figure of a child yet to become an adult.

That licence granted by the depiction of an urinating boy lacking adult self-control—or, better, lacking the self-control associated with oedipalisation into adulthood—was then maximised by the acknowledgement that the boy-child was, in fact, a child god and, thus, twice removed from the constraints placed upon human masculinity and its socially sanctioned regime of visual representations. After all, as feminist art historians have argued, naked deities or allegorical figures were allowed throughout early modernity exactly because they weren't actual people and were thus exempt from the moral codes governing image-making. They were also a great excuse for men to come together in front of naked bodies, whether male or female, as a legitimate form of homosociality that oftentimes masked its underlying homoeroticism (Salomon 1996, 1998; Pollock 1999; Davis 1992, 2010). By inhabiting the space of scatological humour rather than the space of the horrifying monstrous I've discussed above, figures such as Reni's *Drinking Bacchus* got away with symbolic murder, by wittily alluding to that which could threaten the wholeness and cohesion of the modern European subject in the early stages of its development, that is, the kinship between the liquids we expel and the liquids we consume. Through humour rather than horror, early modern pissing figures deflected having to take seriously the threat posed by the Mr Hyde of their Dr Jekyll.

What those figures have also come to show, whether in their early modern versions or in their contemporary iterations—of which there are many—is that it was not so much the formlessness of male bodily fluids or even their circulation that threatened ideals of masculinity but, rather, the *direction* of their flow. As Elizabeth Grosz noted in *Volatile Bodies*:

> Part of the process of phallicizing the male body, of subordinating the rest of the body to the valorized functioning of the penis, with the culmination of sexual activities occurring, ideally at least, in sexual penetration and male orgasm, involves the constitution of the sealed-up, impermeable body. Perhaps it is not after all flow in itself that a certain phallicized masculinity abhors but the idea that flow moves or can move in two-way or indeterminable directions that elicit horror, the possibility of being not only an active agent in the transmission of flow but also a passive receptacle.
>
> (Grosz 1994, 200–201)

Following both Simons and Grosz, it was not just the possibility but the high likelihood that the male body could function as a receptacle for bodily fluids entering it through its orifices that threatened the ideological foundations of the male body as it would come to be conceived throughout the long history of European modernity. Amounting to a threat to the autonomy of the male body by emasculating it, the intake of bodily fluids would also, by extension, threaten the autonomy of the modern European subject and, by analogy, the autonomy of the developing nation-state and of its polity. Yet, despite the fact that early modern Europeans were able to use humour and wit to defer the fears of self-obliterating male penetrability and permeability—of the porosity of the male body—the horrors of dephallicisation would eventually come to be embodied in the figure of the homosexual, always-already effeminate and emasculated by virtue of the openness of his body to the bodies and bodily fluids of others. It was for that very reason that Elizabeth Grosz saw in the figure of the penetrated male a way out of hegemonic, phallic masculinity. In being a "body that is permeable, that transmits in a circuit, that opens itself up rather than seals itself off, that is prepared to respond as well as to initiate", the homosexual body can become a starting point from where to engage in "a quite radical rethinking of male sexual morphology" (Grosz 1994, 201).

It is in relation to this long history of European ideals of autonomous masculine embodiments and subjectivities, in their philosophical, political, scientific, and social dimensions, that I situate contemporary "pig" masculinities. As *masculinities of the threshold*, gay "pigs" ground their masculinity in their holes. Unwholly, they constitute themselves through a radical openness to the bodily fluids of others, an openness that troubles the private/public, inside/outside, and mind/body distinctions that have sustained European culture and politics, from early modern fascinations with monsters and bodily fluids, all the way through the development of the educational, scientific, medical, and legal institutions of liberalism, and culminating with the twenty-first-century paradigms of the self-administering, self-entrepreneurial neoliberal subject who knows and speaks their truth, who works on themselves and their bodies, who self-cares, who is healthy and—most importantly—who realises their potential and succeeds. For even if, as men, gay "pigs" do certainly still benefit from what Raewyn Connell (2005) called the "patriarchal dividend", in their reframing of their masculinity through an excessive and unproductive economy of bodily fluids, gay "pigs" pose a risk to hegemonic forms of masculine embodiment and to their perceived universality and stability. For, as Claire Rasmussen (2011) stressed, "bodies produced by relationships of power can, in turn, challenge the very power relations that make them possible" (138).

Consider *Fuck Holes 3*. Directed by Max Sohl for Treasure Island Media and released in 2015, the video is a hardcore extravaganza of sperm being taken in by all kinds of body orifices. Being the first Treasure Island Media production to feature not only cis gay men but also a trans and a cis woman, the video opens with a quote from its director that simply states "Sometimes a hole is just a hole". Composed of six scenes and a bonus sequence, *Fuck Holes 3* levels the sexual playing field of gay porn by presenting the bottoming models—whether cis gay men, trans women or cis women—as peers in a heroic undertaking. The studio's webstore describes it in the following manner:

> Keep an open mind. FUCK HOLES 3 is unlike anything you have ever seen because it's never been done before. Look at the above 5 holes closely. I bet you can't even tell which are gay, trans or straight.

> FUCK HOLES 3.
> Sometimes a Hole is Just a Hole.

Whilst the promotional text that accompanied the release of the video did obviously overlook the established history of different genders and body types that had already been featured together in independent queer porn, *Fuck Holes 3* was still, when it comes to porn aimed at cis gay male viewers and to Treasure Island Media's catalogue in particular, innovative in its inclusion of trans and female bodies. The video's most intense scene as far as bodily fluids are concerned—cum, in this case—is scene one, titled "Fucking Crazy". Opening with a close-up shot of a bottle filled with a white liquid over which the titles "110 loads" are overlaid, a male voice-over reminiscent of early US TV documentary films is heard saying "Ladies and gentlemen, the story you're about to see is true. The names have been changed to protect the innocent". In the scene, bottoming model Ryan Cummings is set up for a gangbang involving 18 tops in a bedroom in which a digital screen had been placed to serve as what the promo text calls a "digital load taking counter". Crucially, as the promotional narrative continues, Cummings had turned up with a "bottled filled with 110 loads of cum", which were, halfway through the scene, eventually injected into his rectum before other tops continued to penetrate him. With so much sperm being directly ejaculated or injected into his rectum, and with the thrusting movements of all the penetrations making a lot of it be squirted back out onto the bed and the bodies of the models, the smell was, according to the same text written by Sohl, so intense that "a third of them [the tops] went running for the hills [...]. As one guy said do me afterward—'*I didn't sign up for that*'". What I find interesting about the—some would reasonably say—"extreme" nature of this particular scene is the way in which the abject, disgusting smell of such high amounts of ejaculate was presented as having become too much for some, thus adding to the transgressive authorial aesthetics that's been so central to Treasure Island Media's (TIM) brand identity. But not only that, for the scene also portrays Ryan Cummings, with his sexual athleticism, as the hero of the fantasy. Cummings is a man who is eager and can endure, a superman whose masculinity is actualised not by virtue of his penis, which is either covered by a jockstrap or, when visible, overshadowed by his hole—his truly muscular organ and thus, by that logic, the one that confers him his masculinity. After all, Cummings does not only ask for "it" throughout the whole scene, but he can also visibly take it—take it "like a man".

It is in the context of that first scene and of how the heroic masculinity of the bottom is portrayed in it as a function of his porosity to other men's sperm that the logics of the representationally innovative scenes four and five can be better understood—innovative, I should once again stress, for Treasure Island Media's standards and market. Scene four, "Queer. Not for Everyone", stars cis man Rob Yaeger as the top and trans woman Sami Price as the bottom in a sexual pas-de-deux that, obviously, culminates with Price being "bred" by Yaeger, a self-described "omnisexual porn guy" (Yaeger 2015). Calling her "an inspiration" in the video's promotional text, Sohl went on to write of Price that "If the sight of her gorgeous and stunning tits are going to throw you off don't be fooled. She wants the load as much as any other TIM fuck hole".

Scene five, in turn, entitled "Straight. Not for Everyone", features cis woman Siouxsie Q in an intense gangbang scene, being penetrated by Gage Sin, Michael Vegas, Lucas Knight, Gavin Greene, and Jesse James, and taking cum in all her bodily orifices. Promoting the scene on the studio's webstore with claims such as "there are moments you can't even tell it's a chick getting nailed", Sohl eventually describes Siouxsie Q as "a TIM whore. She was perfect and oh my god what a fucking cumdump pig slut. Seriously".

As the title of the video, its framing by Sohl's promotional narrative, and its inclusion of trans and cis women alongside cis men in the bottoming roles highlight, there is a sense in which the figure of the hole—of a "cumdump" hole—becomes the anchor not only of the bottoming cis men's superhuman masculinities, but also the means through which the cis and trans models become admitted to the TIM crew as "TIM whore(s)" just like the others. This functional equivalence of vaginas and rectums as cum-taking orifices in *Fuck Holes 3* is also symptomatic of wider changes that have been taking place in mainstream porn thanks to twenty-first-century studios like Jockpussy, Bonus Hole Boys or FTM Fucker; the algorithmic powers of online aggregators and tube websites like PornHub; and the increasing visibility of a new generation of female-to-male (FTM) trans models such as Luke Hudson, Cyd St Vincent, James Darling or Jade Philips, who—following in the footsteps of porn icons and campaigners like Buck Angel—are making FTM masculinities increasingly visible in mainstream gay pornography and no longer the exclusive purview of niche trans fetish/voyeuristic websites, or of the more politically invested queer indie studios and websites like Courtney Trouble's Queer Porn TV or Shine Louise Houston's Pink and White Productions.

What becomes so evident with the progressive mainstreaming of FTM masculinities in gay porn is that, whilst indeed it may still trouble the expectations of some of its more "traditional" viewers, the models are filmed in the same way as their cis counterparts. Whilst established genres of trans porn aimed at straight male viewers have often presented trans feminine bodies in problematic trans-misogynistic ways under categories such as "tranny" or "shemale" porn, commonly using visual genital "reveal" techniques that construct a pedagogy of desire for trans bodies as desire for the monstrous other—always desirable and horrifying in equal measures (see Steinbock 2017)—the FTM models that we increasingly see featured in gay porn tend to be depicted as just one of the guys.[5] One of the ways in which that is done—in which cis and trans masculine bodies are equalised—is through their ability to endure relentless penetrations and/or to actively welcome cum inside their bodies, an equalisation that, as I'll discuss in more detail in the next chapter, happens thanks to a dephallicisation of masculinity. By either not having a penis or, if having one, having it often covered by a jockstrap and/or not erect, the porn bottoms that we see engaging in "pigsex"—that is, in sex in which the hermetic autonomy of the male body is violated by an often relentless inflow and exchange of bodily fluids and/or a scatological eroticisation of "filth"— actualise their masculinity by exacerbating other qualities that have historically been associated with being a man; namely, endurance, athleticism, or risk-taking (Pronger 1990; Kimmel 1997; Linneman 2000; Lancaster 2002; Connell 2005), all of which have become part of the toolbox of "pig" subjectivities.

In that context, it is because they trouble the narratives of bodily autonomy and mind over body that have sustained modern European masculinities that gay "pigs" and, most importantly, their exchanges of bodily fluids have become a source of contemporary moral, sexual, and technological panics. Whether presented as concerns for the health of gay men or advanced more straightforwardly as unabashed criticism of gay men's promiscuous "lifestyles", the increasing number of think-pieces and news stories in the tabloid press that deal with gay men's "risky" behaviours, PrEP as a "lifestyle" or "party" drug, and/or gay men's consumption of recreational drugs during sex parties facilitated by geolocating hook-up apps (see, for instance, Garcia 2013; Rojas Castro and Girard 2015; Kagan 2015; Hakim 2019; Mowlabocus 2019), all hint at the fact that most, if not all, of those behaviours pose very tangible threats to the idealised masculinities that most boys are prescribed as models for growing up as "proper" men: responsible, self-aware, self-controlled, healthy, capable of rational decision-making and of participating in the life of the polity as citizens. Despite presenting them as both a social and a public health epidemic, those recent panics about unhinged, uninhibited gay male sex in the age of antiretrovirals haven't risen out of concerns with gay men or *their* own conceptions of what living a positive and fulfilling life may be. Instead, they stem from an understandable fear of how some of gay men's sexual behaviours—or, better, how the sexual behaviours of some gay men—may not only actualise forms of masculinity that are dangerously open and porous, but—most importantly—how porous kinds of masculinity may threaten the stability of our privileged form of subjectivity by foregrounding the contingency and instability of that prescribed model body, as well as the ways in which such a body has never really been so much embodied as it has been idealised. In posing a political threat to the survival of the forms of embodied subjectivity upon which European modernity has depended, gay "pigsex" and the "pig" masculinities it catalyses seem to fall within the economy of sexual pleasure without punishment that Michel Foucault discussed in "The Gay Science", his 1978 interview with Jean Le Bitoux, conducted three years before the public onset of the AIDS crisis would call into question his own positioning in that conversation. A remarkable text in which Foucault discusses his disagreement with Deleuze over the latter's continuous embrace of the notion of desire—one which Deleuze infamously borrowed from psychoanalysis whilst radically altering its meaning to rescue it from its reduction to oedipal dynamics at the hands of the latter (see Deleuze and Guattari 1983; also Beckman 2013)—"The Gay Science" also offers some profound insights into the ways in which, for Foucault, it was not homosexuality in itself that was threatening the foundations of Western societies but, rather, the kinds of pleasures that came with it, particularly their relationship to happiness. The reality as he saw it, was not that "licentious practices" were forbidden and criminally punishable. Much to the contrary; they were being and had always been "tolerated and even accepted", even if to different degrees. After all, "prohibited practices are part of the functioning of the law that prohibits them" (Foucault and Le Bitoux 2011, 393; see also Foucault 1977). The core of the problem concerning societal reactions to homosexuality had nothing to do with gay sex in itself but with the fact that homosexuals were not paying for their pleasures with unhappiness:

> [...] this is why, in the end, I believe that two homosexuals, no, two boys who are seen leaving together to go to sleep in the same bed are tolerated. But if they wake up the next morning with a smile on their faces, if they hold hands and kiss each other tenderly and thereby affirm their happiness, then no one will forgive them. What's unbearable is not leaving in search of pleasure but waking up happy.
>
> (Foucault and Le Bitoux 2011, 393)

Fully embracing their sexuality and exploring their pleasures without paying with unhappiness or anguish afterwards—how could one live happily whilst engaging in such depraved acts?—was, however, not the only source of panic for straight society. As Foucault went on to argue in that same interview, the gay sexual subcultures that had been emerging in the USA during the 1970s—the clones—were not so much sustaining the phallocratic regime of Western society but, instead, radically troubling it by devirilising the male body through experimentations with new sexual practices that no longer required the phallic primacy of the erect penis to sustain masculinity. For Foucault, rather than being a form of "monosexual machismo", the clone subculture that developed in the decade preceding the public onset of AIDS did "not coincide with a revaluation of the male as male" (396). Instead, by exploring non-phallic forms of sexual pleasure and by developing relations that were "tender and affectionate" whilst also involving "practices of a communal sexual life", those gay men "[used] the signs of masculinity" in such a way that did not reinforce phallocentrism but did, instead, allow them to "invent themselves, [...] to make their masculine body a place for the production of extraordinarily polymorphous pleasures, detached from the valorizations of sex and particularly the male sex" (396–397).

In hindsight, one could be tempted to retort to Foucault by mentioning the epidemic that was looming at the time of that interview, one that would also end up being responsible for his own death. Indeed, the fact that AIDS was caused by a virus and not by any particular behaviours did not stop a hysteric clampdown on venues that were seen to facilitate gay promiscuity, or large groups of gay men from radically changing their behaviours in order to change their public image, turning themselves into "not-one-of-those-gays". And yet, in the twenty-first-century conjuncture of "post-crisis" (Kagan 2015, 2018), the introduction and widening access to antiretrovirals for treatment and prophylaxis of HIV, the current patterns of recreational drug consumption, the widespread use of geolocating apps for arranging sexual encounters, and the online availability of amateur and professional pornography and the ways in which it has served to both disseminate and shape gay "pig" sexual practices, seems to be leading gay men, once again, to invent themselves and to use their bodies as media through which they can explore a variety of older and new forms of pleasure and sexual sociability. Through that, they are—I argue— picking up on a history that was slowed down but—crucially—not stopped by the AIDS crisis, one in which gay men have experimented with masculinity, with what it means to be a man and to fuck like a man in ways that present masculinity not as the embodiment of an old classical and unchanging ideal—as ideological and political as it is unachievable— but as a process of testing out and playing with the plasticity of bodies and of subjectivities themselves in such ways that new stars may potentially rise on the horizon of twenty-first-century masculinities.

Notes

1

> *Nous sommes les fétichistes du jus. Le sperme nous fait bander. Nous sommes ceux pour qui la capote n'a jamais existé ou presque. Nos fantasmes et notre désir passent au-dessus d'éventuels problèmes de santé! Pour nous, l'échange de fluide est indispensable. La fécondation. Ill n'est plus question de VIH ou de MST. C'est une affaire de partage total. La sexualité*

est immédiate. Le préservatif tue l'essence même de la sexualité, qui est immédiateté. Une sexualité vraie ne peut passer par la mise à distance des condoms. Le sexe, ce sont des glaires, des sécrétions, des muqueuses à vif. La sexualité c'est du sperme, des glaires, de l'urine, de la merde. Donc le safer sex, c'est une autre chose. C'est une sexualité qui prévient. Or, justement la sexualité ne peut pas prévenir. Elle ne peut pas mettre de distance. Elle est fusion. Rien n'est plus fort pour fusionner avec son partenaire que de recevoir ou donner son sperme. Les donneurs ressentent un sentiment total de possession. Une partie d'eux-mêmes, et pas des moindres, est en l'autre, comme une partie de leur âme. Les receveurs gardent le foutre chaud en souvenir de leur amant et de l'acte sexuel. Ils veulent le sentir en eux pour accomplir l'union. Le sperme est l'expression physique la plus puissance de l'intimité.

(Rémès 2003, 41–42).

2

J'ai arrêté de pomper mais je suis resté plié en deux, fasciné par ce que je voyais, la bite que je suçais, ces mains, ces entrejambes, tous ces corps de plus en plus indistincts qui m'entouraient. Je pouvais m'engloutir dans ce magma de mains, de bites, de bouches. Je pouvais me mettre à ne plus rien en avoir à foutre de savoir à qui appartenait quoi, qui était gros, vieux, moche, contagieux. Je pouvais très ben partir, devenir fou, bouffer chaque bite qui passait, devenir une bête, ressortir des heures après, les vêtements déchirés, tachés, nu, couvert de sueur, de salive, de sperme. J'imaginais déjà comment les bourgeois du Trap me regarderaient comme une salope, une traînée. Je me suis redressé d'un bond, les larmes aux yeux. J'ai trébuché jusqu'à la sortie en retenant mon jean avec les mains. Je me suis rhabillé sur le seuil, le cœur battant, sans oser regarder devant moi.

(Dustan 1998, 22–23)

3

Corps phallus, objet de désir, forcément. Corps des autres, de mes amours: caressés, massés, aimés. Libre dans mon corps et ma sexualité. Actif et passif: pénétrant et pénétré. Et ce désir des autres, toujours présent qui me traverse et me scande. Ces corps qui se suivent et se ressemblent, s'enchâssent, s'assemblent, s'emboîtent et s'encastrent. Et lassent. Continuer inlassablement. Courir de corps en cris puisque c'est à travers eux que je m'érige. Gobant l'autre, suçant les âmes et leur enveloppe pour m'en repaître.

Et si le corps et l'agir passaient avant l'esprit et la pensée? J'ai un corps donc je suis. Un désir en chute perpétuelle qui se casse et se tue à chaque rencontre. Puis renaît et bande.

(Rémès 2003, 22)

4 Due to ongoing disputes concerning the copyrights of Bastille's works, it was not possible to obtain a licence to reproduce them in this book. However, a few examples of them are available online at www.eroticartcollection.com/Bastille_X/.

5 It is important to note here that, as Steinbock (2017) also argued, trans women have struggled more than trans men (or trans masculine bodies) for erotic visibility in and out of queer porn. Even if producing their own content or working for studios invested in a queer politics of representation, trans

women in porn still run the risk of their work being received and read through a trans-misogynistic lens. It is no surprise that, in a patriarchal society, trans men and trans masculine bodies encounter less challenges than trans women or trans feminine bodies when it comes to their participation in pornography and sex cultures, and to cultural perceptions of their bodies, sexualities, and sex work.

References

Ahuja, Neel. 2017. "Colonialism". In *Gender: Matter*, edited by Stacy Alaimo, 237–251. Farmington Hills: Macmillan Reference USA.

Bakhtin, Mikhail. 1984. *Rabelais and his World*. Bloomington: Indiana University Press.

Bataille, Georges. 1991. *The Accursed Share: An Essay on General Economy*, Volumes II and III. New York: Zone Books.

Bauman, Zygmunt. 1992. *Mortality, Immortality and Other Life Strategies*. Cambridge: Polity.

Beckman, Frida. 2013. *Between Desire and Pleasure: A Deleuzian Theory of Sexuality*. Edinburgh: Edinburgh University Press.

Beistegui, Miguel de. 2018. *The Government of Desire: A Genealogy of the Liberal Subject*. Chicago: The University of Chicago Press.

Bleys, Rudi. 2017. "Embodied Imagination". In Marc Martin, *Schwein: Bastille Traces*. Paris: Agua.

Buttigieg2020. 2019. "Becoming whole: a new era for LGBTQ+ Americans. www.washingtonblade.com/content/files/2019/10/LGBTQ-white-paper-.pdf [accessed 25 April 2020].

Callen, Anthea. 2018. *Looking at Men: Art, Anatomy and the Modern Male Body*. New Haven, CT: Yale University Press.

Connell, Raewyn. 2005. *Masculinities*. Cambridge: Polity.

Cornwall, Andrea. 2016. "Introduction: Masculinities under neoliberalism". In *Masculinities Under Neoliberalism*, edited by Andrea Cornwall, Frank G. Karioris, and Nancy Lindisfarne, 1–28. London: Zed Books.

Creed, Barbara. 1993. *The Monstrous-Feminine: Film, Feminism, Psychoanalysis*. London: Routledge.

Cresswell, Tim. 1997. "Weeds, plagues, and bodily secretions: A geographical interpretation of metaphors of displacement". *Annals of the Association of American Geographers* 87 (2): 330–345.

Croce, Mariano. 2018. "Desiring what the law desires: A semiotic view on the normalization of homosexual sexuality". *Law, Culture and the Humanities* 14 (3): 402–419.

Davis, Oliver. 2015. "Introduction: A special issue of *Sexualities*: Bareback sex and queer theory across three national contexts (France, UK, USA)". *Sexualities* 18 (1/2): 120–126.

Davis, Whitney. 1992. "Founding the closet: Sexuality and the creation of art history". *Art Documentation: Journal of the Art Libraries Society of North America* 11 (4): 171–175.

Davis, Whitney. 2010. *Queer Beauty: Sexuality and Aesthetics from Winckelmann to Freud and Beyond*. New York: Columbia University Press.

Dean, Tim. 2009. *Unlimited Intimacy: Reflections on the Subculture of Barebacking*. Chicago: The University of Chicago Press.

Deleuze, Gilles, and Félix Guattari. 1983. *Anti-Oedipus: Capitalism and Schizophrenia*. Minneapolis: University of Minnesota Press.

Deleuze, Gilles, and Félix Guattari. 1987. *A Thousand Plateaus: Capitalism and Schizophrenia*. Minneapolis: University of Minnesota Press.

Douglas, Mary. 2002. *Purity and Danger: An Analysis of Concept of Pollution and Taboo*. London: Routledge.

Dustan, Guillaume. 1998. *Plus Fort que Moi*. Paris: P.O.L.

Elias, Norbert. 2000. *The Civilizing Process: Sociogenetic and Psychogenetic Investigations*. Oxford: Blackwell.

Evans, Elliot. 2015. "Your HIV-positive sperm, my trans-dyke uterus: Anti/futurity and the politics of bareback sex between Guillaume Dustan and Beatriz Preciado". *Sexualities* 18 (1/2): 127–140.

Federici, Silvia. 2004. *Caliban and the Witch: Women, the Body, and Primitive Accumulation*. New York: Autonomedia.

Foucault, Michel. 1977. "A preface to transgression". In Michel Foucault, *Language, Counter-Memory, Practice: Selected Essays and Interviews*, edited by Donald F. Bouchard, 29–52. Ithaca, NY: Cornell University Press.

Foucault, Michel. 1978. *The History of Sexuality, Volume I: An Introduction*. New York: Pantheon Books.

Foucault, Michel. 1995. *Discipline and Punish: The Birth of the Prison*. New York: Vintage Books.

Foucault, Michel. 2003. *The Birth of the Clinic: An Archaeology of Medical Perception*. London: Routledge.

Foucault, Michel, and Jean Le Bitoux. 2011. "The gay science". *Critical Inquiry* 37: 385–403.

France 2. 2004. "Débat entre Eric Rémès et Didier Lestrade à propos du sida". Online video, 7:57. From *Tout Le Monde en Parle*, 1 May 2004. Institut National de L'Audiovisuel. www.ina.fr/video/I09034592/debat-entre-eric-remes-et-didier-lestrade-a-propos-du-sida-video.html [accessed 7 November 2019].

Freeman, Elizabeth. 2019. *Beside You in Time: Sense Methods & Queer Sociabilities in the American 19th Century*. Durham: Duke University Press.

Freud, Sigmund. 1962. *Civilization and its Discontents*. New York: W. W. Norton & Company.

Garcia, Christien. 2013. "Limited intimacy: Barebacking and the imaginary". *Textual Practices* 27 (6): 1031–1051.

Gatens, Moira. 1996. *Imaginary Bodies: Ethics, Power and Corporeality*. London: Routledge.

Girard, Gabriel. 2016. "HIV and sense of community: French gay male discourses on barebacking". *Culture, Health & Society* 18 (1): 15–29.

Greenblatt, Stephen. 1982. "Filthy rites". *Daedalus* 11 (3): 1–16.

Grosz, Elizabeth. 1994. *Volatile Bodies: Toward a Corporeal Feminism*. Bloomington: Indiana University Press.

Hakim, Jamie. 2019. "The rise of chemsex: Queering collective intimacy in neoliberal London". *Cultural Studies* 33 (2): 249–275.

Hawkins, Gay. 2006. *The Ethics of Waste: How We Relate to Rubbish*. Lanham: Rowman & Littlefield Publishers.

Hellstrand, Ingvil *et al.* 2018. "Promises, monsters and methodologies: The ethics, politics and poetics of the monstrous". *Somatechnics* 8 (2): 143–162.

Hengehold, Laura. 2007. *The Body. Problematic: Political Imagination in Kant and Foucault*. University Park, PA: The Pennsylvania State University Press.

Hobbes, Thomas. 1996. *Leviathan*. Cambridge: Cambridge University Press.

Jeanneret, Michel. 2001. *Perpetual Motion: Transforming Shapes in the Renaissance from da Vinci to Montaigne*. Baltimore: The Johns Hopkins University Press.

Kagan, Dion. 2015. "Re-crisis: Barebacking, sex panic and the logic of epidemic". *Sexualities* 18 (7): 817–837.

Kagan, Dion. 2018. *Positive Images: Gay Men and HIV/AIDS in the Popular Culture of 'Post Crisis' "*. London: I.B. Tauris.

Kant, Immanuel. 1991. "An answer to the question: 'What is enlightenment?' ". In *Immanuel Kant, Political Writings*, edited by Hans Reiss, 54–60. Cambridge: Cambridge University Press.

Kant, Immanuel. 2007. *Critique of Judgement*. Oxford: Oxford University Press.

Kimmel, Michael. 1997. *Manhood in America: A Cultural History*. New York: The Free Press.

Kristeva, Julia. 1982. *Powers of Horror: An Essay on Abjection*. New York: Columbia University Press.

Lancaster, Roger. 2002. "Subject honor, object shame". In *The Masculinity Studies Reader*, edited by Rachel Adams and David Savran, 41–68. Oxford: Blackwell Publishing.

Land, Nick. 1992. *The Thirst for Annihilation: Georges Bataille and Virulent Nihilism (an Essay in Atheistic Religion)*. London: Routledge.

Leach, Edmund. 1989. "Anthropological aspects of language: Animal categories and verbal abuse". *Anthrozoös* 2 (3): 151–165.

Lebensztejn, Jean-Claude. 2017. *Pissing Figures: 1280–2014*. New York: David Zwirner Books.

Lindisfarne, Nancy, and Jonathan Neale. 2016. "Masculinities and the lived experience of neoliberalism". In *Masculinities under Neoliberalism*, edited by Andrea Cornwall, Frank G. Karioris, and Nancy Lindisfarne, 29–50. London: Zed Books.

Linneman, Thomas. 2000. "Risk and masculinity in the everyday lives of gay men". In *Gay Masculinities*, edited by Peter Nardi, 83–100. Thousand Oaks, CA: Sage Publications.

Longhurst, Robyn. 2001. *Bodies: Exploring Fluid Boundaries*. London: Routledge.

Lyotard, Jean-François. 1993. *Libidinal Economy*. Bloomington: Indiana University Press.

Marcuse, Herbert. 1966. *Eros and Civilization: A Philosophical Inquiry into Freud*. Boston: Beacon Press.

Marsault, Ralf. 2019. "Kinship of fluids". Paper presented at *Gayness in Queer Times*, University of Brighton, 13–14 June 2019.

Martin, Marc. 2017. "Le lacher prise de Bastille". In Marc Martin, *Schwein: Bastille Traces*. Paris: Agua.

Maus, Marcel. 1973. "Techniques of the body". *Economy and Society* 2 (1): 70–88.

McClintock, Anne. 1995. *Imperial Leather: Race, Gender and Sexuality in the Colonial Context*. London: Routledge.

Morgan, Luke. 2016. *The Monster in the Garden: The Grotesque and the Gigantic in Renaissance Landscape Design*. Philadelphia: University of Pennsylvania Press.

Mosse, George. 1996. *The Image of Man: The Creation of Modern Masculinity*. New York: Oxford University Press.

Mowlabocus, Sharif. 2019. "'What a skewed sense of values': Discussing PrEP in the British press". *Sexualities*. DOI: 10.1177/1363460719872726.

Pollock, Griselda. 1999. *Differencing the Canon: Feminist Desire and the Writing of Art's Histories*. London: Routledge.

Pronger, Brian. 1990. *The Arena of Masculinity: Sports, Homosexuality, and the Meaning of Sex*. New York: St. Martin's Press.

Rabinbach, Anson. 1992. *The Human Motor: Energy, Fatigue, and the Origins of Modernity*. New York: Basic Books.

Rasmussen, Claire. 2011. *The Autonomous Animal: Self-Governance and the Modern Subject*. Minneapolis: University of Minnesota Press.

Rees-Roberts, Nick. 2008. *French Queer Cinema*. Edinburgh: Edinburgh University Press.

Rémès, Érik. 2003. *Serial Fucker: Journal d'un Barebacker*. Paris: Éditions Blanche.

Rojas Castro, Daniela, and Gabriel Girard. 2015. "Barebacking in France: From controversy to community ownership? An account of the 'Zone NoKpote' workshops conducted by AIDES in 2009". *Sexualities* 18 (1/2): 158–175.

Salomon, Nanette. 1996. "The Venus Pudica: Uncovering art history's 'hidden agendas' and pernicious pedigrees". In *Generations & Geographies in the Visual Arts: Feminist Readings*, edited by Griselda Pollock, 69–87. London: Routledge.

Salomon, Nanette. 1998. "The Art Historical Canon: Sins of Omission". In *The Art of Art History: A Critical Anthology*, edited by Donald Preziosi, 344–355. Oxford: Oxford University Press.

Schehr, Lawrence. 2009. *French Postmodern Masculinities: From Neuromatrices to Seropositivity*. Liverpool: Liverpool University Press.

Schiller, Friedrich. 2004. *On the Aesthetic Education of Man*. Mineola, NY: Dover Publications.

Shildrick, Margrit. 2002. *Embodying the Monster: Encounters with the Vulnerable Self*. London: Sage.

Siegert, Bernard. 2012. "Doors: On the materiality of the symbolic". *Grey Room* 47: 6–23.

Siegert, Bernard. 2015. *Cultural Techniques: Grids, Filters, Doors, and Other Articulations of the Real*. New York: Fordham University Press.

Simon, William and John Gagnon. 1986. "Sexual scripts: Permanence and change". *Archives of Sexual Behavior* 15 (2): 97–120.

Simons, Patricia. 2009. "Manliness and the visual semiotics of bodily fluids in early modern culture". *Journal of Medieval and Early Modern Studies* 39 (2): 331–373.

Stallybrass, Peter, and Allon White. 1986. *The Politics and Poetics of Transgression*. Ithaca, NY: Cornell University Press.

Steinbock, Eliza. 2017. "Representing trans sexualities". In *The Routledge Companion to Media, Sex and Sexuality*, edited by Clarissa Smith, Feona Attwood, and Brian McNair, 27–37. London: Routledge.

Theweleit, Klaus. 1987. *Male Fantasies: Women, Floods, Bodies, History*. Minneapolis: University of Minnesota Press.

Tziallas, Evangelos. 2019. "The return of the repressed: Visualizing sex without condoms". In *Raw: PrEP, Pedagogy, and the Politics of Barebacking*, edited by Ricky Varghese, 117–141. Regina: University of Regina Press.

Vasari, Giorgio. 1912–1914. *Lives of the Most Eminent Painters, Sculptors & Architects*. London: Macmillan and Co. & The Medici Society.

Winckelmann, Johann. 2013. "Thoughts on the imitation of Greek works in painting and the art of sculpture". In *Johann Joachim Winckelmann on Art, Architecture, and Archaeology*, edited by David Carter, 31–56. Rochester, NY: Camden House.

Yaeger, Rob. 2015. "I am: Rob Yaeger". Treasure Island Media Blog, 18 February 2015. https://blog.treasureislandmedia.com/2015/02/i-am-rob-yaeger/ [accessed 7 November 2019].

3 Self-augmenting masculinities[1]

In opening their bodies to penetration and in welcoming in them matter that is seen as dirty because it is thought not to belong there, gay "pigs" enact their subjectivities through a process of self-intoxication. Nowhere is that more evident than in the eroticisation of bodily fluids—sometimes even the eroticisation of HIV-positive and/or HIV-undetectable bodily fluids—or in the intensification of one's desire, pleasures, and endurance through the consumption of recreational drugs in a sexual play scenarios— what is commonly known amongst gay men as "chemsex" or "PnP" ("Party and Play"). In that context, I will now expand on the notion of porous masculinities introduced in the previous chapter and further it by discussing the role played by the figure of toxicity and intoxicating practices in the becoming-pig of gay men.

Sometimes tattooed with biohazard signs when living with HIV, gay "pigs" embrace intoxication as a practice that is central to the becoming of their sexed masculinities. However, whilst most psychoanalytically inflected critical discussions of bareback sex have claimed such eroticisa- tions of potentially toxic or life-threatening matter to be triggered by a drive towards self-annihilation that, when pursued, results in an intense self-shattering feeling of *jouissance* (Dean 2009; Bersani and Phillips 2008), I draw from Gregory Tomso (2008) to complicate that analysis. Rather than simply seeing "pigsex" as a symptom of the drive to self- obliteration, I claim here that self-intoxicating sex practices are also— and perhaps even paradoxically—life-affirming and self-augmenting. By mediating the self-fashioning of "pigs" and their affirmation of their own subjectivities, "pigsex" can be understood as an ethics of freedom. As a practice that both creates and cares for the self, I intimate, "pig" play is akin to the pursuit of an internal order freed from societal norms which Michel Foucault named an "aesthetics of existence" (1990a, 1990b, 1997). As such, rather than reducing "pigsex" to a mere eroticisation of death, in this chapter I argue that "pigs" embrace life, albeit in complex and arguably contradictory and unresolvable ways—they embrace toxic- ity in order to enact a becoming or augmentation of their (masculine) subjectivities, which they project into a future. Approached in such a way, "pig" play can be seen as an embodied practice of speculative think-ing about the body and its horizons. Yet, whilst doing so, they do, none-theless, undo or obliterate the "human" within the self. Through that, and thanks to such an inhuman sexual ethics, "pig" masculinities them-selves become polluted, they become toxic. Not toxic, however, as neces-sarily oppressive to others but toxic to hegemonic masculinity and to the enduring legacy of the autonomous human subject. By receiving and accumulating toxic matter in their bodies, gay men enact their mutant subjectivities and affirm their bodies as symbiotic entities. They deterrito-rialise themselves and become "pigs", hypermasculine living bodies that—crucially—are "hard 2 kill", as one of the tattoos on the abdomen of porn model PigBoy Ruben clearly states.

*   *   *

Released in 2017, Shu Lea Cheang's cyberpunk queer sci-fi film *Fluidø* tells the story of a speculative "post-AIDS" world set in the 2060s, one in which HIV underwent a mutation in its last human carriers. As a result, the latter—now known as "Ø GEN"—are able to produce mutated HIV-positive bodily fluids that, upon contact with the skin of HIV-negative humans, cause an intense and addictive high. As the titles at the start of the film inform the viewer, "Fluidø is the 21st century high. What the white powder was for the 20th century". In one of the scenes, for instance, a group of Ø GENs masturbate on a circular stage reminiscent of a strip club, surrounded by clients. As the intensity of the scene increases, AS, the Sexecologist—one of the Ø GENs—tells Jean-Pierre, a male client who's sitting in front of her and masturbating: "Softly, no need to be hard … mmm … fabulous, you got a soft-on … no need for an erection … so … soft." As the Ø GENs eventually cum all over their clients, these experi-ence a strong psychological and physical high, represented in the film through intense muscular contractions, self-touching and vocalisations of pleasure that come across as highly sexual, as if they were having the most intense full body orgasm. Whilst the narrative of the film focuses on the black market farming and distribution of the new bio-narcotic named "DELTA", and on the authoritarian government's new war on drugs for which it enlists a drug-resistant army of replicant law enforcers, what interests me for the purposes of my argument here is the way in which the dystopian cyberpunk world of *Fluidø* imagines a "post-AIDS" future in which HIV has mutated from killer virus to drug of choice in such a way that the bodily fluids of Ø GENs become a highly sought psychosexual commodity, one that fundamentally changes the ways in which people experience sexual pleasure. If we put aside the most futuristic traits of the filmic world of Cheang's cyberpunk extravaganza, we can easily come to realise that, at its core, *Fluidø* is closer to the reality of our antiretroviral-fuelled sexual subcultural worlds than we might, at first viewing, have expected. In order to expand on this idea and explore the role played by practices of intoxication in contemporary "pig" play, I would like to turn to *Viral Loads*, Treasure Island Media's controversial 2014 porn video.

Since its creation in San Francisco in the late 1990s, Treasure Island Media, also known by the acronym TIM, not only has become one of the most famous gay porn studios operating in the antiretroviral age, but it is also one that has received substantial amounts of scholarly attention, its popularity having risen due to the ways in which it embraces bareback sex, presenting the exchange and accumulation of bodily fluids—as well as their potential health risks—as targets of libidinal investment. The infamous popularity of such scenes is, however, not only a consequence of what we see men getting up too. It is also the result of how articulate Paul Morris, the founder of the company and one of its pornographers, has been every time he has spoken about his work. For instance, in "No Limits: Necessary Danger in Male Porn", the speech he delivered at the World Pornography Conference in Los Angeles in 1998, Morris defended his work by positioning it as documentary filmmaking, as a trustworthy record of contemporary gay male sexual practices. Distancing himself from the work of mainstream studios, which he regarded as producing "hyper-real fantasies" with "very little truth-content", Morris ([1998] 2011) claimed that:

> The positing of sex and eros as things that occur in hyper-real worlds removes them from the mess of viruses, germs, test-results, imperfections and real intimacy (physical or emotional). Sexworlds like those of Falcon and Titan are arid paradises that are inhabited by unexcited actors who move through tableaux that call for replications of sex. The "safety" that is enabled through the creation of other worlds for perfect sex is a safety of relative lifelessness for the viewer.

The hyper-real safety that Morris diagnosed in what was mainstream porn in the 1990s was, in his view, created through its depiction of "perfect" bodies, hyper-scripted and staged sex scenes, and—most importantly—its use of condoms, all of those being features that, to him, were at odds with the real lives of gay men, that "mess of viruses, germs, test-results, imperfections and real intimacy". In an offensive waged against mainstream porn of the late 1990s, Morris set up Treasure Island Media to document what "real" gay sex and intimacy was supposedly about. Namely, the embracing of risk and the rejection of condoms, which he saw as a form of political, transgressive sex. Accordingly, gay men who engaged in bareback sex were, to him—and as already mentioned before—the legitimate heirs of the gay liberation movement due to their refusal to abide by the codes of behaviour that had made gay sex acceptable to mainstream culture. His porn videos were, therefore, put forward as documentaries of an ongoing gay sexual revolution against assimilation into hegemonic straight morality.

Still, Morris's role as a documentary filmmaker is not as straightforward as he claimed, for as porn scholars have argued, porn is less about documenting reality and more about producing a reality-effect through a "complex interplay between authenticity and artifice" (Paasonen 2011, 17). Porn is "authentic" because, after all, it is a record of sexual acts that have indeed taken place. But it is also artificial inasmuch as each scene is performed and often especially lit for the camera, with performers and cameramen positioned in such a way as to grant the viewer maximum visibility and a mediated sense of physical closeness to the mediated sex that, as Susanna Paasonen (2011), Eliza Steinbock (2016) and others have argued, plays an important role in the development of the viewers' own sexual subjectivities and experiences of embodiment. As Steinbock (2016) wrote, arguing for a haptic dimension that was missing from Linda Williams's field-defining early porn studies scholarship and the latter's visual essentialism, "although it may suggest a mimetic relationship to reality, clearly porn also functions as an inter-subjective social space to explore and produce our sexual bodies" (65). An example of the techniques used by Paul Morris and other contemporary pornographers to overcome the "difficulty of vision alone to capture raw sex" (Dean 2009, 134) are the use of subtitles describing what cannot be seen, compromise money shots (when the top pulls the penis out in order to make the ejaculation visible), reverse money shots (when the bottom pushes out the semen in his rectum), unedited ambient sounds, cameramen intentionally visible in the shot, and even the occasional presence of the cameraman's voice speaking off-camera as the action unfolds. All such techniques are used to produce and reinforce the intended effect of documentary realism and of resonance between the bodies on screen and the bodies of viewers.

Yet, what strikes me in Morris's 1988 speech, delivered only two years after combination antiretroviral therapies and viral load testing were introduced to successfully manage HIV infection, is that it shows an understanding of contemporary gay male subjectivities and sexual practices, as well as their politics, taking place at the intersections of the body with viruses and bacteria, medical discourse and clinical practices, and pharmaceutical research. More recently, in an interview with Paasonen, Morris expanded on that point and on Treasure Island Media's role in such a context:

> TIM is two things, basically. We're a developing and living archive of real male sexual experience. And we're a laboratory that performs experiments that the men involved in our community propose. You could say that we're a genetic laboratory exploring the viral sexual symbiosis of human and viral DNA. For the most part, gay porn pretends to represent experience without peril, experimentation without damage. Most gay porn hides behind a facade of "safeness." But in my case, the men in my work are considered and prized for being

damaged, for having taken what conservative gays deem "the ultimate risk" and lost. In a world increasingly dominated by the medical gaze, to willingly live in symbiosis with a virus is seen as irrational and socially expensive. I see it as necessary and revolutionary.

(Morris and Paasonen 2014, 217–218)

With this statement, Morris claimed TIM's porn to be more than an ethnographic record of the sexual practices of twenty-first-century gay men. To him, TIM should also be seen as a creative, future-orientated, and necessary research enterprise invested in the production of new chimeric bodies. Posited as a contemporary form of symbiogenesis whereby human and nonhuman bodies not only touch one another but also fuse together, raw sex became TIM's research method for experimenting with the limits of our bodies and what they might one day become.

Now, it is likely that Morris's statements are a crucial part of the very successful marketing strategy of his studio through which he sells dreams of a transgressive sexual utopia at least as much as he sells pornography. Still, his idea that HIV seroconversion might lead to new forms of human-viral symbiosis is not so far-fetched, even if not that dissimilar from the future we see portrayed in the cyberpunk world of Cheang's *Fluidø*. As recent studies in immunology have shown, the incorporation of retroviral genes into human DNA is an observable phenomenon that hints at the co-evolution of humans and retroviruses. For instance, Frank Ryan (2004) noted how, as early as the 1970s, scientists had already identified retroviral genetic material built into the genome of mammals, including humans. Thanks to a long process of co-evolution that involved the incorporation of viral genetic material into the germ cell lines of human hosts, some retroviruses developed a survival strategy based on vertical rather than horizontal transmission. In other words, the genes responsible for coding the synthesis of viral proteins became part of the human genome and started being passed down by parents to offspring. Through that, ancient retroviruses stopped having to infect new hosts in order to secure their own survival. Instead, the survival of their genetic material was secured by human reproduction itself. Given that those ancient retroviruses had once been highly contagious viruses similar to HIV before they became coded into the human genome, it is not hard to speculate on a possible albeit distant future when HIV itself could become written into our human DNA, another step in the co-evolution of humans and retroviruses.

Such a possibility also makes sense in light of recent studies on acquired immunity, which argued that, in order to be successful, pathogens need to balance their virulence with their infectivity. What that means is that a pathogen cannot be so virulent that it ends up killing its host before the latter gets a chance to transmit it. Instead of pathogens and hosts evolving separately—the former to kill faster and the latter to become more efficient at defending itself against infection—both the pathogens and the immune systems of their host species need to co-evolve. That process, research has shown, has more to do with an increase in their levels of tolerance to one another than with an escalation of a war-like zero-sum game where one side needs to be defeated for the other to survive (Hedrick 2004). What those recent developments demonstrate is that the paradigms that sustain immunology have come a long way since immunity was first discovered. As authors like Ed Cohen (2009) and Roberto Esposito (2011) have argued, the modern body has been understood as a private territory with borders in constant need of defence against foreign invasion. In Cohen's words, "the modern body aspires to localize human beings within an epidermal frontier that distinguishes the person from the world for the duration which we call a life" (2009, 7). Thanks to the work of early immunologists, immunity came to be seen as a mechanisms whereby a body establishes its biological self—its identity—and protects its integrity through a process of clear discrimination between self and non-self, that is, a clear differentiation between what belongs in the body and what is foreign to it. Importantly, the emergence of the ideas of immunity-as-defence occurred at the same time as wider medical discourses and institutions were being developed to govern and preside over the production of the subject, by managing the truth of the self in its difference from the other—what Michel Foucault (1978, 1983, 1990c, 2003a, 2003b, 2005) named processes of governmentality and subjectivisation.

However, thanks to the developments in contemporary immunology I've just mentioned, the clear border between self and non-self that had been so central to modern understandings of immunity and to the maintenance of a clearly demarcated self has become blurred as a result of what Alfred Tauber (2000) called the "ecological sensibility" of contemporary biology (244). According to Tauber, the body is no longer conceived as a discrete closed unit but as an ecosystem, and immunity ceased to be understood as a defence against foreign invasions and is now thought to be more of a process of interfacing—of mediated touch and exchange—in which foreign matter can be tolerated and incorporated in the interest of the organism and of its survival, thus potentially impacting the evolution of its species. As a consequence, biological bodies are now thought to be heterogeneous, partially incorporating external entities, and seen to exist in a co-constitutive relationship with their surroundings.

Still, despite all that, Paul Morris's desired "vital symbiosis of human and viral DNA" will, at best, only take place in a very distance future, perhaps a future not very dissimilar from Cheang's *Fluidø*. At worst, it is nothing but an intentionally controversial form of self-promotion by a pornographer who has created a myth for himself out of the controversial nature of his pornographic videos and public statements. Nonetheless, if we frame Treasure Island Media's videos within what Paul Preciado called the "pharmacopornographic regime" we cannot so easily discount Morris's words nor the ways in which his work both documents and feeds into the continued production of new forms of sexed gay masculinities that have toxicity and practices of self-intoxication at their core.

By "pharmacopornographic", Preciado (2013) means "the processes of a biomolecular (pharmaco) and semiotic-technical (pornographic) government of sexual subjectivity" (33–34) that define contemporary biopolitics, arguing that contemporary subjectivities are produced and maintained thanks to a system of chemical, semiotic, and technological prostheses that attach and plug themselves into bodies, in-forming them as they do so; that is, giving them both their form and their meaning. Building on Teresa de Lauretis's (1987) notion of "technology of gender" (1–30), Preciado (2013) argued that "the pharmacopornographic regime functions like a machine of somatic representation in which text, image, and the corporeal spread though the interior of an expansive cybernetic circuit" (180) and are responsible for creating the "toxic-pornographic subjectivities" (35) of our contemporary cyborg-like bodies.

Such linguistic, imaginary, and material plug-ins operate as catalysts in processes of subjectivisation, intervening within and feeding back into the body conceived as an interface. In that context, as one of a myriad of prostheses in-forming contemporary subjectivities through mediations of desires and pleasures, pornographic texts code meanings and value systems and in-corporate them in the bodies of particular sexual-linguistic communities such as gay "pigs". As a "sexual vernacular" (Patton 1991), pornography is an important source for understanding how contemporary subjectivities are coded, performed and—at times—hacked. Such an avenue of enquiry, however, must not only take into account what happens on-screen but it also ought to consider the discursive environments and institutions that surround and frame the sex we see depicted. It is in that context that, departing from Paul Morris's discussion of his work, I will build on his video *Viral Loads* in order to examine the ways in which it re-coded the toxicity of bodily fluids at the dawn of the antiretroviral age, when fears of HIV infection amongst gay men were still very much present in the popular consciousness, and before "U=U" ("Undetectable = Untransmittable") was clinically confirmed and started informing sexual health campaigns.

Released in 2014, *Viral Loads* gathered media attention due to the ways in which the video appears to eroticise HIV transmission. Its title refers both to the technical clinical term used to name the number of viral particles in a millilitre of HIV-positive blood, and to the usage of the word "load" amongst gay men as another name for ejaculate. *Viral Loads* thus not only promises to show us men sharing their loads with one another, but it also wants us to know—or at least to believe—that such loads are viral, that alongside semen they also carry HIV.

The video opens to the sound of a storm and a rotating globe with the words "TIM GLOBAL" written on it, followed by TIM's pirate-like logo of a black-and-white skull above two crossed swords. Once the sound changes to a meditative electronic drone, a variation of TIM's logo appears on screen. Here, the skull mutates into the head of a jester through the addition of a four-pointed hat reminiscent of the motley attire of Medieval and Renaissance court entertainers. The insignia is completed by the Latin words "IOCARE SERIO ET STUDIOSISSIME LUDERE" written in a thick serif typeface around the jester skull. The whole thing conveys the overall impression of being a powerful sigil, one that suddenly comes alive when the skull's eyes light up in bright red.

Before discussing the scenes, it is worth reflecting on the unique presence of this symbol both at the start of the video and on the front cover of its DVD release. The symbol sets *Viral Loads* apart from all other Treasure Island Media releases, which tend to only use their regular logo and, unless they're thematic compilations of existing scenes, always have production shots on their front covers. The *Viral Loads* insignia and its usage as the single image on the DVD front cover thus frames this particular porn video as a stand-out item in the studio's catalogue.

"Iocare serio et studiosissime ludere", meaning "to jest in seriousness and to play in the greatest earnest", is a phrase associated with Marsilio Ficino's 1496 commentary on Plato's *Parmenides*. Appearing at the start of Ficino's preface to the work, the phrase concludes its opening sentence, which translates as:

> It was the custom of Pythagoras, Socrates and Plato to conceal divine mysteries everywhere beneath figures and veils, to modestly dissimulate their wisdom, in contrast to the sophists' arrogance, to jest in seriousness and to [play] in the greatest earnest.
>
> (Ficino 2012, 33)[2]

Discussed by Renaissance scholars, this passage has been read as an example of how, according to Ficino, philosophical wit had been used by Socrates to conceal and protect the higher truths of ancient theology from those who were considered underserving of them (Knox 1989, 121–123). That approach to philosophical method was part of a wider Renaissance interest in the wisdom of fools and in the connection the latter were seen to establish between the lowest and the most admirable, between body and soul, appearance and reality, the grotesque and the beautiful. Or, as John Lepage (2012) put it, "the unspeakable folly of human existence, the madness that in order to glimpse the truth we must indulge in fictions or follow the imagination wherever it takes us" (79).

Paul Morris's allusion both to Ficino's Neoplatonism and to the figure of the jester at the start of *Viral Loads* complicates the pornographer's earlier views that stressed the documentary nature of his work. By hinting at *Viral Loads* as an exercise in philosophical wit, Morris seems to wilfully take up a new role, that of the wise fool. No longer embracing pornographic texts simply as a truthful record of reality, he hinted at a figure of

Figure 3.1 Treasure Island Media, *Viral Loads*, 2014. DVD front cover.
Courtesy of Paul Morris.

rhetoric known for dissimulating truths with appearances, perhaps telling us that, underneath the cover of his pornographic fantasy, he was offering us something else, a different grasp on reality. Through the intertextuality of the insignia with which he decided to open *Viral Loads*, Morris invited us to look beneath the veil of pornography and its depiction of raw sex, to seek what kinds of thinking may be hiding in there. Not only that, but in requiring us to decipher the symbol, the pornographer-as-jester appears to be have asked us to prove how deserving we are of the hidden knowledge he will have buried in his work. As he put it in an interview with *Vice* published after the release of the video:

> The point of *Viral Loads* was for those people to whom it would make sense to look at it, say it, own it, and fucking move on. Fucking move on! In 20 years, there will be references to HIV, and young gay men will astonish and horrify people who are now in their 20s when they say, "What the fuck are you talking about?
>
> (McCasker 2014)

With that statement, Morris hinted at the double status of *Viral Loads* as both a pornographic text and some sort of manifesto for a "post-AIDS" future. To him, eroticising HIV and fantasising about its transmission appeared to be a means to foreground the structures that discipline our bodies and our pleasures. Further adding to the intertextual complexity of *Viral Loads*, the promotional text for the video on the studio's webstore is also rather opaque. It reads:

> Mansex is a virus, one that uses men as its host. Some try to resist it. Others embrace it as the source of life and meaning. We live and breed the sex-virus, to pass it on to every random anonymous dude we meet and fuck. It's how we reproduce, man.
>
> We shoot viral loads every time. Our jizz ain't for making babies. Or sex spreads like wildfire, squirting out of one man's dick, shooting deep inside another, then another and another.
>
> Join in, buddy. You'll never look back.

What is really being said here? If, as its title implies, *Viral Loads* is about the eroticisation of HIV transmission, why did Morris not name the actual virus? Instead, he equated "mansex" with "virus" and used the compound noun "sex-virus", allowing for multiple ways of decoding the text, including the one in which it is not HIV but (masculine) sex itself that "spreads like wildfire" and reproduces without babies. Interestingly, if we take up that reading, Morris's wise fool rhetoric starts unfolding in sharp contrast to the antisocial positions that have gained momentum in queer scholarship over the last decade or so, and even if Morris himself has claimed, during one of our conversations, that he feels drawn to queer endorsements of negativity.

Calling for an embrace of the death drive, Lee Edelman (2004) rejected politics on the grounds that all political projects, being future-orientated, necessarily inhabit heteronormative forms of temporality. They require heterosexual reproduction and depend on the figure of the Child to whom the future is seen to belong. Against such antisocial or anti-relational stance—and even against his own declared allegiance to Edelman's work—Morris's quote above appears to allude to an alternative way in which the future may still be thought through contemporary queer forms of relationality and intimacy. In what I read as a rejection of Edelman's reduction of queerness to the death drive, Morris appears to call for new future-orientated forms of queer communion, fuelled by "mansex" spreading "like wildfire" and "jizz" that isn't used for "making babies". Here, just like in his interview with Susanna Paasonen (Morris and Paasonen 2014), the pornographer appears to be claiming that his is a business that takes up a hedonistic present in order to fashion new queer modes of embodiment and communal futures. In that way, and even if the antisocial turn in queer studies embraced the relationship between queerness and death that had been taken to its limit by the AIDS crisis, Morris still appears to hint at the possibility of new futures, even if their emergence may require a flirtation with death. In that way, the promotional text for *Viral Loads* seems to make death and the possibility of life coalesce in the same instant, just like AIDS never really managed to eradicate the creative potential of queer life forces. As Jack Fritscher wrote in his obituary to his friend Allen J Shapiro, artist and one of the founders of *Drummer* magazine, who died of AIDS complications in 1987:

> … with so much death this side of Venice, the world gives little safe access anymore to unbridled Desire, but Desire's memory burns in my heart and mind. I know, I swear I know, despite the growing rolls of the dead, the world has not heard the end of us. If and when the last one of us lies dying in some cold fluorescent hospital, I guarantee, I do, I do affirm, the last sound he will hear, echoing from down the long corridor, the sound that will cheer his ears and his valiant heart, will be the first cry of a brand-spanking neonate, a new little baby boy born as we were, gifted innately with our special ways of love, and in him, in that boy child, our kind will find a new Adam and begin the beguine all over again.
>
> (Fritscher 1987)

With that in mind, I would now like to turn to the defining scene of *Viral Loads*. Entitled "Blue's Man-worship Gangbang", a scene in which Blue Bailey, the bottoming model, is fucked bareback by a large number of men. It opens with a close-up of a pighole inserted in Bailey's rectum and the hand of another man with most of its fingers inside it. The close-up dissolves to a bedroom, where Bailey is in bed, on his fours, sucking one man and surrounded by several others. The camera cuts to one of the other men walking towards the foreground with a jar full of a white, creamy substance, which he extracts with a large pipette and inserts into Bailey's rectum through the opening in the pighole. "Fuck yeah, fill it up … keep going … drink it up" can be heard uttered in the background under an echoing sound effect.

After that, a jump cut is applied and signalled by the titles "one hour earlier". Starting with a slow-motion sequence set to electronic music in which Bailey is seen kissing one man, viewers eventually learn that the scene actually kicked off with Bailey being gang-fucked whilst various men kissed and masturbated one another in the background, waiting for their turn with him. As increasing numbers of men fuck and ejaculate inside him, cum is seen dripping out of Bailey's rectum, only to be licked and eaten by Max X, a model whose only role seems to be making sure no cum is wasted. There is a strong sense of relentless giving and exchanging of bodily fluids here, heightened by the apparent consecutive "loads" some of the men are seen depositing inside Bailey, often accompanied by subtitles such as "Tom's second load" or "Logan's third load", and by the almost immediate transfer of those fluids out of Bailey's rectum and into Max X's mouth.

The scene eventually leads back to the jar sequence that had opened it. In this iteration, however, the words "poz cum" can be read on the lid of the jar before its contents are injected into Bailey's rectum, a clear attempt at circumventing the narrative problem of the invisibility of HIV noted by Tim Dean (2009) in his discussion of bareback porn. The scene closes with Bailey and Max X kissing cum off each other's mouths followed by a headshot of Bailey smiling as laughter is heard echoing in the background.

Interestingly, it is not until the bonus sequences that the whole narrative becomes complete by making use of yet another jump cut. It is only then, after six unrelated scenes, that the viewers are eventually shown cum being collected to fill the jar seen in the gangbang scene. Making use of an uncharacteristic 3×3 split screen, we see nine men sat on chairs, filmed only from their necks down and masturbating into the jar, adding their contribution to what, according to the press pack, were "200 poz loads". Just like the words "poz cum" had been deployed to overcome the invisibility of HIV, anonymity functions here in much the same way; namely, to strengthen the affective charge of the fantasy of HIV infection. By not showing the faces of the men in this last sequence, Morris intensified the aesthetics of transgression he pursued with *Viral Loads*. Considering that the vast majority of TIM models are clearly recognisable by their faces and listed on its online roster, Morris's decision to play with anonymity in this instance further contributed to the reality-effect he was seeking. Particularly so given that the scene was filmed in a legal context that allowed criminal prosecutions for willingly or consciously exposing someone to HIV and potentially infecting them (Lazzarini *et al.* 2013; Ashford 2015). Invisibility and anonymity—absences that serve as proxies for the presence of HIV—thus strengthened the sexual fantasy of toxic bodily fluids portrayed in *Viral Loads*. Given that none of the actual sex scenes in the video are fundamentally different from most other scenes in TIM's catalogue, the controversy surrounding *Viral Loads* is not just the result of the sex we see but, rather, of its style and the sophisticated ways in which Morris, the witty jester, made use of intertextuality to play with presence and absence, visibility and invisibility. By doing so, he alluded to what Linda Williams (2014) described as the "perpetual push and pull between on/scenity and obscenity as a part of the neoliberal dilemma of an ever-expanding market for all sorts of sexual representations" (38). The truth-effect of the video, however, is disrupted by the realisation that Blue Bailey was already living with HIV and with an undetectable viral load at the time the "poz cum" scene was shot. Concealment, this time of the model's serostatus, was used again to benefit the fantasy or, as Bailey himself put it, to "hype [the video] up" (Clark-Flory 2014). Even if that were not the case, medical evidence still suggests that the virus itself can't survive long outside the body (CDC 2019).

To my mind, then, what *Viral Loads* offers beneath its play of artifice and reality is a rich text through which to think the role played by the figure of toxicity and practices of intoxication in the development of gay "pig" masculinities and the ways in which the latter complicate modern understandings of the body and of the autonomous subject. My position here resonates both with Morris's manifested interest in human-viral symbiosis discussed above and with Gregory Tomso's (2008) view that barebacking supplements masculine subjectivity through the accumulation of foreign matter in the body. *Viral Loads* used pornographic and narrative devices both to reassert masculinity as ideal and to queer it through intoxication. On the one hand, by heroically enduring relentless penetrations and accumulations of bodily fluids, Blue Bailey reiterated masculinity as athleticism and endurance. On the other hand, and as Byron Lee (2014) noted in relation to the masculinity of bareback bottoms, by reframing masculine athleticism as relentless bottoming, "what was once an act of effeminacy is now a masculine act" (110). Further to that, *Viral Loads* reproduces masculinity whilst nonetheless queering it through both the penetrability of Bailey's body and its radical porosity to matter that, because it is foreign, is conceived as intoxicating to the self-sameness of the modern subject. Blue Bailey's body offered us a fantasy of hyper-masculine embodiment albeit one that was predicated on its radical openness to a threatening outside.

Performances of masculinity such as Bailey's gain a particular relevance in the context of the biopolitics of combination antiretroviral therapies, administered as Treatment-as-Prevention (TasP) or Pre- and Post-Exposure HIV Prophylaxis (PrEP and PEP). After all, as Blue Bailey noted, most HIV-positive models working in porn live with undetectable viral loads thanks to antiretroviral regimes (Clark-Flory 2014). Notwithstanding the fantasy of HIV transmission in *Viral Loads*, the reality is that, thanks to antiretrovirals, the bodies we saw exchanging semen with one another were likely to exist outside the positive/negative binary upon which the seroconversion the video eroticised would depend. Constituted as a third term between positivity and negativity, HIV undetectability simultaneously increases sexual freedom whilst subjecting the body to increasing biomolecular control. In other words, whilst undetectability allowed a queering of Bailey's masculinity through a relentless embrace of penetrability and porosity to foreign matter, the biopolitics of antiretroviral drugs re-inscribed Bailey's subjectivity within the realm of the masculine as a heroic form of life, at once allowing his exposure to risk and chemically protecting him from it.

It is in the context of such posthuman becoming—one in which the affordances of flesh, desire, and pleasures are at once increased by foreign matter and semiotic chains, and recaptured by economies of life and (self-)care—that *Viral Loads* can be read as a kind of jester's wit, a pornographic fantasy that alludes to important changes in how gay male subjectivities are being embodied and performed in the age of antiretrovirals. Thanks to the technoscientific developments that have been taking place since the late 1990s, the masculinities performed in *Viral Loads* cannot be fully captured by earlier understandings of bodies as enclosed spaces and toxicity as something that ought to be avoided at all costs, or else. Instead, *Viral Loads* enacts masculinity through opening the body to a seemingly endless number of "loads" presented as foreign and intoxicating matter. At the same time, however, those bodies remain protected as standing reserves of life and labour by being chemically reconditioned with antiretrovirals.

Rather than having their subjectivity dependent on a clear separation of self and other, the masculine bodies we see in *Viral Loads* suggest themselves as perverse realities—they are porous, penetrable, multiple, and self-constituted in their openness to strangers. In operating their boundaries not as closed borders but as interfaces, they veer away from modern understandings of the human as a discreet self-enclosed unit. That is, even if their masculinities are made possible thanks to antiretroviral drugs, even if the biopolitics of the latter may still perpetuate the sovereignty of the self-administering neoliberal subject, they may also allow for those same bodies to fashion themselves differently (see Schubert 2019). In order to develop this point and further clarify how exchanges of bodily fluids constitute an enactment of intoxication that simultaneously troubles, reshapes and reaffirms masculinity, I would like to bring up Leo Bersani's recent work on bodily receptivity.

In *Receptive Bodies*, Bersani (2018) explored the role of penetrability and receptivity vis-à-vis the production and maintenance of selfhood. Focusing on activities such as breathing in and out, eating and defecating, as well as sexual penetration, Bersani noted that the human body, from its intrauterine origin to its postnatal existence, is always characterised by a dual process of reception and expulsion. It was, however, in sexual penetration that Bersani narrowed down his argument. To him, and whilst "penetration violates the bodily boundaries of selfhood" by having an external object—living or non-living, a penis or a dildo—penetrate the body, it is "neither exchange, nor is it fusion" due to the ways in which the penetrating object "must alternate each of its moves forward with a partial retreat or withdrawal", therefore always necessarily having to leave after entering the body (86). This idea of impossible exchange or fusion is further reinforced by Bersani's claim, familiar in psychoanalytical theory, that the *jouissance* of sexual climax is "solipsistic" even when achieved with an other—that orgasm is an "explosive implosion" (87–88). In short, for Bersani (2018), one always cums alone. As he wrote:

> Our climatic aloneness is both instinctual and willed, as if an act presumed to be one of great openness to the other were repudiated or "taken back" at the moment when a total self-absorption might also be one of total self-exposure. The exposed face of orgasm violates a fundamental privacy of being, and it must be hidden by a somewhat gratuitous, or belated, gesture of great modesty, a silent proclamation of psychic chastity.
>
> (88)

As I will clarify in the following chapter, whilst I do think that there are important practices and experiences of exchange and communion enacted in "pigsex" due to the ways in which gay pigs eroticise bodily fluids well beyond the moment of orgasm, making bodily fluids rather than the penis the targets of libidinal investment, I still think that Bersani's argument can offer us a way to better understand how "pig" play is intoxicating to subjectivity in such a way that it opens it up for augmentation. Where my position differs from his, however, is that—unlike him—I believe that the self-augmentations associated with the human body's receptive qualities passes through a series of practices that make the latter emerge as always-already multiple, singular-plural, and constituted in its porosity to foreign matter. Even if, as Bersani argued, *jouissance* is always solipsistic—an "explosive implosion" as he put it—the augmented self we find ourselves with at that moment is augmented through additions from the outside, always-already a Self + 1. "There is no solitary *jouissance*", as Jean-Luc Nancy wrote (Nancy and van Reeth 2017, 17). In that way, we can understand how, in *Viral Loads*, Blue Bailey became more masculine and heroic the more loads he took. Rather than withdrawing into himself during the gangbang scene, Bailey's hypermasculine "pig" subjectivity was progressively loaded into him by the men who penetrated him.

In "Receptivity and Being-In", the fifth chapter of *Receptive Bodies*, Bersani reflected on Peter Sloterdijk's *Spheres*, namely Sloterdijk's critique of psychoanalysis's paradigm of object relations. In *Bubbles*, the first volume of his magnum opus *Spheres*, Sloterdijk (2011) referred to the work of Thomas Macho to highlight the role played by what the latter called "nobjects" in the formation of the subject. Whilst psychoanalytical theory grounds the development of the self on the latter's relationships with objects from birth—where objects are understood as existents posited in relations of alterity to the subject—Sloterdijk sees the formation of the subject initiating *in utero* well before the cut away from the mother that psychoanalysis sees as inaugurating selfhood. Macho's notion of "nobject" offered Sloterdijk a conceptual framework to approach the subject—as well as the relationships between the latter and its surrounding environment—without having to rely on the assumption of a primordial split that would kickstart the development of the subject as an autonomous being (Sloterdijk 2011, 467). A paradigmatic example of that relationship between the pre-subject and a nobject is the intimate "fluidal communion" between the foetus and the placenta in the medium of blood inside the womb which, to Sloterdijk, represents the primordial microsphere serving as the model for all subsequent intimate relationships on which the post-natal development of the subject will be based (295). For Sloterdijk, the structuring of the subject is always a "'structuring' through *inhood*" (541). In other words, before being

> assumes the character of being-in-the-world, it already has the constitution of being-in. [...] This principle of the intimate relationship space should make it clear why a life is always a life-in-the-midst-of-lives. Being in, then, should be conceived as the togetherness of something with something in something.
>
> (541–542)

As such, to him, the development of the self takes place within a topology of spheres through which the subject moves and in which it is included, from the micro-spheres of the primordial soup and the womb to the macro-spheres of global systems and the cosmos: "What we call growing up consists of these strenuous resettlings of smaller subjectivities in larger world forms" (56). The ontological priority given by Sloterdijk to alternating relations of content and container—whereby the experiences of closeness and intimacy required for the development of the subject are relationships of incorporation—means that his topology of spheres spatialises the subject in a manner that is radically different from the cartography of object relations in which psychoanalytical theory is grounded. Whilst, in the words of Klaus Theweleit (1987), Freud "[refused] to concede that the ego lacks definite boundaries, except in an inward direction" (252), leading on to Bersani's claim that *jouissance*, "worked up to with the other, is itself solipsistic" (2018, 88) and to the development of the anti-relational strand of queer theory with its privileging of the death drive, self-shattering and masochism (see Ruti 2017), for Sloterdijk (2011) the whole process of subjectivisation is not marked by the boundary principle that sustains psychoanalysis's

relations of self and other. Instead, it is defined by a permanent "consubjec-
tive intimacy" (96) whereby it is the constant penetration of the subject by
external worlds that is responsible not only for the development of the
former but also, crucially, for its augmentation:

> Does not every unneglected child realize the advantage of being born
> only thanks to eudemonic nipples, good candy spirits, conspiratorial
> bottles and drinkable fairies that watch discreetly by its bed, occasion-
> ally entering the interior to nurse it? Does a sum of advantageous
> invasions not hollow out a love grotto within the individual, with
> enough space to house the self and its associated spirits for life? Does
> not every subjectification, then, presuppose multiple successful pene-
> trations, formative invasions and interested devotions to life-enriching
> intruders? And is not every feeling of offensive self-positing injected
> with anger over missing the chance at being taken?
>
> (96)

Whilst Bersani recognised in Sloterdijk's project some of his own investment in developing a theory of closeness, of receptivity to alterity and thus
of Being-With, he was ultimately concerned about Sloterdijk's favouring of
fluidal communion and blood. Sustaining Bersani's concern were the ways
in which the German philosopher had, in 2016, infamously spoken against
Germany's policy of openness to Middle Eastern refugees fleeing ISIS ter-
rorism on the grounds that openness to the outside must not result in the
destruction of the inside (Bersani 2018, 104). Bersani's understandable reticence vis-à-vis fluidal communion highlights an issue at the heart of
Sloterdijk's thesis. Namely, that penetration and incorporation are
required for the formation and augmentation of the subject but only
insofar as the subject and the penetrating worlds exist within the same
sphere and, from there, within increasingly larger concentric ones. In other
words, whilst penetration and fluidal communion are welcomed, they are
so only as long as the security of the spheres within which they take place
isn't disturbed by adjacent differently centred spheres with different internal developmental pathways—say, a Middle-Eastern sphere. Yet, whilst
Bersani's criticism of Sloterdijk's position on the refugee crisis is one that I
certainly endorse, I do not agree with his view—in response to Sloterdijk's
thesis—that "any reference to blood communities at the level of macro-
spheres immediately evokes the most sinister moments of modern Western
history" (Bersani 2018, 103); namely, the horror of the violence carried
out by fascist states in the name of ethnonationalist projects grounded on a
supposed purity of blood and soil. For, despite Sloterdijk's deeply troubling political position regarding refugees, I still think his work can
offer an important set of conceptual tools to help us gain a better grasp of
the increments in masculinity—of the self-augmenting of masculinities—
that appear to be an outcome of gay "pig" sexual practices. Unlike

psychoanalytically informed anti-relational queer thinkers such as Bersani (2018), to whom the "orgasmic subject turns away from the partner who has taken him or her to climax but who is deserted at the climactic instant" (88), Sloterdijk's emphasis on the development of the subject through penetration, incorporation, and fluidal communion can offer us a richer understanding of the processes of "pig" subjectivisation.

To be clear, I do not aim to argue against Bersani's understanding of the solipsistic nature of orgasmic *jouissance*. I still think his view, shared by many others, is useful to understand the "explosive implosion" that men undergo during ejaculation. However, not all pleasures of sex are orgasmic pleasures; much to the contrary, as practitioners of BDSM, edging, fisting, or needle play can attest to. Because his position privileges phallic ejaculatory orgasms, it does not offer any kind of tools with which to approach the registers of pleasure and incremental subjectivisation of cum-thirsty, load-taking bottoms, nor the pleasure both tops and bottoms experience in the expanded temporality that follows ejaculation and that often involves exchanges of ejaculate amongst the models, as seen in *Viral Loads* as well as in many other contemporary porn videos.

In order to explore what, to me, is one of the fundamental transformations that have happened at the level of both pornography and gay sex after the introduction of antiretrovirals—namely, the veering of libidinal investment away from the phallic cumshot and towards cum itself and the extended sexual temporality of its exchange—I would like to attend to Murat Aydemir's work on ejaculation and its meanings. In so doing, I aim to show how masculinity is being reconfigured not so much at the moment of ejaculation as one may initially have expected, but through the expanded temporality of exchanged bodily fluids understood as a self-augmenting practice of intoxication.

In *Images of Bliss*, Aydemir (2007) presented what was the first comprehensive study of the meanings with which we have loaded representations of ejaculations and ejaculate. Calling ejaculation a "significant discharge", Aydemir started by asking why, in Lacanian psychoanalysis, the image of ejaculation appeared "precariously displaced" by the psychoanalyst's over-reliance on the figure of the Phallus. Whilst, for Lacan, the Phallus remained the anchor of all signification, Aydemir claimed that the structure of contemporary pornography appears to anchor meaning and masculinity elsewhere:

> Contemporary feature-length hard-core video and film pornography, both straight and gay, calibrates and celebrates masculinity in terms of the narrative temporality and visibility of male orgasm. The genre presents the so-called cum, pop, or money shot, the simultaneous visualization and narration of ejaculation, as its height of signification, the irresistible juncture where significance, pleasure, and masculinity are united.
>
> (Aydemir 2007, 93)

Even if, as Lacanian scholars in queer and feminist traditions have insisted, the Phallus ought not to be reduced to the penis, it is still the case that, when it comes to signifying masculinity, it is the penis that takes on the role of master signifier. In Lindon K. Gill's words, "the penis is a synecdoche for the phallus, which is in turn a synecdoche for masculinity" (2018, 102). Further, as Eliza Steinbock and others have argued, such a hegemonic technology of masculine signification has tended to make the presence of trans bodies in mainstream pornography subject to a genital epistemology of "the reveal" (Steinbock 2016, 2017), a practice that sits rather comfortably within the genre, given pornography's defining "principle of maximum visibility"—its "on/scenity" (Williams 1999). In a pornographic context in which narrative and affects are primarily dependent on the maximum visibility of genitals, masculinity becomes reduced to the male sex. In line with such favouring of the penis as the entry point for the signifying chain that reads as masculinity, the cumshot—visual evidence of the function that actualises the penis as Phallus—becomes the privileged means by which the masculine body is enacted, the foremost sequence that provides pornographic enactments of masculinity and masculine pleasure with their anticipated formal closure. It is for those reasons that, in what I read as a complication of psychoanalytical arguments on the self-shattering nature of orgasmic *jouissance*, Aydemir (2007) was able to argue that:

> On the one hand, the cum shot can be seen as the furthest reach to the disintegration of masculine subjectivity—from coherent character to assorted images and pieces, from subject to bodily matter, and from agency to effect—and finishes the progressive slide, or drop, away from realistically motivated action. On the other hand, the cum shot also shunts the narration back to the story level, so that its constituting elements or pieces are recuperated, redomesticated, through the character's subjective face, his name, and his agency. In that sense, the cum shot works to save male subjectivity from the pornographic lapse into a fragmented, pleasurable, amorphous, and bodily condition

(97)

And yet, notwithstanding the ways in which, following Aydemir, the cumshot functions as a synecdoche for masculinity in mainstream porn—especially heterosexual porn—that narrative function becomes complicated in gay porn, and even more so in the gay porn produced in the antiretroviral age. As I've already argued above when discussing *Viral Loads*, contemporary gay porn scenes tend to extend well beyond the cumshot, with intense sequences of cum exchange amongst the performers being often framed as the target of libidinal investment by bottoms who are commonly heard saying things like "fuck it in", or tops who go on to lick the cum out of the bottom's rectum (i.e. "felching") and spit it back into their mouths (i.e. "snowballing"). Such a temporal extension of gay porn scenes also speaks to the recent emergence amongst gay men of a phenomenon which "Mark"—a gay man and porn model I interviewed in Los Angeles— described as "making the rounds getting as many loads as they can". That is, bottoms traveling from private home to private home in an attempt to take several loads in a row, sometimes over a period of a whole weekend fuelled by sex-enhancing drugs like crystal methamphetamine, GHB/GBL, mephedrone, etc. That practice, one in which bottoms, whether on or off screen, delay their own ejaculation in order to chase tops for yet another load and take pleasure purely in collecting those, suggests that the masculinity of gay "pigs"—and here I'm referring specifically to "pig" bottoms— is performed and embodied in a very different manner, one that does not privilege phallic regimes of masculinity nor cumshots as the fulcrum of its actualisation, of masculinity *cumming* into being.

In order to develop that claim, I would like to return to Aydemir's work, particularly his discussion of John Elliot's 1990 gay porn *Lunch Hour*. Focusing on a dreamed orgy sequence in Elliot's video, Aydemir identified four ways in which the scene extends the image of the cumshot well beyond its traditional role as the pivot of the sexual sequence. Those are, (1) the multiplication of cumshots by increasing both the number of participating men and the number of different angles from which the same ejaculation is shown; (2) the video looping of the same cumshot; (3) the occasional ejaculation onto the camera lens itself, a choice that breaks the forth wall, as it were, and thus troubles the temporality of the narrative fantasy; and (4) the staging of self-reflexive cumshot sequences that expose the constructed nature of porn by highlighting the presence of "the transparent but impenetrable screen that connects, yet separates [both] performer and viewer, [and] substance and vision" (Aydemir 2007, 126). To those four strategies used to expand the temporality and narrative function of the cumshot beyond its classical role in pornography, I would also add, from "pig" porn, the exchanges of ejaculate amongst the models as well as the continued penetrations even after ejaculation. The implications that has for the construction and mediation of masculinity in gay pornography are significant. As Aydemir (2007) noted in his discussion of the extended cumshots in *Lunch Hour*:

> [These cum shots] seize on the produced, constructed, material, and visible image rather than performing the ideological reproduction of masculinity. For if ejaculation is exposed as a performance and a construction that is entirely conducive to the image, to a material visuality, then the gendered subjectivity that the execution of the cum shot should prove cannot but become less important.
>
> (126)

Building on his claim, and given the specific ways in which cumshots are being further reframed in contemporary gay porn through a process of both temporal and spatial extension, I would like to argue that the weakening of their role as anchors of mediated phallic masculinities opens up an alternative narrative space where contemporary "pigs" become actualised through a process of *self-augmenting anality*. This self-augmenting form of anality goes on to trouble the binary logics of active/passive and impermeable/permeable that had been central to the development and crystallisation of hegemonic Western gender roles.

In an article where he discussed the cumshots in the videos released by Treasure Island Media and their relationship to masculinity, Byron Lee (2014) noted the ways in which, unlike previous porn scripts, it is not ejaculation but the transfer of ejaculate amongst participants that marks the end of a sex scene and thus its narrative and erotic climax (108). Yet, in Lee's argument, that shift did not lead to a queer performance of hypermasculinity as a way to "compensate for what is interpreted as a gender misalignment" (110). Given the pivotal role of the cumshot in anchoring masculinity and in elevating the erect ejaculating penis to the symbolic role of Phallus, a performance of hypermasculinity—understood by Lee as exaggerated masculinity—would likely require an equally exaggerated performance of ejaculation in order to grant, through a logics of compensation, a space in the house of masculinity for the gender-misaligned body of the "pig" bottom. What we see in Treasure Island Media's porn, however, is rather different. Focusing on how TIM bottoms read as masculine despite their performance of what was once seen as an emasculating act—namely, being penetrated—Lee's argument is that the barebacking bottoms of contemporary porn make use of other qualities traditionally associated with masculinity—that is, athleticism and endurance—in order to turn their being penetrated into a masculinising act. In contemporary gangbang scenes, "[receiving] ejaculate is also introduced as a skill", with bottoming being "also positioned as an athletic act that requires preparation" (109). What this allows, in my view, is for masculinity to be remediated and refracted away from its impermeable hegemonic phallic regime and towards a more porous anal model. In being sexual athletes who are able to endure multiple consecutive penetrations and internal ejaculations, "pig" bottoms actualise their masculinity through relentlessly pursuing and taking in load after load.

In a way that resonates with Lee's argument, Gregory Tomso (2008) highlighted what he sees as "some important differences in the ways sadomasochism and viral sex [sex that fetishises HIV] disrupt the formation of male sexual subjects" (274). Whilst sadomasochism has normally been theorised through a psychoanalytical lens of self-shattering *jouissance*, for Tomso "viral sex is not so much a shattering force as it is an additive one" (274). Privileging a quasi-economic reading of practices of accumulation and exchange of semen, Tomso framed gay bareback sex as an economy of excess, one that resembles Georges Bataille's theorisation of the role of unproductive expenditure and gift-giving in what the French philosopher termed a "general economy" (Bataille 1988). For Tomso, it is exactly that economic logics that subverts neoliberal economics by taking the commodity fetishism upon which the latter depends—materialised here in the assignment of an excess of symbolic value to the material reality of sperm—and carrying it past the limit point of neoliberal biopolitical rationality. Whereas neoliberal economics requires the deterritorialising force of commodity fetishism in order to create surplus value and to grow capital through the creation of new desires, neoliberal biopolitics reterritorialises and thus governs that process by ensuring health and life aren't threatened by the disruptive force of new desires and pleasures. In balancing *deterritorialising economics* and *reterritorialising biopolitics*, neoliberalism is able to ensure continuing growth and capital accumulation by, on the one hand, creating desire for new commodities and, on the other, maximising and prolonging the lives of subjects so they continue to produce, reproduce, and consume. As Tomso (2008) concluded:

> The metaphors of bugs and gifts that mark the intransigence of HIV are harbingers of a future in which HIV has not been vanquished by biomedicine and public health. Instead, they function as an imposition, one that insists on making HIV more ubiquitous. They are a sign of the fragility of time, acting counter to the future seen through the biopolitical and neoliberal optimization of life. Coming to terms with the enormity of HIV and AIDS means imagining a time when large numbers of bodies may not be fully optimized for work, for rational living, or for liberal "happiness."
>
> (281)

Whilst there is still a subsection of the gay male population that eroticises HIV transmission and whose sexual practices fall more closely the logics of Tomso's argument (see, for instance, García-Iglesias 2019), the introduction of TasP and PrEP protocols mean that bareback sex is, by far, not the exclusive domain of those who have come to be known as "bugchasers" or "giftgivers". Still, his emphasis on the additive logics of condomless sex can still illuminate the formation of the wider "pig" masculinities we have seen developing in the age of antiretrovirals, offering us a framework with which to understand them that is an alternative to both the psychoanalytically informed framework of *jouissance* (e.g. Bersani and Phillips 2008; Dean 2009) and the reduction of "pigsex" and "pig" masculinities to a sexual politics of abjection (Halperin 2007). Whereas the former sees "pigsex" as a self-shattering flirtation with death, the latter approaches it as a queer practice of "transmutation of social humiliation into erotico-religious glorification" (Halperin 2007, 76), one that re-empowers homosexuals and allows us to appropriate the discourses that abjected us in the first place by inverting the system of values that sustained them—in short, to turn *their* shit into *our* gold. Tomso's economic model, on the other hand, can help us frame "pigsex" in a way that better accounts for how gay "pigs" see their sex as life-affirming without having to defer back to the language of oppressors to do so.

An economic model of excessive consumption—of addition, of more and more, of conjunction (and ... and ...)—resonates with the testimonies of some of my interview participants. Interviewees like "Martin", "Anthony", and "Mark"—experienced porn models—all highlighted the desire to receive multiple penetrations and "loads" as a feature of contemporary gay male sex lives. "Martin", whom I also interviewed in Los Angeles, offered some rather well articulated insights into those practices and their relationship to constructions of masculinity, both within and outside porn. In a rather long exchange that is, nonetheless, illuminating in its nuance and detail, he said, when I asked him about the shift of emphasis away from penises and towards cum:

MARTIN: [...] what's naughty now is cum swapping and what makes it hot ... what was naughty then was just having gay sex. So it wasn't necessary to take it all the way but obviously as a community and as the world has moved on and moved forward just having gay sex is not a big deal anymore. They have gay sex on TV shows that are featured on, you know, CBS ... it's not a big deal to have gay sex anymore so we've got to take it to the next level of what is naughty, what are you getting away with, what are you doing that you probably shouldn't do or what is like compromising your moral compass ... well it's cum and not just cum but celebration of cum—cummy faces, cummy butt holes, ass to mouth [...]

JOÃO: What is it about the cumming inside? Not that you can necessarily even rationalise it ...

MARTIN: So it's about, especially as a pure bottom like myself, it becomes about the connection and the dominance, right? And so if you're dominating me and you're coming inside of me, you're leaving a part of yourself inside of me ... it is no different than when a dog pees on a tree. I wish that I could say it in a way that was less maybe like animalistic than that, but it's not. It's just ... it's exactly the same thing; you have claimed me. Now, maybe you've only claimed me for 10 seconds because I'm in a sex club and someone is coming up right behind you and they're going to claim me as well. But during that time, you have claimed me with action, but you have also left your mark inside of me. That's it, on a physical guttural animalistic level, on a level that is spiritual, which I believe is always existing, even though we ... even if we admit they're not, there's always some sort of spirituality exchange as well. You literally left the seed of yourself inside of me. And so there's something you know, like women, straight women will sometimes get turned on when a gay guy or when straight guys will say to them, I'm going to put a baby in you. [...] And there's no difference between that and being a bottom in gay sex, you want that level of dominance, "I'm going to leave this, I'm going to leave my DNA inside of you, and you know what you're going to do in return? You're going to fucking take it. I'm not going to swallow your load, you're not going to come at me when I walk out of this apartment that might even be your apartment ... I'm going to leave my DNA in your guts, I'm going to leave my DNA in the most sensitive tissue part of your body and you are going to know me, you're going to know who I am on a spiritual and physical level in the deepest part of your bowels. And then I'm going to wipe my dick off on your towel and then I'm going to fucking leave." And that is so hot; that is so hot, you know what I mean? Especially, that's why a lot of bottoms don't need to cum. They don't get hard during sex, they don't need to finish. Now, that's a controversial statement; to each their own. And myself, that's it; I want that level of dominance. And I get turned on by the fact that you do not blow me, you do not jerk me off, you do not care if I'm hard or not, you don't give a shit. Because, not from a selfish point of view where I think less of myself or I think I deserve less. But it turns me on from that dominating point of view. And so I guess, to answer your question in the shortest term possible, is just ... it's a level of dominance; cum is about dominance.

JOÃO: And so the more—I guess—the more loads one takes, the more ...

MARTIN: Yeah, well, if you're taking lots of loads from different people, then you're not submitting to a person, you're submitting to the night; you're submitting to the sex, you're submitting to the theme of the evening. And if the theme of the evening is "I am a bottom and I am here to please the world", well, that's how you feel more in an orgy or gang, but you're like "I am here to please mankind", you know what I mean? [...] Well, then you want as many loads [...] I am happy to be a beta male to every alpha male within a 10-mile radius. Then you want ... that you want as much cum as you possibly can, you want as many partners as you possibly can to cum and dominate you because you're having sex in that capacity. You're having sex with midnight. You're not having sex with the guy, you're having sex with the night. And it is up to the circumstances of the moon that night how many people you get, how much cum ... I'll be filming a scene this weekend, a bukkake scene ... bukkake is when a bunch of guys cum all over your face at the same time. And my goal is going to be ... in this scene and anytime that I've had a bukkake in real life, my goal is to have my face covered in semen, not to swallow a ton of loads so much as to have literally as much of my visage covered in semen as possible because I want to wear the mask of alpha beta. I am *the* best beta male possible. I am wearing literally a kabuki mask, you know what I'm sayin'? It's like a cape; I'm a superhero. And I want to look right up at the camera with my eyes closed and at least one load dripping off my chin and smile and say "look how great of a beta I am; look how good of a bottom I am." It is a trophy that you hold up to the camera, you smile and you say "I would like to thank the Academy."

"Martin"'s account of his occasional desire to take in a high number of "loads" is telling in how it presents such practice as *both* an instance of submission to an "alpha" male ("I am a bottom and I'm here to please the world") *and* a display of skill that sets him on a pathway to augment himself ("It's like a cape; I'm a superhero"). Interesting, too, is the way in which he claimed that his behaviour and desires have nothing to do with his self-perception as someone who thinks little of himself, a position that—were he to maintain it—would more easily lead to an explanation of cum-collecting as being an enactment of negativity. It is, after all, in his words, the high number of loads that he takes that makes him superhero-like; the more loads he takes, the more of a sexual athlete he becomes. To him, it is that anal athleticism, endurance, and eagerness—his anal hunger—that also sustains his own masculinity as a pig bottom in front of the camera. When I asked him about how he performs masculinity on a porn set, he answered:

MARTIN: You have to not come at it from a point of being masculine or feminine. That's how you think historically it was. Now it's gotten to a point where it's a matter of submissive versus dominant. And so you want to aggressively take the dick. Now a way to do that is to accept the dick in a way that is submissive, but also you want more, you're hungry. But then you also can't look too hungry. So you can't look like you're a greedy bottom. You can't tell them what to do. You can't say "oh fuck me". But you also have to say "I need it". You know, you have to beg for the dick, worship the dick but not insist that they give you more of the dick or insist that they give you cum whenever you're ready for cum. Because then you're you can't take … you can't emasculate at all … you cannot take any power, but you have to aggressively—and I guess you can't really find a way to type this out—but the difference is feminine moan would be [moans whilst increasing pitch]. Now there's a time and place for that which is when you're getting absolutely destroyed when you're getting jack hammered. But that is … that moan is specifically timed out like that, it's why it's partially acting because you are waiting strategically to give what I call the "bitch moan". The bitch moan has to come toward the orgasm. All moans before that have to sound like a masculine man who has worked … Basically I use the same moan in the beginning of the porn that I use toward the … toward working out like if I'm lifting weights and it's too heavy, that grunt is what I have to give, you know what I mean?

What we can read in "Martin"'s account of both his own personal life and his performance on set is, all differences between the two notwithstanding, an understanding that his own masculinity as a pig bottom is produced through an enhancement or augmentation of himself to a superhuman level with every new "load". Here, the hegemonic modern Western understanding of penetrability as a passive and emasculating practice is not only rejected but reframed as an active performance, as something one does or works on—a form of labour in which it is the anal sphincter, with all its actual and virtual affordances, that becomes the main tool of the trade. Just like he lifts weights with his arms, "Martin" also actively takes "loads" with his ass; and both exercises build him up. In their being framed in such ways, the "loads" that are collected by "pig" bottoms appear, following the work of Lee and Tomso, pornographic representations, and the accounts of my own research participants, as catalysers of masculinity resembling Sloterdijk's (2011) usage of Macho's concept of "nobjects" as media that "fulfill the function of the living genius or *intimate augmenter for subjects*" (467, my emphasis). That is, unlike objects—things that confirm the subject by being placed in relation to it (Kesel 2009; see also Inwood 1992, 203)—nobjects are not so much put in relation to the subject in order to confirm it but are instead added to it, changing it through intimate contact. The relationship between ejaculate as nobject and the "pig" bottoming subject is thus not one of co-constitutive opposition as in psychoanalytical theories and accounts of fetishism but it is, instead, one of transformative "fluidal communion" (Sloterdijk 2011, 295), a relationship of "togetherness of something with something in something" (542).

A similar understanding of the developmental nature of these intimate practices was also articulated by "Bill", a gay man in his late 20s who lives in Berlin and has worked in porn production. "Bill" is also deeply involved in the gay fisting scene as a versatile fist "pig" and a substantial number of his friends are also fisters. When we were talking about prolapsed rectums and how they are often fetishised and displayed as trophies within the gay fisting community, "Bill" said the following:

BILL: [...] I think it's interesting ... a lot of guys are, like, trying to get one [a prolapse]. But it's like, they probably naturally don't have one, right? It's like, I think there's a certain degree ... a definite, like ... you either have one or you don't but there's maybe a middle ground where you can train it to just, like, come out. [...]

JOÃO: What makes it sexy? [...] What does it make you feel when you see it?

BILL: [...] It's like this act of, like, truly like, letting yourself go and showing like, the deepest part of yourself physically. [...] And then I think it's, for me, that's like, maybe a deep subconscious real turn-on—to have that, like, real vulnerability with someone else. And like, then, to do the act of, like, licking and sucking on it and stuff like that, then it's like, fully embracing it. Like, to me, that's like … the hottest thing is, like, when a guy is willing to do that to mine, where it's like, he's really willing to like, go there with me.

Just like "Martin", who understood his role as a cum "pig" bottom to be one that involved athleticism and was prize-worthy, "Bill" too saw prolapsed rectums as something one can gain through practice and that is then perceived within the fisting community as a trophy of sexual achievement. Later in the conversation, he mentioned how his own prolapse sometimes made him feel like he was the "party clown", when it'd come out and his playmates would gather around to "stare at it". In the fisting community, then, there is a sense in which developing a prolapse grants fist "pigs" a superhuman-like status, just like taking countless "cum loads" did for "Martin". That is also particularly evident in the various sexually explicit Twitter accounts that fistees use to publicly display their latest achievements in rectal prolapse athletics.

In their investment in anal pleasure, permeability, and athleticism, gay "pigs"—as well as their pornographic representations—bring to mind Guy Hocquenghem's (1993) discussion of how "an annular desiring system would abolish the phallic hierarchy" (146; see also Hocquenghem 1995). Reacting against the role of the Phallus in the creation and maintenance of both identity formations and the heteropatriarchal capitalist social order, and drawing from Gilles Deleuze and Félix Guattari's *Anti-Oedipus*, Hocquenghem (1993) claimed that:

> To reinvest the anus collectively and libidinally would involve a proportional weakening of the great phallic signifier, which dominates us constantly both in the small-scale hierarchies of the family and in the great social hierarchies. The least acceptable desiring operation (precisely because it is the most desublimating one) is that which is directed at the anus.
>
> (103)

Divesting from the penis and investing in the anus—which, for Hocquenghem, was revolutionary due to the ways in which it overturned the Oedipal institution—mirrors the recent changes in the form and syntax of gay porn and sex play that I've been discussing. Such changes, I contend, have allowed for a reframing of gay masculinity away from the erect penis and the phallic event of the cum shot, and towards the receptive and muscular anus—with its capacity to take in dick after dick, fist after fist, load after load—making *self-augmenting anality* the medium through which "pig" subjectivities are actualised as forms of enhanced, superhuman masculinity. As "Martin" noted, pig bottoms "don't need to cum. They don't get hard during sex, they don't need to finish". Yet, their soft penises notwithstanding, their masculinity is still transformed through augmentation to make them superhero-like.

There seems, however, to be a tension between "Martin"'s arguably individualistic account of his "load"-taking—that is, how disinterested he claimed to be in the tops that fuck him, preferring instead to have "sex with the night"—and Hocquenghem's (1993) understanding of homosexual desire to be a way of forming collectives that, precisely in its being "opposed to the usual 'social mode' [...] would cause the collapse of both the sublimating phallic hierarchy and the individual/society double-bind" (1993, 110). If the phallic orientation of Oedipal development delivers us the private/public and dirty/clean divides that have sustained the hegemony of the bourgeois social order, then anal homosexual desire may undo those very same divides and deliver us a new form of relating to one another collectively, in line with what Hocquenghem (1993) called "primary sexual communism" (111) and Dennis Altman (1983) idealised as "A sort of Whitmanesque democracy, a desire to know and trust other men in a type of brotherhood far removed from the male bonding of rank, hierarchy, and competition that characterizes much of the outside world" (79–80).

"Martin"'s account also echoes the narrative of contemporary porn videos produced by studios such as Sketchysex, famous for its fantasies of US "bros" in their 20s, living in shared flats and in permanent need of dick and "loads". Set in said flats amidst TVs that never seem to stop playing porn, empty cups and beer bottles on dirty floors, and sounds and shots of hook-up apps like Grindr being used to arrange sex, Sketchysex's trademark videos depict "no load refused"-types of gangbang scenes in which bottoms are fucked by tops who keep on arriving through the unlocked front door—what Charlie Sarson (2019) described, following Tien Yeo and Tsz Fung (2018), as a "conveyor belt system" (6) of sexual partners. In Sarson's cautionary words, though:

> Those performers in question taking on the role of the bottom are often heard to demand from those fucking them that they 'want their load', to 'cum in my hole', and, as soon as one of the active performers has done so, for the bottom to then declare that he 'needs another dick'. With regards to aforementioned notions of community formation, there is little of the sort at stake in these videos.
>
> (6)

How are we then to understand this tension between, on the one hand, a practice that, in its self-augmenting nature, may indeed be framed as an individualistic and competitive pursuit (of the exact kind that Hocquenghem had associated with sublimated homosexuality and the hegemony of the Phallus); and the alternative view that conceives of those same practices—and their contemporary actualisations in "pigsex"—as having the potential to create conditions of possibility for new experiences of communion to emerge that may trouble the hegemony of heteropatriarchy and capitalism? In his afterword to Hocquenghem's work, Paul Preciado (2009) wrote the following:

> *Homosexual Desire* is an instruction manual on how to operate an anti-system orifice that is installed in each and every body: the ANUS. Precise, offensive, vital, it is a revolutionary machine, highly manageable and devised for collective use.
>
> (148–149, my translation)[3]

Exploring the tensions between individual and community that seem to shape conflicting experiences of gay sex and "pigsex" in particular, at times appearing to lead men down a path of individualistic hedonism, other times sending them toward new horizons of collective becoming, in the following chapter I will attempt to argue my way out of that impasse.

Notes

1 Sections of this chapter have been published in *Porn Studies* (Florêncio 2018).
2 "*Pythagorae Socratisque & Platonis mos erat ubique divina mysteria figuris involucrisque obtegere, sapientiam suam contra Sophistarum iactantiam modeste dissimulare, iocari serio & studiosissime ludere*" (Ficino 1962, 125). Whilst Maude Vanhaelen's translation (Ficino 2012, 33) uses the phrase "to jest in seriousness and to joke in the greatest earnest", I chose instead to substitute "to joke" by "to play", following Michael Allen's translation (1986, 438), as "to play", is more fitting for my argument concerning "pig" sex play.
3
> "El deseo homosexual *es un manual de instrucciones para hacer funcionar un orificio anti-sistema instalado en todos y cada uno de los cuerpos: el ANO. Preciso, ofensivo, vital, es una máquina revolucionaria altamente manejable y pensada para su uso colectivo*".
>
> (Preciado 2009, 148–149)

References

Allen, Michael J. B. 1986. "The second Ficino-Pico controversy: Parmenidean poetry, eristic, and the one". In *Marsilio Ficino e il Ritorno di Platone: Studi e Documenti*, edited by Gian Carlo Garfagnini, 417–455. Florence: Leo S. Olschki Editore.
Altman, Dennis. 1983. *The Homosexualization of America*. Boston: Beacon Press.
Ashford, Chris. 2015. "Bareback sex, queer legal theory, and evolving socio-legal contexts". *Sexualities* 18 (1/2): 195–209.
Aydemir, Murat. 2007. *Images of Bliss: Ejaculation, Masculinity, Meaning*. Minneapolis: University of Minnesota Press.
Bataille, Georges. 1988. *The Accursed Share: An Essay on General Economy*, Volume I. New York: Zone Books.

Bersani, Leo. 2018. *Receptive Bodies*. Chicago: The University of Chicago Press.

Bersani, Leo, and Adam Phillips. 2008. *Intimacies*. Chicago: The University of Chicago Press.

CDC. 2019. "HIV transmission". www.cdc.gov/hiv/basics/transmission.html [accessed 9 November 2019].

Clark-Flory, Tracy. 2014. "When HIV is a turn-on". *Salon*, 15 April 2014. http://salon.com/2014/04/15/when_hiv_is_a_turn_on/ [accessed 9 November 2019].

Cohen, Ed. 2009. *A Body Worth Defending: Immunity, Biopolitics, and the Apotheosis of the Modern Body*. Durham: Duke University Press.

Dean, Tim. 2009. *Unlimited Intimacy: Reflections on the Subculture of Barebacking*. Chicago: The University of Chicago Press.

Deleuze, Gilles and Félix Guattari. 1983. *Anti-Oedipus: Capitalism and Schizophrenia*. Minneapolis: University of Minnesota Press.

Edelman, Lee. 2004. *No Future: Queer Theory and the Death Drive*. Durham: Duke University Press.

Esposito, Roberto. 2011. *Immunitas: The Protection and Negation of Life*. Cambridge: Polity Press.

Ficino, Marsilio. 1962. *Opera Omnia*. Torino: Bottega d'Erasmo.

Ficino, Marsilio. 2012. *Commentaries on Plato, Vol. 2, Pt. I*, edited and translated by Maude Vanhaelen. Cambridge, MA: Harvard University Press.

Florêncio, João. 2018. "Breeding futures: Masculinity and the ethics of CUMmunion in Treasure Island Media's *Viral Loads*". *Porn Studies* 5 (3): 271–285.

Foucault, Michel. 1978. *The History of Sexuality, Volume I: An Introduction*. New York: Pantheon Books.

Foucault, Michel. 1983. "Afterword: The subject and power". In *Michel Foucault: Beyond Structuralism and Hermeneutics*, edited by Hubert L. Dreyfus and Paul Rabinow, 2008–226. Chicago: University of Chicago Press.

Foucault, Michel. 1990a. *The History of Sexuality, Volume 2: The Use of Pleasure*. New York: Vintage Books.

Foucault, Michel. 1990b. "An aesthetics of existence". In Michel Foucault, *Politics, Philosophy, Culture: Interviews and Other Writings, 1977–1984*, edited by Lawrence D. Kritzman, 47–53. London: Routledge.

Foucault, Michel. 1990c. "The return of morality". In Michel Foucault, *Politics, Philosophy, Culture: Interviews and Other Writings, 1977–1984*, edited by Lawrence D. Ktrizman, 242–254. London: Routledge.

Foucault, Michel. 1997. "On the genealogy of ethics: An overview of work in progress". In Michel Foucault, *Ethics: Subjectivity and Truth*, edited by Paul Rabinow, 253–280. New York: The New Press.

Foucault, Michel. 2003a. *Abnormal: Lectures at the Collège de France, 1974–1975*. London: Verso.

Foucault, Michel. 2003b. *The Birth of the Clinic: An Archaeology of Medical Perception*. London: Routledge.

Foucault, Michel. 2005. *The Hermeneutics of the Subject: Lectures at the Collège de France, 1981–82*. Basingstoke: Palgrave Macmillan.

Fritscher, Jack. 1987. "Al Shapiro, A. Jay, & Harry Chess (The passing of one of Drummer's first daddies)". In Correspondence to Dick Kriegmont, 17 July 1987. A. Jay Papers, GLC 117. James C. Hormel LGBTQI Center, San Francisco Public Library, San Francisco, California.

García-Iglesias, Jaime. 2019. "Wanting HIV is 'such a hot choice': Exploring bug-chasers' fluid identities and online engagements". *Deviant Behavior*. DOI: 10.1080/01639625.2019.1606617.

Gill, Lindon K. 2018. *Erotic Islands: Art and Activism in the Queer Caribbean*. Durham: Duke University Press.

Halperin, David. 2007. *What Do Gay Men Want? An Essay on Sex, Risk, and Subjectivity*. Ann Arbor: The University of Michigan Press.

Hedrick, Stephen. 2004. "The acquired immune system: A vantage from beneath". *Immunity* 21: 607–615.

Hocquenghem, Guy. 1993. *Homosexual Desire*. Durham: Duke University Press.

Hocquenghem, Guy. 1995. "To destroy sexuality". In *Polysexuality*, edited by François Peraldi, 260–264. New York: Semiotext(e).

Inwood, Michael. 1992. *A Hegel Dictionary*. Oxford: Blackwell.

Kesel, Marc de. 2009. *Eros and Ethics: Reading Jacques Lacan's Seminar VII*. Albany: State University of New York Press.

Knox, Dilwyn. 1989. *Ironia: Medieval and Renaissance Ideas on Irony*. Leiden: E. J. Brill.

Lauretis, Teresa de. 1987. *Technologies of Gender: Essays on Theory, Film, and Fiction*. Bloomington: Indiana University Press.

Lazzarini, Zita *et al.* 2013. "Criminalization of HIV transmission and exposure: Research and policy agenda". *American Journal of Public Health* 103 (8): 1350–1353.

Lee, Byron. 2014. "It's a question of breeding: Visualizing queer masculinity in bareback pornography". *Sexualities* 17 (1/2): 100–120.

Lepage, John L. 2012. *The Revival of Antique Philosophy in the Renaissance*. New York: Palgrave Macmillan.

McCasker, Toby. 2014. "A porn director stirred up controversy by making a movie centered around HIV". *Vice*, 12 May 2014. www.vice.com/en_us/article/yvqbgm/director-paul-morris-believes-hiv-should-be-part-of-gay-porn/ [accessed 6 November 2019].

Morris, Paul. 2011. "No limits: Necessary danger in male porn". *Treasure Island Media Blog*, 15 November 2011. https://blog.treasureislandmedia.com/2011/11/no-limits-necessary-danger-in-male-porn/.

Morris, Paul, and Susanna Paasonen. 2014. "Risk and utopia: A dialogue on pornography". *GLQ* 20 (3): 215–239.

Nancy, Jean-Luc and Adèle van Reeth. 2017. *Coming*. New York: Fordham University Press.

Paasonen, Susanna. 2011. *Carnal Resonance: Affect and Online Pornography*. Cambridge, MA: The MIT Press.

Patton, Cindy. 1991. "Safe sex and the pornographic vernacular". In *How do I Look?: Queer Film and Video*, edited by Object-Choices Bad, 31–63. Seattle: Bay Press.

Preciado, Paul. 2009. "Terror anal: Apuntes sobre los primeros días de la revolución sexual". In Guy Hocquenghem, *El Deseo Homosexual*, 133–172. Santa Cruz de Tenerife: Melusina.

Preciado, Paul. 2013. *Testo Junkie: Sex, Drugs, and Biopolitics in the Pharmaco-pornographic Era*. New York: The Feminist Press.

Ruti, Mari. 2017. *The Ethics of Opting Out: Queer Theory's Defiant Subjects*. New York: Columbia University Press.

Ryan, Frank. 2004. "Human endogenous retroviruses in health and disease: A symbiotic perspective". *Journal of the Royal Society of Medicine* 97: 560–565.

Sarson, Charlie. 2019. "'The neighbourhood cums: Ding dong! Dick's here!': SketchySex and the online/offline culture of group sex between gay men". *Porn Studies*. DOI: 10.1080/23268743.2019.11592698.

Schubert, Karsten. 2019. "The democratic biopolitics of PrEP". In *Biopolitiken: Regierungen des Lebens heute*, edited by Helene Gerhards and Kathrin Braun, 121–153. Wiesbaden: Springer VS.

Sloterdijk, Peter. 2011. *Spheres, Volume I: Bubbles*. Los Angeles: Semiotext(e).

Steinbock, Eliza. 2016. "Look! But also, touch!: Theorizing images of trans eroticism beyond a politics of visual essentialism". In *Porno-Graphics & Porno-Tactics: Desire, Affect, and Representation in Pornography*, edited by Eirini Avramopoulou and Irene Peano, 59–75. Goleta, CA: Punctum Books.

Steinbock, Eliza. 2017. "Representing trans sexualities". In *The Routledge Companion to Media, Sex and Sexuality*, edited by Clarissa Smith, Feona Attwood, and Brian McNair, 27–37. London: Routledge.

Tauber, Alfred. 2000. "Moving beyond the immune self?" *Seminars in Immunology* 12: 241–248.

Theweleit, Klaus. 1987. *Male Fantasies: Women, Floods, Bodies, History*. Minneapolis: University of Minnesota Press.

Tomso, Gregory. 2008. "Viral sex and the politics of life". *South Atlantic Quarterly* 107 (2): 265–285.

Williams, Linda. 1999. *Hard Core: Power, Pleasure, and the "Frenzy of the Visible"*. Berkeley: University of California Press.

Williams, Linda. 2014. "Pornography, porno, porn: Thought on a weedy field". In *Porn Archives*, edited by Tim Dean, Steven Ruszczycky and David Squires, 29–43. Durham: Duke University Press.

Yeo, Tien and Tsz Fung. 2018. "'Mr Right Now': Temporality of relationship formation on gay mobile dating apps". *Mobile Media & Communication* 6 (1): 3–18.

4   The cummunion of strangers

Treasure Island Media's (TIM) owner Paul Morris is both a deeply fascinating and a frightening man. With a personal, academic, and professional history that I've only managed to partially piece together during our several hours-long conversations in his office in San Francisco, Morris has come across as an extremely well-read and articulate pornographer and thinker. Having managed to divert all my attempts at recording an actual interview with him and preferring instead to have me turn up to Treasure Island Media at any time and unannounced during my stay in the Bay Area ("I'm not a dentist, I don't make appointments", he had told me on an email), Morris gave me open access to the rather welcoming and relaxed office he shares with a few staff, a couple of dogs, a fridge exclusively dedicated to storing bottles of poppers, rows of shelves holding sex toys and TIM's stock of porn DVDs, and an impressive bookshelf holding titles that covered everything including early modern philosophy; ritual, magic and the occult; art, poetry, fiction, and music; and queer theory. There, he invited me to sit through interviews of prospective porn models, allowed me to pet the office dogs, introduced me to all his staff (after insisting that I pick a new name for myself for "why would you not want a chance to make yourself anew?") and—most importantly—sat with me in his windowless office where we spent hours talking, often with him talking *at* me. He told me about his views on the exceptionality of gay men and gay sex, on hedonism, on the power and nature of Eros, and on queer temporality, always somehow managing to bring all that to bear on a discussion of beauty—we talked about beauty a lot. Between that and asking me rather probing questions about my family background, the small Portuguese village where I was grew up, the English university town where I work, my coming-out, my first sexual experiences both alone and with others, my current sex life, my relationships, my lovers, my boyfriend, and my boyfriend's work, he would end our meetings with an abrupt "I think this is enough for today; see you again next week?" before giving me a hug and sending me on my way after a last cuddle with one of the dogs. Suffice to say that, every single time, I left the office both mesmerised and intrigued—whilst, on the one hand, there was a sense in which a lot of what he had said could have been deeply calculated and acted out in order to paint a particular self-aggrandising picture of himself for me, on the other hand, and as time went by and we had more meetings, I could not but feel that underneath his frightening, self-assured persona, there was a deep generosity, honesty, and commitment to what he sees as the ethical and political potential of gay sex to forge queer ways of being in a straight world—a belief in our duty to embrace what to him is some kind of queer essence shared by all gay men, if only we free ourselves from the chains of heterosexual culture.

Who was this man who would come across as some kind of guru of gay sex, who would talk of gay men as if we were the avant-garde, who would give me his detailed views on some of queer theory's most canonical books and postulates, and who would never shy away not only from disagreeing with me but also from doing so in a raised tone that would sometimes scare me, sometimes tease out the submissive side of my psychosexual persona. Funnily enough, he would often insist on how Eros is something that drives not only the forging of—in his words—"a collective mind" during and through sex, but also the forging of a collective mind through conversations like ours. Ultimately, to him, our meetings were enactments of the erotic. So whilst I was certainly frightened, mesmerised, and suspicious in equal and still unresolved measure, I couldn't help feeling drawn to the rather convincing and confident manner in which he would place his work in relation to cultural artefacts as diverse as Poulenc's Concerto for two Pianos in D minor, Dawn Shadforth's video for Kylie Minogue's "Can't Get You Out of My Head", Hitchcock's 1948 classic *Rope*, Indonesian gamelan music, or the individual illustrations and plot in *Pleasure Park*, issue 20 of Tom of Finland's famous magazine of gay erotica *Kake*, from 1980.

Towards the end of our last meeting, Morris told me he had been wanting to show me something. He turned to his computer and played me a porn scene that, according to him, managed to capture something he'd been waiting for 15 years to document. Not only that but, apparently, once he was first shown the final edit, he immediately knew he'd have to overlay the music of Franz Schubert on it. And that he did. The sequence, a special edit of scene five of TIM's DVD release *Sick Fucks* from 2016, opened with a written warning on a black background: "Do not watch this video more than once. Repeated viewings are not recommended." As soon as the warning disappeared, we were right in the middle of the action, with a close-up shot of Jack Darling fucking Murphy Maxwell, shot with a familiar porn up shot, the camera behind the top at the level of his lower thighs as he penetrated the bottom. Maxwell was laying on his back on a bed moaning in pleasure, and as the cameras—I eventually noticed there were three of them—moved around him and Darling, I realised the latter was pissing inside Maxwell's rectum. "Fucking fill me up", the bottom said, one camera closing in on his face. As the scene continued with cameramen entering and exiting the frame at various points, Darling grabbed a kitchen pan, placed it by the bed, and Maxwell squatted over it, pushing out the urine the top had pumped inside him. Once he did so, the camera closed in on his face and, with a cheeky smile, Maxwell said "Fuck! I'm a fucking pig … I'm a fucking pig!" after which he and the cameraman laughed. "It's true!" he added, with a delightfully cheeky, child-like smile. Once Maxwell returned to his original position laying on his back on the bed, Darling started to slowly push Crisco into his rectum whilst the bottom inhaled poppers, his head out of focus in the middle-ground of a frame more concerned with closing in on Darling's hand lubbing-up Maxwell's sphincter than on the little bottle the bottom held close to one of his nostrils. With both orifices—his nose and his anus—functioning there as gateways to pleasure, only one of them was the clear star of the show.

At this point, as Darling continued to lube-up Maxwell's ass and eventually managed to insert his whole fist into him, the unexpected occurred: gently, the second movement of Schubert's String Quintet in C Major (D. 956, Op. 163) started playing, competing with Maxwell's increasingly loud moans for the viewer's aural attention. When I asked Morris what had come first, Schubert's Adagio or the final edit of the scene, he reassured me that the scene had been edited before he decided to lay the music over it. Whether or not that had been the case—and I have no reasons to suspect it hadn't—the affective charge of the increasingly intense fisting scene became amplified by the equally increasingly intense affective charge of Schubert's music. At that moment, it became harder for me to doubt what Morris's had told me earlier in that meeting, that he had finally managed to find, capture, and edit together that one sex scene he'd been searching for over the previous 15 years, a scene that he immediately realised to be Schubert's score, completed two months before the composer's death, transposed to pornography. At this point, it is useful to make a detour to reflect more carefully on the musical progression of Schubert's famous Adagio as it accompanied and resonated with the unfolding of the fisting scene.

Writing about Schubert's quintet, John Gingerich (2000) noted how it draws forth "extreme existential states" (619), invoking both "convivial fellowship and tortured interior monologue" (631). In his view, "Schubert has bequeathed to us, instead of a heroic narrative of telos, music of tremendous courage in its refusal to shrink from the remembrance of loss or from the self-dividing consequences of introspection" (631). When zooming in on the second movement of the piece—the one Morris chose to accompany the porn scene I've been describing—Gingerich spoke of it as being "the most extreme illustration in Schubert's entire instrumental oeuvre of an 'utopian' or 'static dream tableau'" (621). Further, he continued, the "ways in which the music compels rapt attention whilst submerging the usual conscious processes of listening are closely akin to immersion in the vivid presentness of a dream" (623). The Adagio was composed in a ternary (A-B-A) form, with the first section evoking "a painful radiance" and "deep tranquility", traits that, as Gingerich noted, have been "conventionally associated with profound happiness" (623). The second section, on the other hand, opens with an abrupt shift in intensity and harmonic contrast, jumping from *pianissimo* to *fortissimo* and from E major to F minor in such a way that "the breathlessness of the melody, combined with the continuously febrile accompaniment, give the whole of the B section a tinge of desperation, even of hysteria" (625). Despite their contrasts, however, both A and B sections have the character of an "internal monologue" and if the former alludes to the temporality of a "dream of impossible bliss", the latter is "a compulsive outpouring of protest, pain, anguish, and sorrow" (625)—affects that manage to somewhat still linger on the transformed line of the second cello after the reassuring return of section A completes the ternary form.

What interests me in Gingerich's analysis of Schubert's "true swan song" (631), is not just his framing of the piece around ideas of memory, interiority, temporality, and utopia, but also the ways in which the adagio returns, in its third section, to the "deep tranquility" and "painful radiance" of the first albeit not without having been transformed or modulated by the "protest, pain, anguish, and sorrow" of the middle section. As a musical utopia where remembrance, sorrow, pain, fellowship, and bliss coalesce, the second movement of Schubert's quintet seems to me to resonate with Lee Edelman's (2004) queer negativity of self-obliteration whilst still insisting on the creative possibility and ecstatic potential that can be enacted through queer body practices approached as carnal speculations on futurity (Muñoz 2009). For all intents and purposes—for all *my* intents and purposes—Schubert's music appears to offer a vision of flowers sprouting through the crevices of crumbling internal and external walls, of ruins as spaces of decay from which life still insists on growing. It doesn't get queerer than that.

At this point I would like to return to the video itself. As both the Adagio and the fisting started, the cameras moved around Darling, the top, and Maxwell, the bottom, going back and forth between close-ups of the fisting action and of Maxwell's face, which reflected the rising intensity of the scene—his eyes rolling back into his head, his facial expression and moans seeming increasingly out of control. Amidst the arguable violence or stress that may often be associated with sexual practices such as fisting and fist "pigs" ' investment in extreme bodily sensations that to viewers and participants alike can come across as an indiscernible mixture of pleasure and pain, a few moments in the video did take me back by surprise, triggering a rather physical reaction that wasn't so much sexual as it was aesthetic—it resonated in me like an encounter with sublimity. At one point, soon after the music had started and Maxwell's contorted expressions of pleasure increased in intensity, one of the cameras zoomed out from a close-up of the penetration to slowly show the hand of the bottom gently placed around the waist of one of the cameramen, drawing him into the action as a fellow traveller in a shared journey. Soon, and maybe as a result of that hand having been gently placed on his lower back—an inviting gesture that is certainly not unfamiliar to any gay man versed in the etiquette of sex clubs or darkrooms—the cameraman took the place of Darling and started fisting the bottom, the beak of the bird tattooed on the inside of his forearm moving progressively closer to the lubbed-up gaping gateway to Maxwell's secret interior. At that point, Darling joined in, slowly inserting his hand where the hand of the cameraman already was, in a double-top, double-fist sequence that, rather than coming across as violent, evoked instead feelings of care, comradery and shared intimacy amongst the three men. Maxwell responded with intense grunts and moans, sniffing a red hanky sprayed with ethyl chloride as Schubert's first violin started playing a brief sequence of high As with hard, loud attacks that contrasted with the legato motives that had immediately preceded them. With the scene drawing to a close, the fisting cameraman returned Maxwell's sphincter back to Darling and Schubert's Adagio returned to its first section modified—dare I say loosened up—by what had come before. The frenetic intensity of the music and the fisting gave way to a progressive return to "deep tranquility" and "impossible bliss", with Darling eventually inserting a large butt-plug in Maxwell's ass whilst saying, in the most caring and tender of tones, "you got it … you got it, brother. You got it". The scene closed with the top fucking the bottom with both his penis and his hand simultaneously, a sequence of gratification of both self and other, Darling's dick rubbing up against his own hand inside Maxwell's welcoming hole.

As we watched the scene in his office, Morris and I remained completely silent, in what can only be described as a state of absorption. As far as I was concerned, I was deeply taken back by the intensity and sublimity of what I was watching, unable to say anything, incapable of articulating it in words. I certainly had never expected to react in such a way to a porn video, to having a porn video convey such a sense of ineffability, of immensity or a quasi-religious experience of transcendence, my body resonating with the "painful radiance" and "impossible bliss" conveyed both by Schubert's Adagio and by Maxwell's contorted facial expressions of the kind of pleasure one must feel when one's body is sensed to be melting into a myriad of tiny dancing electron-like particles radiating light into the void. The whole thing brought to mind a passage from a letter Harry Hay—the communist gay activist founder of the Mattachine Society and the Radical Faeries—had written to his lover Jim Kepner in 1963, a passage that my own lover had read me in bed only a couple of months prior:

> I think we are like two electrodes which, when charge with the same current, are prone to spark in response to one another and thus to

fuse, at top heat of pure efficiency, until the given charge is spent: whereupon the two electrodes return to ionic [quiescence] to prepare for the next charge and consequent renewal of spark.

(Hay 1963, 1–2)

My mind moved from image to image, from thought to thought, revisiting what I had just watched in a failed attempt to fully capture it in words. I glanced at Morris and saw him wiping tears off his face with paper tissue. He returned my gaze. As I struggled to articulate a response to the video, the only thing I was able to say was "Wow; I'm speechless …" He answered: "I knew you'd get it. I'm glad I was able to share this with you." He paused for a moment and then said, "I think this is enough for today. See you again next week?"

I left Treasure Island Media's office and decided to make the 40-minute walk back to my apartment in order to try to organise my thinking. What was it about that video that triggered such a strong reaction in me? How did those men who, according to Paul, had never met before the shoot, manage to engage in such an intense sexual encounter, where roughness, surrender, and care appeared to be present in equally high measure? How did those strangers approach one another as "brothers"? Or—more interestingly perhaps—what does seeing them address one another as "brother" do to our understanding of structures of kinship, sexual sociability, and communion? What ethics can be derived from that? A few weeks later, after I was back in the UK and decided I wanted to write about the video he'd shown me in San Francisco, I emailed Morris asking him about it— had it been released? Did it have a title? His reply was both less and more helpful than I expected. He wrote: "The fisting scene was, I believe, appended as a bonus track on the DVD that had the full scene. As far as I can recollect, it had no title. How can you name something like that?" Despite his inability to name that particular video and the kind of intimacy and communion it depicted, I couldn't help recalling an earlier conversation I had had with him, one that focused on Tom of Finland's work, and on an yet-unpublished article Morris had emailed me afterwards, one in which he discussed Tom's "Pleasure Park".

"Pleasure Park" is a narrative series of drawings that opens with one man entering a "men only" park named "Pleasure Park", encountering another man masturbating on a bench, engaging in sex with him, and subsequently being joined by other men, one at a time, until the story ends with an amalgam of countless bodies having sex together. The story comes across as a narrative of additive seriality—of n + 1—one in which each new man resembles the other in facial features and body type (the standard Kake character in Tom's work), with their individuality being minimally marked by the different clothing they wear—military uniforms, cowboy attire, workwear—the different hair, the occasional moustache. In that way, Tom's "Pleasure Park" and the sex it depicts can be seen to foreground as its lead characters not the men themselves but the transversal logics of the libidinal force that cuts through them and connects them in an assemblage: $1+1+1+1....$ It is not so much about the men understood as individualised parts of a whole but about the creative power of the serial impetus that drives them together in their collective *becumming*.

Morris makes similar points in his article, engaging Tom's "Pleasure Park" to argue for what he sees as the exceptionality of gay male sexual sociability as a queer world-making practice. Two claims stand out in his essay. First, that all the different men depicted are the same regardless of the differences that may identify them as individuals; and, second, the claim that, by having their bodies come together and resonate in the same "erotic 'bandwidth'", those men, with their bodies plugged into one another, submerge themselves in some kind of pre-cognitive, pre-individual, "single mind" (Morris n.d.). One paragraph of his text synthesises both points through musical analogies (again, music emerging as a central rhetoric device in Morris's thinking about gay porn and gay sex). He writes, in a passage that is worth quoting in full in order to better grasp that analogy:

> Two compositional elements are maintained through the sequence of drawings. The first is that of exciting newness kept at high pitch by the successive entrance in each frame of essentially the same entity (one handsome, muscled man): a repetitive beat, a mantra, a chant, a stutter, the repetition of an hypnotic and minimal melodic fragment. The second and more significant element is the constellated development into sexual constructs of the assembled and growing group of men. If "Pleasure Park" were music, the first line perhaps would be the rhythm of the piece and the second would be the harmony. Each "note" (that is, each man) has a complex envelope, a distinct entrance and timbral continuity that enables the "rhythm" and "harmony" to develop. The identity of each man and of the group itself can be read musically: men are presented in their ornamented (costumed) anonymity as mutually equivalent elements in a (consonant and sexual) composition.
>
> (Morris n.d.)

I could not but notice how Morris's argument had a certain Deleuzean flair to it, perhaps unsurprising given how Deleuze himself had often also drawn from music and music theory to inform his philosophical work. To me, the anonymity that Morris highlighted in Tom's men as equivalent "notes" in a composition brought to mind the way in which Deleuze stressed the primacy of the conjunctive "AND" in the formation of multitudes. As the French philosopher noted to Claire Parnet:

> It is not the elements of the sets which define the multiplicity. What defines it is the AND, as something which has its place between the

elements or between the sets. AND, AND, AND—stammering. And even if there are only two terms, there is an AND between the two, which is neither the one nor the other, nor the one which becomes the other, but which constitutes the multiplicity. This is why it is always possible to undo dualisms from the inside, by tracing the line of flight which passes between the two terms of the two sets, the narrow stream which belongs neither to the one nor to the other, but draws both into a non-parallel evolution, into a heterochronous becoming.

(Deleuze and Parnet 1987, 34–35)

By focusing on the "AND", Deleuze wrote against humanism and the latter's prioritisation of the autonomous subject. The "AND" shifts our attention towards the productive power of a conjunctive force—which both Deleuze and Morris associated with desire—to produce machinic assemblages in relation to which the individuation of a being—the subject's process of subjectivation—is not an *a priori* but an *a fortiori*, the arrest of the many in the one that's responsible for stratifying being out of an ontologically prior process of becoming. Talking about Being as such is thus always to talk about being singular-plural (Nancy 2000), the impetus of desiring-production operating as a transversal force that Charlie Blake (2011) defined, after Deleuze and Guattari, as "a system of lines of flight and creativity that criss-cross the univocity of Being so as to enable and bring to actuality new assemblages, new concepts, new affects, and new interminglings and comminglings of bodies" (183).

Deleuze, the philosopher: "You are always an assemblage for an abstract machine, which is realized elsewhere in other assemblages. You are always in the middle of something; plant, animal or landscape" (Deleuze and Parnet, 1987, 112–113). Morris, the pornographer: "The driving phallic energy becomes monstrous in its translation into this transhuman amalgam. And these men become inhuman in their submersion in a single mind" (Morris n.d.).

Yet, despite their conceptualisation of desire as a connective force, Morris and Deleuze's views diverge on how they see the pleasure of the collective orgasm that a story such as Tom of Finland's "Pleasure Park" is normally expected to culminate with. I say "normally" because there is a sense in the series that the many-headed sex machine doesn't really stop, its last image still showing ongoing group sex even as the man with whom the story started appears to leave the park, moving towards the foreground of the image—towards the viewer looking in—and leaving behind the orgy that continues despite himself. For Morris, the desire that brings men together in "Pleasure Park" has the potential to culminate in mass orgasmic *jouissance* with the power to "destroy societies, upturn all property, end capitalism, swallow and digest everything human", thus leaving us with "a world vastly improved in terms of human satisfaction, a world where universal satiation as a ruling and organizing principle [would have] supplanted greed and compulsive competition" (Morris n.d.). For Deleuze, on the other hand, the idea of the satiation of desire through pleasure and release in orgasm is a betrayal of the creative force of desiring-production by submitting it to the logics of lack, the psychoanalytical lack against which both he and Guattari engaged their schizoanalytic philosophical project. In the name of desiring-production, Deleuze privileged the affirmative economies of "disavowal and suspense" that he saw sustaining masochistic desiring-plateaus (Deleuze 1991, 32), and decried the libidinal economies of the negative that he associated both with the "rotten idea" of pleasure (2001, 96)—responsible for interrupting desire (1997, 53)—and with the reaffirmation of the Oedipal institution through the "inflation of the father" encountered in sadism (1991, 68). Whilst for Morris the pornographer, sexual pleasure—more precisely gay male sexual pleasure—has the power to undo the human, for Deleuze the philosopher, only suspended desire with no pleasurable resolution could offer us such thing, for every time desire is satiated it reinstitutes the subject (of lack) and thus the human.

However, there is a sense in which Deleuze's distaste for pleasure—one that led to a famous disagreement between him and his friend Foucault (Deleuze 1997; Foucault and Le Bitoux 2011)—can be seen to still maintain part of the psychoanalytic apparatus he and Guattari aimed to undo. As both Frida Beckman (2013) and Charlie Blake (2011) noted, whilst rescuing desire from the psychoanalytical logics of lack by affirming the unconscious as a factory and desire as desiring-production, Deleuze still left untroubled the psychoanalytical understanding of orgasm as surrender to lack—the *petite-mort* driven by a body's desire to return to an inorganic state (Freud 1989), or the self-shattering *jouissance* arising from a flirtation with the Real (Lacan 2008). Against this position, both Beckman and Blake used Deleuze against himself, arguing that, rather than simply reinstituting the Oedipal subject of psychoanalysis, sexual pleasure can indeed help us better understand Deleuze's own conceptualisation of the body and the subject as foldings in univocal Being; how, in the dynamics of desire and pleasure that culminate in orgasm, *the body individuates itself by opening itself to the multiple*, by simultaneously sedimenting itself as beach sand and abandoning itself to the oceanic pull of the sea in the threshold space of the shore, a rhythmic pattern—or, in Morris's words above, a "stutter"—"from coming to becoming and from becoming to coming" (Blake 2011, 197)—what I would call a *becumming*. Consider now the following passage from Erik Rémès's *Serial Fucker*, one in which the author describes the experience of gay sex in darkrooms:

> We fuck with a stranger. A body. That is to say, above all, a cock or an ass that one does not necessarily see in the moist half-light. A stranger without identity, without history and without tomorrow. A relationship to another without an other. A relationship without name nor

verbal language. Meat. Serial, we go from one body to another, then to a third again, until no longer thirsty. [...]

In some darkrooms, bodies come and go, lend and exchange. Then it emerges, a true sexual communism. And even the oldest or the ugly have (or should have) their chance. And so much the better for them.

(Rémès 2003, 28, my translation)[1]

What we see in the additive group sex scenes depicted in both "Pleasure Park" and Rémès's account of darkroom sex cannot be fully reduced to a specular narcissistic system whereby the one always relates to himself at the level of the imaginary, where each man confirms himself simply through relating to an other who functions as a mirror-image returning back to the subject the image of himself that he desires. Instead, what we have is a more complicated scene, an assemblage where the subject relates to *different timbres or hues* of an immanent sameness—sailor Kake to army Kake to cowboy Kake to labourer Kake to policeman Kake—in such a way that each man cannot be reduced to a self-enclosed interiority that precedes its encounter with others nor by an *a priori* lack but, rather, by his capacity to extend into the other as he himself emerges as singular-plural, evoking new *cummunal* worlds as he does so (Tuhkanen 2002). By noting the tension—the unresolved coexistence—of sameness and differ-ence in "Pleasure Park", where every man is and is not a copy of himself, we can start to figure out the complex ways in which the one relates to the multiple—the singular to the plural—in those scenes of group sex play, evoking Tim Dean's reading of what Leo Bersani's called the "inaccurate self-replication" of the gay clone (Dean 2013, 126).

Drawing attention to the ever-growing number of hanky codes used by clones to signal different sexual preferences, Dean (2013) argued that clones are not just a subset of the gay male population built around visual resemblance and a shared erotic ideal, but they are also "subject to end-lessly proliferating differentiations" based on what they like to get up to sexually (127–129). Following Lacan, Dean noted how the imaginary alienation and potential misrecognition that will inevitably take place amongst look-alike clones as a result of their wide variety of sexual tastes has the potential to shatter the ego, for what at first appeared identical suddenly emerges as different. According to that logic, and rather than reassuring the subject of his identity, clones function instead as imaginary "allegorical figures" (126), as "superficial instances of a more profound [ontological] sameness that de-individuates subjectivity" (132). The poten-tial of this argument, as I read it, is that hypermasculine clones, in having what Dean called an "intuitive grasp of the workings of desire *tout court*" (129), open up a different pathway for thinking forms of communion that are not so much predicated on the assumption of a recognisable pre-existing identity confirmed and shared in our encounter with others. Instead, those alternative forms of communion take as their grounds the inevitability of misrecognition and alienation amongst individuals who are always-already the same yet different, singular yet plural, one yet many, even as they *cum* together.

To explore those ideas further, I would like to draw from Gayle Rubin's ethnography of the infamous San Francisco fisting and SM club, the Catacombs. Writing about the club, which opened in San Francisco in May 1975 (Fritscher 1978), Rubin (2004) noted the ways in which transgression of bodily boundaries and explorations of extreme forms of sexual pleasure were, in the club, not only approached as forms of sexual sociability but also created the conditions of possibility for various kinds of intimate friendships to emerge and be fostered through a shared investment in a specific kind of sexual exploration, and a ritualistic approach to rough sex as a means towards affective transcendence, all framed by a collective investment in care, intimacy, and trust amongst men who would often first meet as strangers. In Rubin's words:

> At the Catacombs, even brief connections were handled with courtesy and care. And there was a particular kind of love that emerged from the slings. Sometimes that love only happened in "the back" [the playroom]. Just as often, it extended out into the everyday world. The Catacombs facilitated the formation of important friendships and lasting networks of support. Many of the men who frequented the Catacombs found relationships there that have sustained them through time, nurtured them with affection, cared for them in sickness, and buried them in sorrow.
>
> (139)

Rubin's claims would not have been foreign to the gay men who had been to the Catacombs and taken part in some or all of the practices that often happened there. As a piece by Jack Fritscher published in *Drummer* in 1978 had already noted:

> The Catacombs fosters a family aspect that a guy won't find at the anonymous tubs where if he has some difficulty, strangers will step over his body. At the Catacombs, people are not only permissive, they responsibly look out for each other.
>
> (Fritscher 1978, 10–11)

Even today, after AIDS sexual panics have led—directly or indirectly—to the closure of many such spaces during the 1980s, the Catacombs included, similar dynamics and forms of sexual sociability and intimate friendship can be still be found in gay sex clubs and darkrooms around the world, particularly after the introduction of antiretrovirals started to progressively do away with the spectre of death that used to haunt our sex. Whether in London, Berlin, New York, Los Angeles, or San Francisco, whether in clubs or sex parties organised in private apartments or rented playrooms, "pigsex" appears to have picked up on where the clones of the 1970s left us. A pursuit of extremes of pleasure, transgression, experimentation, and intimacy that is always-already mediated either chemically (antiretrovirals, Viagra/Cialis, crystal meth, GHB, MDMA, etc.) or visually (professional and amateur porn), "pigsex" constitutes, as I've mentioned before, what Evangelos Tziallas (2019), writing about barebacking, called the "return of the repressed" (120). "Pigsex" returns us to forms of sexual sociability that were, to a certain extent, put on hold or pushed underground in the aftermath of the AIDS crisis and the spectre of actual death gay sex started carrying with it. Thanks to chemical and visual mediations, pre-AIDS forms of sexual sociability have now returned with a vengeance, bringing gay men together and catalysing forms of intimacy and more or less lasting bonds that cannot be fully captured by the normative discourse of "rights" that has come to dominate LGBTQ+ politics since the 1990s.

During my fieldwork I have come to experience many instances of those forms of *becumming* together. I remember, for instance, one night in the basement darkroom of a Berlin bar where I had gone to meet a friend. After a few drinks upstairs, we decided to have a wander downstairs to see what was going on. After a few minutes of walking around in almost pitch-black dark, using hands to navigate both the space and the bodies around us, my friend and I started playing with one another in one of the rooms that was then still empty. Soon after we started having sex, as if some inaudible mating call had been broadcast by our conjoined bodies, several other men entered the room and formed a circle around the two of us. Whilst most of them stood there playing with themselves, others started getting closer to us, so close that I eventually felt the hand of one of them being gently placed on my back, just like Maxwell had done with the cameraman in the fisting video I described earlier. I couldn't see his face in the dark, but I do clearly remember the feel of his hand inviting himself in. I grabbed it and pulled him towards us.

Invitations and advances aren't, however, always accepted. Gay men still make choices about what they will accept doing and with whom, choices that are oftentimes based on the worst kinds of prejudices and standards of what or who counts as sexually appealing. After all, gay men, too, are subjects of their historical moment and hegemonic systems of value. For that reason, I could be led to agree with Leo Bersani's response to Dennis Altman's claim that bathhouses (and, by extension, any public or semi-public spaces of gay sex) are inherently democratic. According to Bersani:

> Anyone who has ever spent one night in a gay bathhouse knows that is (or was) one of the most ruthless, ranked, hierarchized, and competitive environments imaginable. Your looks, muscles, hair distribution,

size of cock, and shape of ass determined exactly how happy you were going to be during those few hours, and rejection, generally accompanied by two or three words at most, could be swift and brutal, with none of the civilizing hypocrisies with which we get rid of undesirables in the outside world.

(2010, 12)

Yet, whilst there are indeed many instances of rejection in contemporary spaces of communal gay sexual play, I don't think those have to be inherently or even "generally [...] swift and brutal" simply because gay sex spaces aren't themselves inherently democratic. What I do believe, however, is that something is taking place in those spaces—something that is being catalysed, i.e. sped up, by cocktails of recreational and/or prescription drugs—that has the potential to help us imagine new experiences of communion and thus invoke, to quote Deleuze and Guattari (1994), "a people to come" (176). It is there that I think what has come to be known as "pigsex" and "pig masculinities" may, in their shift away from an exclusive eroticisation of looks to a privileged eroticisation of practices—of fluid exchange and boundary transgression—allow us to conceive different modes of relating to others that are not predicated on the sameness of what gay men *are*, on their cloneness, but on the self-augmenting resonances of what they *do* with one another.

Another experience from my fieldwork helps illustrate that point: one Sunday evening, having been at one of the Berlin clubs with my lover since the morning—chatting with one another and with friends and acquaintances, visiting the darkroom every once in a whilst, dancing, sitting by the bar with a drink or sharing drugs—an incident took place that caused some commotion and drew my attention. A mid-30s-looking guy, muscled and hairy in all the supposedly "right" places and in the supposedly "right" amount, violently pushed away some other guy who had been trying, insistently, to hook up with him. The guy in question was certainly not muscled nor was he hairy; he was a slightly chubby and smooth guy who was also visibly wasted. After that drew my attention, I asked some friends what had just happened. At that moment, a friend of a friend—also very muscled and who was friends with the guy who had violently rejected the other—said, in an extremely annoyed tone, something along the lines of "you may not want to fuck someone but you don't need to be a dick!" His reaction surprised me. Here he was, one of those guys who, judging by Bersani's account and certainly to many of us, occupies the proverbial top of the gay food chain—a muscled, hairy, mid-30s to early-40s hypermasculine male—coming in to defend a guy who looked nothing like him, criticising his own friend for having acted in such violent way. Or, at a different club a few days earlier, as I was involved in some one-to-one light play with a German guy who had taken a fancy to my trainers, another guy, possibly drunk or high, kept on coming up to us and trying to grab the guy I was with. Every single time he approached us—and they were many—the guy I was with kept on smiling at him, chatting to him, and politely declining his invitation, gently lifting the hands that kept landing on him. Whilst at first I felt uncomfortable, I eventually became fascinated by that situation and by the level of care, respect, and empathy that was still being invested in a moment of saying "no; thank you"—miles away from the "swift and brutal" rejections Bersani wrote about and which are nonetheless still around today, as the first incident I described shows. So how exactly can the forms of hypermasculine "pigsex" I've been discussing give rise to care, to a set of practices that, as Joan Tronto (2013) noted, are normally deeply gendered as "women's work" (68)?

In a passage of his 1978 interview with Le Bitoux in which he addressed the emergence of the gay "clone" and the SM and fisting scenes that were being associated with the emergence of hypermasculine gay subjectivities in the 1970s, Foucault painted an interesting picture of the phenomenon. He said:

> [These men] use the signs of masculinity but not at all to return to something that would be of the order of phallocratism or machismo, but rather to invent themselves, to allow themselves to make their masculine body a place for the production of extraordinarily polymorphous pleasures, detached from the valorization of sex and particularly the male sex.
>
> (Foucault and Le Bitoux 2011, 396–397)

Whilst I am not fully convinced that gay hypermasculinity and "pigsex" as they have unfolded in tandem with one another won't necessarily return us to machismo, I do think that there is a disruptive potential in contemporary "pig" masculinities and "pigsex" that, as Foucault noted, passes through a detachment from the male sex, by which I mean, along with Guy Hocquenghem, a departure away from phallic sexuality to anality. Such a move has the potential to undermine the Phallic order that, in psychoanalytic studies of the modern bourgeois libidinal economy at least, have made "private cleanliness" [*propreté privée*] the grounds of "private property" [*propriété privée*] (Hocquenghem 1993, 98). By that same token, and with identity emerging as the private property of individuals—*my* identity, *my*self—in a phallogocentric order, it is only "any social use of the anus, apart from its sublimated [bourgeois] use, [that] creates the risk of a loss of identity" and, therefore, a threat to our most private of properties (101). An anal mode of desire and sexuality, which is not so much about a refusal of the penis as one of many sexual organs, but more about a turning of the anus and of anal activity away from the domain of the most private (e.g. defecation) to the domain of the public, the pleasurable and the sociable, has important consequences for thinking new horizons of communal possibility. By refocusing our psychosexual organisation on the anus as a

porous a-hole, we should be able to speculate on what anal forms of communion may look like and to what extent they may be able to dispense
both with the identitarian logics of "community" and with understandings
of the commons that have historically seen the latter as property, even if a
shared one.

Writing about *communitas*, Victor Turner associated it with the feeling
of belonging that individuals experience during the liminal stage of a ritual.
Whereas outside the space-time of that stage of a ritual the world is struc-
tured and organised—i.e. governed—during the liminal phase the pre-ritual
boundaries between individuals and well as the hierarchies amongst them
are blurred, allowing for the group to emerge as an unstructured, undiffer-
entiated, "community, or even communion of equal individuals who
submit together to the general authority of the ritual elders" (Turner 1995,
96). Drawing from Arnold van Gennep's classification of the three phases
of rites of passage, Turner (1995) pointed out that the latter are characterised by a first stage—"separation"—in which individuals or groups are
detached from the social structure, followed by a second stage—"margin"
or *"limen"*—in which the ritual subject appears as having ambiguous,
unclassifiable characteristics. Finally, a third stage—"aggregation"—
returns individuals back to the social order, albeit transformed by the
ritual experience they went through (94–95, 129).

Turner's study of ritual processes could, at first, look like a fitting
frame to understand ritual-like events such as "pig" play. After all, gay
sex play tends to involve planning, preparation, oftentimes travels to a
specific location (a private apartment, a sex club, a darkroom, etc.), and
then a return to the everyday world at the end of an intense sexual
encounter with one or more men. Taking up that position would also be
supported by studies of rave and clubbing subcultures such as Sarah
Thornton's (1995) landmark study *Club Cultures*, in which the author
drew from the same paradigm of ritual studies to investigate how feelings
of belonging were being developed amongst clubbers, and how clubbers
conceived of their clubbing lives vis-à-vis their everyday lives. The
problem with such an approach if one is to consider the ways in which
feelings of communion may play a part in a progressive politics is that the
logics of liminality, just like those of Bahktin's carnivalesque, are socially
conservative. That is, their primary function is to maintain order rather
than troubling it. According to such a view, the phenomena under analysis
would eventually be reduced to pure hedonistic escapism, something
people do to let off steam, as it were, before returning to life as it still is.
Crucially, in so doing, community thus conceived would reaffirm the
status quo, allowing for subcultural practices to become integrated into it
rather than challenging it. Furthermore, the idea of community itself not
only replicates dominant patterns of heteropatriarchal thought by being
dependent on ideas of kinship and (social–) reproductive futurism (Berlant
and Warner 1998) as well as on conceptions of empty linear time (see,

e.g. Zimmerman 2018), but it is also substantially different from what Berlant and Warner (1998) saw as the queer project of world-making and its irreducibility to the logics of identity and recognition of the one in the other:

> By queer culture we mean a world-making project, where "world," like "public," differs from community or group because it necessarily includes more people than can be identified, more spaces than can be mapped beyond a few reference points, modes of feeling that can be learned rather than experiences as a birthright. The queer world is a space of entrances, exits, unsystematized lines of acquaintance, projected horizons, typifying examples, alternate routes, blockages, incommensurate geographies. World making, as much in the mode of dirty talk as of print-mediated representation, is dispersed through incommensurate registers, by definition *unrealizable* as community or identity.
>
> (558)

Berlant and Warner's reticence vis-à-vis appeals to community as the grounds of politics—of progressive politics—is also echoed in the work of Miranda Joseph (2002) who argued against the liberal position that sees experiences of belonging and community as fundamental to establishing alternatives to contemporary regimes of power. Developing a critique of the ways in which authors like Giorgio Agamben and Jean-Luc Nancy have attempted to re-signify community away from its tendency to create a homogeneity that erases the political affordances of the particular and the different, Joseph claimed that any attempts to rescue community from universalising narratives ought to also take into account the ways in which discourses of community have been central to the survival of capitalism. "Before any progressive or resistant reimagination of community will be efficacious", she wrote, "we need to account for the relentless return of the dominant discourse and practice of community" (xxxi). Rather than seeing community as inherently a form of resistance or as a collective shield against the violence of capital, Joseph contended that the lingering romantic longing for community as the other of modernity was not only necessary for the development of modern capitalism, but that capitalism itself, through its performative logics of production and consumption, has been central to the continued production and survival of communities. Giving as one of many examples the ways in which the LGBTQ+ "community" not only developed through but also catalysed forms of queer consumption, and how LGBTQ+ agendas are today part and parcel of liberal political and managerialist discourses, Joseph claimed that because community is "constituted as the site of values, of fetishized identities, of culture"— and is therefore seen as "autonomous from capital"—not only does it "operate as a supplement to capital" but it also "enables exploitation", for communities are constituted as autonomous units, that is to say, as autonomous sets of producers and/or consumers that are separate from one another and thus can't empathise or even care for one another (172). However, despite what can be read as scholarly cynicism vis-à-vis lived experiences of community and the actual material relations upon which they depend, Joseph did, nonetheless, concede that, due to the high dependency of capital on actual communities and community narratives—and, therefore, due to the "great deal of agency [that] resides with the producers of community"—there is still scope to "make our collectivities more disruptive rather than less" (172). One of the ways in which that can happen, she argued, is by "imagining, articulating, and constituting disruptive or displacing social formations, active collectivities, that do not depend or insist on the closures and oppressions of community or pretend that difference in itself is resistance" (172).

The difficulties of relying on dominant understandings of community in order to conceive queer forms of communion such as "pigsex" are also evident in Tim Dean's monograph on barebacking subcultures. Whilst, on the one hand, Dean (2009) rightfully highlighted the potential of "pigsex" to draw strangers together whilst keeping them estranged—that is, "without necessarily domesticating the other's otherness" (180)—at the core of his argument there still lay an understanding of community that required something—that is, HIV—to be shared amongst its members. According to his account, homosexual men "breeding" one another allow for a biosocial form of group membership to develop amongst them whilst not denying them their status as strangers to one another (92–96). In Dean's argument, dominant conceptualisations of community still linger even if queered: whilst, on the one hand, "by transforming relational affines (lovers) into consaguines (siblings) and by confusing relations of consanguinity with relations of descent, bareback 'breeding' irrevocably contaminates the elementary categories of kinship" (93), on the other hand, it still depends on the presence of HIV as a form of private property that is shared by all, a commons upon which a community of barebackers is constructed and a certain level of recognition is allowed to take place amongst strangers. The problem with such an approach is that it lays way too much emphasis on the sharing of HIV as the material grounds for a sense of collective belonging amongst barebackers. In the current age of antiretrovirals, especially, thanks to HIV undetectability and Pre-Exposure Prophylaxis, increasing numbers of gay men engage in bareback sex without HIV ever becoming part of the equation, whether as something to be pursued or as something worth risking in the pursuit of queer forms of belonging. Let's remember that, as I've already discussed, the ways in which "pigsex" has been represented in porn and framed by my interviewees, is less a means to an end—that is, less about seeking to *have* something in common—and more about an eroticisation of bodily porosity in itself; less about sharing something with another and more about troubling bodily autonomy through opening oneself to the other, the target of libidinal investment being the process rather than its end result. If, in Dean's analysis, HIV is the object of desire—Lacan's *objet petit a* promising a temporary coalescence of the body into a whole and the ensuing confirmation of the ego—in antiretrovirally mediated "pigsex", HIV is mostly out of the picture and is thus no longer able to anchor an imaginary pursuit of communal integration through bodily infection. Instead, what gay "pigs" eroticise is processual in nature—not only a doing (instead of a thing) but a doing that comes into being through the undoing of the body itself, through the relentless transgression of its boundaries. Gay "pigs" become themselves the more they undo themselves. Antiteleological at its core, "pigsex" thus falls under the broader umbrella of sex play as recently theorised by Susanna Paasonen (2018)—a set of practices that instead of being grounded on lack and the pursuit of its ever-failed fulfilment, do instead function by opening the body to new "carnal horizons of possibility" (8). Therefore, and if the introduction of combination antiretroviral therapies has made HIV-positive bodies uninfectious and HIV-negative bodies uninfectable, a new conceptualisation of *communitas* is needed in order to theorise the ways in which "pigsex" brings gay men together, the political implications of such modes of collective pleasure and speculative experimentation with bodies, and the kinds of communal queer worlds they may index.

In his study of community, Roberto Esposito (2010) troubled dominant definitions of the term by analysing the etymology of *communitas*. For the Italian philosopher, the definition of community that dominates modern and contemporary political and philosophical debates—one that resembles that of Victor Turner—is highly contradictory. According to that dominant paradigm, what is shared by the members of a community is both private property of each individual and also, paradoxically, something that belongs to all. Against such deeply contradictory definition, Esposito highlighted the following:

> In all neo-Latin languages [...], "common" [...] is what is *not* proper [...], that begins where what is proper ends: "*Quod commune cum alio est desinit esse proprium.*" It is what belongs to more than one, to many or to everyone, and therefore is that which is "public" in opposition to "private" or "general" [...] in contrast to "individual" [...].
>
> (3)

The Latin maxim quoted by Esposito, "*Quod commune cum alio est desinit esse proprium*" stresses the paradox at the centre of taken-for-granted notions of community. Attributed to Roman rhetorician Quintilian, that sentence translates into English as "what we share with another ceases to be our own". The paradox is thus evident: community cannot be thought as the totality of those who have something in common—say, a shared HIV status—because it already implies that, somehow, individuals who share their possessions end up losing them. What starts by being private so that it can be shared becomes public once shared, and it is thus by definition no longer owned by any of the individuals doing the sharing. Going back to Turner, if individuals were to discover their shared humanity through ritual or social drama, they would then have to let go of that same humanity they thought to possess in the first place. In short, by claiming things like "I am you", "we are one", "we are Europeans", etc., one is actively disposing of whatever it is that makes oneself and the other two modes of the same substance, two individuals of the same kin.

As a consequence, rather than being gained, in *communitas* there is always something that is given away. Esposito (2010) stressed that aspect by once again going back to the etymon of the term and noting that the meaning of *"munus"* from which *"communitas"* derives oscillates between "duty" or "obligation" and "gift". *Communitas* is thus not about possessing something that the other also possesses and, therefore, forming a community around that shared possession. Instead, *communitas* is fundamentally about owing something to the other, about an unconditional duty of giving. Against Turner, *communitas* "doesn't by any means imply the stability of a possession and even less the acquisitive dynamic of something earned, but loss, subtraction, transfer. It is a 'pledge' or a 'tribute' that one pays in an obligatory form" (5). As such, the "common" in *communitas* is not the property of all by being the property of every single one; it is, instead, the "voiding [...] of property into its negative" (7). As Esposito (2010) explains:

> In the community, subjects do not find a principle of identification nor an aseptic enclosure within which they can establish transparent communication or even a content to be communicated. They don't find anything else except *that void, that distance, that extraneousness that constitutes them as being missing from themselves*; [...] Therefore the community cannot be thought of as a body, as a corporation [...] in which individuals are founded in a larger individual. Neither is community to be interpreted as a mutual, intersubjective "recognition" in which individuals are reflected in each other so as to confirm their initial identity; [... the community] isn't the subject's expansion or multiplication but its exposure to what interrupts the closing and turns it inside out: *a dizziness, a syncope, a spasm in the continuity of the subject.*
>
> (7, my emphasis)

Therefore, community, as theorised by Esposito, complicates the sharing economy that Dean saw taking place in bareback sex. For Dean (2009), barebackers forge a queer home economics whereby heterosexual senses of kinship grounded on consanguinity still survive their being queered by gay men who share HIV. Even if the subjects of Dean's ethnography did

indeed see themselves as belonging to the same kin, to the same community of equals, due to the shared nature of what they had in common—i.e.,
HIV—the issue, in my view, is more complicated than that. Because community always implies some degree of sacrificial giving, the subject who is
giving risks obliterating itself; community threatens with self-disintegration
or self-subtraction at the same time as it promises hospitality. And that
paradox, according to Esposito, was at the centre of the emergence of
modern theories of immunity, which attempted to counter-balance the self-
obliterating pull of *communitas* by means of a protective defensive layer
erected around its edges. For instance, in Hobbes, what all men had in
common was a capacity not only to be killed but to kill one another.
Hence the Hobbesian project of the Leviathan state, a state that immunises
subjects against the potentially self-obliterating bonds they risk maintain-
ing with one another, progressively atomising each subject and replacing
those horizontal social relations with the vertical relations of immunisation
through obedience that would come to form the bond between each citizen
and the state (Esposito 2010, 11–14).

In the context of gay "pigsex", that argument acquires very tangible
dimensions: if, without antiretrovirals, the relentless exchange of bodily
fluids may, as Dean suggested, have indeed led to a sense of belonging and
kinship developing amongst gay men, that sense of kinship and belonging
would eventually become life-threatening, with men risking a very real and
ultimate form of self-obliteration in the pursuit of *communitas*; that is, an
AIDS-related death. Against that threat to life posed by AIDS—and the
consequent threat to the maintenance of healthy populations understood
by the state as reserves of consumer- and labour-power—antiretrovirals
entered the scene as a form of immunisation against death by *cummuning*,
thanks to their ability to halt the replication of HIV amongst HIV-positive
mean—by making them HIV- undetectable *and* untransmittable—and by
allowing HIV-negative men to internalise a protective prophylactic layer
through PrEP, one that protects them against incorporating the very thing
that would, in Dean's argument, served as the material substrate for
kinship amongst barebackers. In Esposito's words, "if community is so
threatening to the individual integrity of the subjects that it puts into relation, nothing else remains for us except to 'immunize us' beforehand and,
in so doing, to negate the very same foundations of community" (2010,
13). Following that line of reasoning, it isn't surprising to feel that a
certain sense of mourning is present in Tim Dean's later revision of his
argument, which he published in 2015 in an article entitled "Medicated
Intimacies". In that article, which revisited bareback sex amongst gay men
in the aftermath of the introduction of Treatment-as-Prevention (TasP)
and Pre-Exposure Prophylaxis (PrEP), Dean (2015a) drew from Paul
Preciado to claim that "raw sex does not exist" (224). In a hyper-mediated
culture such as ours, one in which every aspect of our lives is heavily saturated not only with images but also often with irreconcilable meanings and

narratives that all compete to become anchoring points for our senses of self, our understandings of our relationships with others, and our sense of our place in the world, the rawness—i.e. unmediated nature—of the condomless sex pursued by increasing numbers of gay men remains a fantasy desired but never realised, a fantasy that gay men have created to compensate for a certain sense of increasing inauthenticity of our lives (Dean 2015a). Noting the slower-than-expected uptake of PrEP by gay men when it became available in the USA, Dean (2015a) went on to speculate that, for some gay men at least, taking PrEP may constitute a betrayal of the very anti-normative rationale of their barebacking practices. If barebacking emerged, in *Unlimited Intimacy* (Dean 2009), as a subcultural sexual behaviour that attempted to reject the compulsion towards social assimilation and normalisation driven by mainstream LGBTQ+ politics, the refusal to take PrEP may be explained in those same terms. That is, by deciding not to take PrEP, gay men are rejecting the state's intervention in their own bodies and the paradigms of health and forms of sanctioned sexual sociability it promotes. However, and as some recent studies have argued, even whilst doing so gay men still have a complex and fluid relationship with antiretrovirals (see, e.g. García-Iglesias 2019), with the risk of contracting HIV, and with how those two come to bear on their own identities in ways that complicate Dean's claim that refusing to take PrEP and embrace risk can be understood as a form of subcultural resistance. Further, and as Dean (2015a) also noted with reference to Foucault and Preciado, even before antiretrovirals were introduced, sex was already heavily mediated (by drugs such as the contraceptive pill, hormones, recreational drugs, pornography, and clinical and legal discourses on sex). Modern sex has always been mediated sex, and so the possibility of sex being "raw" can only operate in the realm of fantasy, whether amongst gay men who reject PrEP or amongst those who take it.

I would, however, like to attend to the closing section of "Mediated Intimacies" where, writing about the new category of HIV-undetectability brought about by antiretrovirals and its consequent disruption of the positive/negative binary, Dean (2015a) wrote that "the category of 'undetectable' could not be more ironic, since it relies on surveillance at the bimolecular level by an entire apparatus of medical power. Nothing could be less raw" (241). Whilst I certainly do not dispute the complexity of the regimes of biopower that sustain what Preciado (2013) called the contemporary "pharmacopornographic era", I think Dean's apparent dismissal of the symbolic systems that guide gay men's engagement in "raw" sex is unproductive and indeed strange for a theorist of sexual behaviour who is so indebted to Lacanian psychoanalysis. After all, if indeed the rhetoric barebackers used to articulate their sexual practices was so fundamental to Dean's ethnography of barebacking subcultures in *Unlimited Intimacy*, why is it that the ways in which "raw" sex is now thought by younger generations of gay men do suddenly seem less worthy of taking seriously when trying to understand forms of gay male sexual sociability and communion in the age of antiretrovirals? Furthermore, if Dean (2015a) drew so heavily from Preciado's work, why did he overlook the potential for biopolitical resistance that Preciado associated with the hacking of the very same molecular technologies that are today being deployed as tools for the biomedical surveillance and control of bodies? For, as Preciado (2013) wrote:

> In terms of political agency, subjection, or empowerment do not depend on the rejection of technologies in the name of nature, but rather on the differential user and reappropriation of the very techniques of the production of subjectivity. No political power exists without control over production and distribution of gender brocades. Pharmacophornographic emancipation of subaltern bodies can be measured only according to these essential criteria: involvement in and access to the production, circulation, and interpretation of somato-politic biocodes.
>
> (129)

By attending to the above paragraph, it becomes easier to recognise that the tensions between freedom and surveillance are more complicated than Dean's argument in "Mediated Intimacies" seems to imply. Granted, the deployment of antiretrovirals should be seen as part of a longer history of molecularisation of biopolitical surveillance and control; and, sure enough, on a material level no sex can ever be "raw" sex. "Rawness", just like the documentary aesthetics used in so much contemporary gay porn, is an epiphenomenon of our pharmacopornographic era, the result of a hyper-mediated culture producing a desire for authenticity and unmediation which are, in turn, synthesised and delivered in highly artificial and mediated forms, a phenomenon not dissimilar from the ways in which "Nature" did not predate but was instead produced as an after-effect of European industrialisation and Romanticism's Edenic nostalgia (see, for instance, Latour 1993; Cronon 1996; Morton 2007; Daston 2019). And yet, acknowledging those dynamics does not mean that the phenomena to which they have given rise aren't meaningful to people's lives in how they function as symbolic vectors in the production of selves and worlds. Such a view is also supported by Preciado's own understanding of the pharmaco-pornographic body as a "techno-organic interface, a techno-life system" that is not so much docile as it is the "materialization of *'puissance de vie,'* 'power of life'" (2008, 113). In such a line of thinking, whilst biomedical practices and state institutions attempt to surveil, code, and regulate the body, its power can still overflow the constraints of those apparatuses and create mutations and unexpected worldings through hacking of the very same technologies whose deployment regulates the material and semiotic flows that coalesce to produce contemporary bodies. Thus, for Preciado (2008), the re-appropriation of those technologies of control for emancipatory projects is at the core of what he calls a "*gender-copyleft* revolution" (115).

Given Preciado's argument, it is useful to draw attention to the various socio-political contexts in which PrEP has been introduced and circulated, as well as the differing ways in which state institutions and discourses have facilitated or not access to the drugs. In the USA, for instance, Gilead's Truvada was approved by the Food and Drug Administration (FDA) to be used as Pre-Exposure Prophylaxis in 2012 (Dean 2015a, 228) and made accessible in the US healthcare market through complicated health insurance plans and local payment options that restricted its access to only a fraction of the target demographics. In the UK, PrEP is, at the time of writing, still only being offered by the National Health Service on an ever-expanding trial basis despite both the High Court and the Court of Appeal of England and Wales having judged, in the landmark court case *National AIDS Trust v NHS England* of 2016, that provision of PrEP falls within the powers of the NHS under the National Health Service Act 2006 (Maine 2019). Therefore, whilst it is true that clinical and epidemiological research has recommended that PrEP is included in national strategies to end HIV, economic, demographic, and political factors still make its provision and uptake very patchy and/or slow, even in large-economy countries (PrEPWatch.org; Pebody 2018; Crary 2018; Maine 2019). As a result, and in resonance with what happened during the peak of the AIDS crisis in countries like the USA, buyers' clubs have been set up in places like Germany and the UK to make PrEP drugs, often imported from India at a much lower cost, accessible to as high a number of people as possible, thus circumventing the restrictions imposed on access by state institutions and policies, health insurance providers, and the profit-making interests of pharmaceutical companies like Gilead (Prepster.info; IwantPrEPnow.co.uk; Samuel 2018). With gay men and activist networks doing it for themselves, the current picture of PrEP uptake by gay men around the world seems to include at least as much of the re-appropriative tactics of Preciado's "copyleft revolution" as it does of the regimes of surveillance and control that Tim Dean associated with Pre-Exposure Prophylaxis and Treatment-as-Prevention.

If we attend to the nuances and tensions in the ways in which antiretrovirals are conceptualised, promoted, distributed, and consumed today, we can commence to grasp them not simply as molecular technologies deployed to make unruly bodies docile, but also as drugs that can be appropriated and used to catalyse new embodied senses of self and forms of sexual sociability that escape the parameters of the "healthy" body of modern medicine, and the docile "responsible" body of condom morality that emerged thanks to the association of AIDS with sex during the 1980s. Otherwise, how are we to understand the backlash against the so-called "Truvada whore"—the gay man, understood as a PrEP-taking HIV-negative bottom—onto whom the source of all the moral panics associated with the mythic AIDS Patient Zero have become transferred in the age of PrEP (Calabrese and Underhill 2015; González 2019)? How are we to understand claims such as those by Michael Weinstein, the President of the AIDS Healthcare Foundation, who in 2014 told the Associated Press that Truvada, taken as PrEP, was a "party drug" (Crary 2014; Barro 2014)?[2] How to make sense of the words of the *New York Times* conservative gay columnist Andrew Sullivan who, in 1996, associated the end of AIDS promised by antiretrovirals with an increase in hedonism and reckless sexual behaviour fuelled by drug cocktails of antiretroviral *and* recreational drugs in gay circuit parties (Sullivan 1996; see also Race 2015; n.d.). Even if Sullivan's views on sex appear to have mellowed in the years that passed since he wrote "When Plagues End", only as recently as June 2019—and on the occasion of the celebrations of the 50th anniversary of the Stonewall Riots—he still published a piece in the *New York Magazine* calling on gay men to start "getting on with our lives, without our sexual orientation getting in the way", apparently the "sanest approach to being gay" (Sullivan 2019). Or how to see anything other than sexual puritanism in James Kirchick's June 2019 article for *The Atlantic*, in which the American neoconservative columnist announced the end of the "struggle for gay rights" and made the unfortunate claim that "AIDS enforced a maturation on the gay community, and a tempering of the previous decade's sexual excesses" (Kirchick 2019). When taking into account the standpoints of the likes of Weinstein, Sullivan, and Kirchick, it doesn't become difficult to understand how PrEP, despite the ways in which it functions as molecular control in contemporary biopolitics, also carries within it an excess—or the affordance of an excess, of a sexual excess—that is seen to threaten the very foundations of Western societies and their sanctioned forms of sexual intimacy, kinship, and sociability. If, as Paula Treichler (1999) has shown, AIDS was seen by some as bringing about the demise of homosexuality they desired—or, at least, of homosexual promiscuity—then promiscuity and, with it, its associated moral panics appear to have returned in the age of TasP and PrEP (González 2019; Tziallas 2019).

   In that context, I would like to bring up the club scene that is presented to viewers 25 minutes into Robin Campillo's award-winning 2017 film *120 Battements par Minute*. In it, a group of gay men is seen dancing in a club to pumping house music, the camera never really able to convey much more than fragments of their moving bodies—heads, chests, arms in the air—and a sense of a pulsating, de-individuated, impersonal multitude. As the camera pulls its focus away from the body fragments, the dust particles suspended in the air become increasingly perceptible as the club lights hit them. As the beat of the music continues, the particles in the foreground of the image progressively morph into tiny copies of HIV on their way to infect CD4 cells. As Gary Needham (2019) has pointed out, the scene—thanks to the affordances of digital post-production technologies—offers us an occasion of the "plasmaticity of dissolving and morphing from bodies in the club, to particles in the air, to plasma, to cell and virus". This notion of "plasmaticity", which Needham drew from Kristin Whissel's work on digital effects and Eisenstein's work on animation, speaks to cinema's ability to blur boundaries between bodies and taxonomic systems through the morphing of one into the other, claiming cinema as a topological space. For Needham (2019), therefore, the digital technologies behind the plasmaticity of that club scene could potentially make *120 Battements par minute* "the start of an 'HIV cinema' rather than an 'AIDS melodrama' ".

The blurring not only of bodies and scales but also of inside and outside that we see in the scene presents a very strong and original proposition on the dynamics of communion with which I'm concerned here. Not only that but, I'd argue, they also allow us to reframe the forms of sexual sociability that are being mediated by antiretrovirals and pornography and enacted in group "pigsex." What I find fascinating about that short sequence is the way in which HIV is indexed by the image not so much as something that exists within specific men but as a material existent that cuts across the dancing bodies, some kind of connective tissue or substrate within which bodies themselves dance. If we were to speculate forwards those blurred relationships between inside and outside—those economies of scale and the continuity between the micro- and the macroscopic—to the antiretroviral age, it would be conceivable to imagine the molecules that cut across bodies, that sustain the dancing of bodies, being no longer viral but antiretroviral, no longer HIV but the tenofovir-efavirenz compounds found in Truvada, the PrEP drug of choice. After all, antiretrovirals do, today, sustain both the dancing of bodies and their mingling into one another through relentless exchanges of bodily fluids that, thanks to the prophylactic molecularisation of HIV biopolitics, cease to be potentially life-threatening and become, instead, life-affirming experiments in intimate world-makings. In order to explore this point, I would like to go back, once again, to the gangbang scene in Paul Morris's *Viral Loads*, which I've discussed in Chapter 3.

When it was released in 2014, *Viral Loads* led to media furore for the ways in which it supposedly fetishised HIV transmission, with the title referring to both the phrase used to describe the number of HIV copies in a millilitre of HIV-positive blood, and to the use of the word "load" as slang for ejaculate. Building on the two different meanings of its title, *Viral Loads* set itself to present a pornographic fantasy involving HIV-positive semen. However, as I've argued in the previous chapter and elsewhere (Florêncio 2018), the video shouldn't be read in such straightforward way. Instead, it could be approached as a piece of moving-image rhetoric aimed at causing controversy and polemic whilst, at the same time, making viewers realise that their fears of HIV infection are, after both TasP and PrEP, anachronic. Furthermore, despite all the rough and athletic sex we see depicted in the video, there is still a sense in which that space of "piggy" group sexplay is still a space of care and of communion. Just like with the fisting scene with which I opened this chapter, in *Viral Loads* we also see giggles, laughter, smiles, passionate kissing, etc. Added to that, bodily fluids—more specifically cum—are also seen *circulating* between bodies, not only being gifted by tops to bottoms but also being then passed back from the bottoms to the tops through "felching" and "snowballing", in a general economy of excess (Bataille 1988) that cannot be captured by a logics of profit or the means-to-an-end of biological and/or social reproductive imperatives. Instead, they seem to rely on unproductive expenditure and pleasure for pleasure's sake. If, as Murat Aydemir (2007) noted, Bataille associated the introduction of private property with the development of what he called the "restrictive economy" of bourgeois modernity (218); and if, as we've already seen, that same phenomenon of individualisation of property also brought about the private/public binary that separated what belongs to the body from what doesn't belong to it, then such excessive and relentless circulation of bodily fluids across bodily boundaries not only inaugurates a new understanding of the pharmacopornographic body but also troubles the very foundations on which modern understandings of community have depended. In "pigsex" bodily fluids are not so much owned so they can be shared with others as a sexual commons; they are, instead, owned by nobody in that it is their circulation rather than their collective ownership that brings gay "pigs" together and sustains their experiences of sexual intimacy and sociability. If, as Lauren Berlant (1998) argued, experiences of intimacy link the vulnerability of the lives of individuals with the "trajectories of the collective" (283), and if modern bourgeois societies were predicated on a displacement of forms of intimate sociability from public to private domains (284), in what ways do the contemporary forms of public and group "pig" sex—predicated on relentless exchanges of bodily fluids freed from the spectre of AIDS—produce *cummunion* as a queer world-making project (Berlant and Warner 1998)? In short, how do bodily fluids bring men together?

That topic of connection kept on coming up during the interviews I conducted with gay men whilst researching this book. For "Mark", for instance, being able to connect with the men he had sex with was fundamental. When talking about his sexual life, connection was important to him:

> Well like, with the bondage stuff … I mean, I think I was just searching for just like connection. Like, we all search for connection. Like, nobody wants to be lonely. I think that's, like, why anybody has sex.

When I asked him whether it was easy to build connection in fleeting casual sexual encounters, he continued:

> I'm not someone who will just, like, stick my ass up in a glory hole and take loads all night. Like, that's not exciting to me. Like, I wanna

be like, I wanna see everybody that's fucking me. I want to be like, engaged with them. I wanna be like meeting up with ten people or, you know, like, the piss and the sweat and the spit. Like, I want it all to be like, there. That's the appeal for me. It's not … um … it's not hiding it in that way.

Crucially, exchanges of bodily fluids seemed, to him, fundamental to achieving that desired experience of connection with sexual partners, a view that became evident from his reflection on his consumption of scat porn and eventual engagement in scat, i.e. coprophagic, sex play:

I think [scat] was like, it was like consuming … um … like just, I guess like … it's the domination element. But then it's also like, it is oddly like, it's oddly like a weird connection thing. Like I really loved like seeing a guy's, like, mouth on a butt hole. And then, like, you didn't even necessarily see the shit, but he would just be, like, you'd see it go down, you'd see the resistance and you'd see him take it in. And, like, and then being so turned on and like disgusted at the same time. And like the guys in porn would be like that. […] and then obviously when it was, like, these really beautiful guys doing this really ugly, gross thing, it was just like, for some reason, like all those wires crossing was hot to me.

What becomes interesting about his argument is that feelings of both disgust and desire occur simultaneously in response to bodily excretions. Rather than having one being replaced by the other, the tension between those two pre-cognitive, affective responses to excreted matter appears fundamental to the development of the sense of connection he associated with scat play. That is a view that he also manifested in relation to what he saw as the increasing popularity of piss play in the aftermath of the introduction of antiretrovirals:

It's odd, like, I've kinda noticed, […] just over the past few years, like, there's been more guys […] more guys want to piss inside me. Or, like, ask me if that's something I want. […] and then I'm like, you know, and I think it is like, that is a connection thing. It's weird, like, "will you allow men to do this to you?"

Asked whether that tended to involve power-play or BDSM scenarios, a context in relation to which piss would become a form of humiliation, "Mark" had a more complicated view of it:

No, not … the last two times I did it, it was just like, "come over and fuck me; I want raw sex". Okay, and then they get here and "what else are you into?", "kind of also into piss, also into whatever", and then, I mean, like, I had sex a few nights ago here. And it was this like, kinda sweet, whatever, white guy from Santa Monica ... asked if I was into piss and like, you know, like, raw sex. And I was like "okay", and he came and then he asked if he could piss inside me and I was like "okay, sure". And he really, really went for it. And then he, like, fucked me and it was really hot. And, you know, it's like, piss everywhere, whatever. And then he came out ... he like, was finishing ... he was like, "Oh, that's the first time I've ever done that". [laughs] Okay ... "Yeah, like ever, like pissing inside someone and, like, doing that. [...] But in a weird way, it was just like, it's just like an added layer. I mean, I think it's like, now if cum by itself is kind of harmless and it's not a taboo anymore, like, adding the piss in there kind of becomes something else a little bit, you know? [...] I think it's like for guys, it's like if, you know, everybody's gonna let you shoot a load in their ass now, then, like, who's gonna let you piss in their ass too, you know?

Porn model Brian-Mark's framing of scat in his 2003 interview with the *Chicago Reader* also resonates with "Mark"'s views:

"Let's see," says Brian-Mark, ticking off a list of things he's done on film. "Water sports, boot worship, leather scenes, bondage, scat—big-time, lots of brown [slang for scat]. I really love the smell and taste of a man's butt, because it's very animal. It's like feeding from somebody. You really are taking them in."

He pauses for a moment. "Here's the problem with fetishes: if you say you're into piss or scat, they think you want everybody's piss or everybody's shit, and most of the time it's a very special thing. It's a head space that I have to go to, and it's very intimate."

(Knight Jr. 2003)

In the context of both "Mark" and Brian-Mark's tying of scat and piss play with the enactment of intimacy and connection, I would like to refer to Mary Douglas's famous definition of dirt as "matter out of place" (2002, 44). What we see in "Mark"'s testimony as well as in all the examples I've been discussing in this chapter—the Treasure Island Media videos, Tom of Finland's "Pleasure Park", even the clubbing scene in Campillo's *120 BPM*—is matter that ought to *either* be kept inside the body *or* be disposed of privately losing its place and becoming matter of public exchange, matter that is seen to exist where it shouldn't, constantly being made to cross bodily boundaries and never being stopped by the latter. Whilst, as Douglas (2002) and others have argued, the encounter with bodily fluids understood as private matter made public and, therefore, out of place, tends to trigger feelings of disgust and horror for the ways in which they threaten the stability of the body and, by extension, of the autonomous subject (Kristeva 1982; Menninghaus 2003), in "pigsex" exchanges of bodily fluids are sought out by gay men, eroticised, and exchanged well beyond the orgasm as a means towards connection and intimacy. By focusing on fluid exchanges, gay "pigs" shift the erotic focus away from the culminating resolution of the orgasm and coalesce as a multitude in which impersonal bodily fluids work as connective tissue. Just like Deleuzean assemblages come together not according to some given properties of their constituent parts but thanks to the productive force of the AND that lies between them, gay "pigs" come together less because of their private identities or personal qualities they may have in common but, rather, thanks to the fluids that circulate between them. If, as claimed above, displaced bodily fluids are dirty and abject, if they are threatening to the wholesomeness of the subject, that is because they intoxicate the subject by putting him in intense proximity to an other. As Tim Dean (2015b) claimed when writing about piss play:

> Gay identity is so marketable because it seals off queerness into safely autonomous units, whereas piss is a sign of connection that destroys the fiction of autonomy. Your fluids inside me become my fluids that I offer for recycling into you. Our bodies become porous to each other through the medium of piss. And that is why piss play is both sexually exciting and a provocation to ethics: Piss dramatizes my porosity to the other, whereas disgust seals me off from connection with other bodies. Disgust consolidates my identity by erecting barriers against others' materiality.
>
> (124)

Using Dean's work on piss to refract "Mark"'s views on piss and scat play, it becomes possible to argue that the intimacy and connection that is sought through exchanges of bodily fluids in "pigsex" does not so much circumvent disgust as a self-defence strategy against self-dissolution. Instead, it faces disgust and the associated threat to the autonomy of the subject and pushes through it. Only in that way can we understand "Mark"'s highlighting of the co-existence of disgust and pleasure during exchanges of excreted matter, namely faeces. In other words, the desire to open oneself to the other can only be pursued through a disgusting and horror-inducing undoing of the self (Kristeva 1982). In *cummuning* with an other, the self and its private qualities or properties are sacrificed. *Cummunion*, the enactment of our porosity to the other in "pig" play, is always-already the doing of self-intoxication, for only through a self-intoxicating event can *communitas* come into being—hence Esposito's study of the ways in which immunity has come to protect individuals from the centripetal self-obliterating force of *communitas*. For, as Jean-Luc Nancy (2016) has also put it, intoxication draws us into the knowledge of the "existence and proximity of an outside, of a ruptured barrier through which everything can flow" (12), thus leading us to feel the "vertigo of the infinitely near" (41), of existing as "nothing in itself, nothing but relation, nothing but the shattering of the identical and the one-in-itself" (Nancy 2013, 10). Unlike Lacan, to whom desire and *jouissance* were primarily understood from within a psychoanalytical paradigm of object relations (Kesel 2009), for Nancy (2013) there is nothing that precedes the relating: "desire, properly speaking, has no object. What desire desires is not objected by it, is not placed before it as though opposite to it, but rather is part of its desiring movement" (13). If nothing precedes the relating, if there is nothing but the relation itself, then the *cummunion* we are seeking is not a coming-together predicated on shared commons but always and primarily a *commoning*, an active social relation, a doing-in-common rather than a being-in-common (De Angelis 2017). This, and the understanding that bodily fluids are self-intoxicating—that is, that they threaten the autonomy of the subject by bringing it into a relation of radical intimacy with the outside, by folding the outside in—serves to illuminate the tension found by Esposito (2010) between community and immunity:

> In the community, subjects do not find a principle of identification nor an aseptic enclosure within which they can establish transparent communication prevent a content to be communicated. They don't find anything else except that void, that distance, that extraneousness that constitutes them as being missing from themselves; "givers to" inasmuch as they themselves are "given by" *[donati da]* a circuit of mutual gift giving that finds its own specificity in it is indirectness with respect to the frontal nature of the subject-object relation or to the ontological fullness of the person (if not in the daunting semantic duplicity of the French *personne* which can mean both "person" and "no one").
>
> (7)

If indeed the body politic is achieved by diverting the threatening horizontal relations of community and replacing them with the vertical relations of immunity between part and whole—citizen and state—that protect the self-citizen against what is foreign to it and thus potentially life-threatening (Esposito 2010, 11–14), the *cummuning* of "pigsex" manages to reappropriate the technologies of biopolitical molecular immunity (antiretrovirals) to ensure the survival of the subject whilst nonetheless still allowing it to engage in self-intoxicating experiments of radical porosity to alterity. Whilst, on a biomedical level, the subject remains protected from actual death, on a symbolic level these group sex encounters have the capacity to reframe the ways in which the subject relates to an other and its foreignness. After all, the space of sexual intimacy is always a space of excess, one in which the self is found tending towards its own destabilisation (Nancy 2017). No longer predicated on the identification of a set of *a priori* private qualities to be shared with an other; no longer requiring the

recognition of the self in the other; no longer being but doing-together—
cumming together—"pigsex" becomes an important case study for thinking beyond existing formations of place, community and belonging, at a
time when ideologies of state immunity are being recovered by contemporary nation-states to justify the closure of their borders to foreign "aliens".
As Mel Y. Chen (2012) noted:

> Thinking and feeling with toxicity invites us to revise, once again, the
> sociality that queer theory has in many ways made possible. As a rela-
> tional notion, toxicity speaks productively to queer-utopian imagining
> and helps us revisit the question of how and where subject-object dis-
> positions should be attributed to the relational queer figure.
>
> (207)

Chen's drawing together of the toxic and the queer in the name of a political investment in queer world-making disavows modern and contemporary
discourses on community and belonging predicated on allegiances to the
"natural", the "pure" and the "proper", all terms that are used to police
the order of things by giving the latter their designated rightful place. Just
like bodily fluids should be kept inside the body in order not to infect or
intoxicate the bodies of others in which they don't belong, so do the queer
need to be either kept in the margins of the social body or shaped back
into the norm—through marriage, family, and the cultivation of the impermeable, autonomous and whole body. As Alberto Sandoval-Sánchez
(2005) wrote, in a way that foregrounds the relationship between the
abject and toxic queer, and the bodies of both individuals and the state,
"[abject] bodies are repulsive because they manifest and inflict a confusion
of boundaries which punctures, fractures, and fragments the assumed
unity, stability, and closure of the identity of the hegemonic subject and
the body politic of the nation" (547). Those abject bodies—in which
Sandoval-Sánchez included not just the bodies of the queer but also those
living with HIV, those who are Black, and those who are migrants (548)—
threaten the stability of the body politic and its sanctioned forms of citizenship by establishing themselves through displacement—displacement
from the Oedipal triangle, from whiteness, from the logics of blood and
soil of the "fatherland". For them, "home" is not constituted through
identification and recognition of the self in the other. Instead, it is a place-
less home, a home that emerges through an incorporation of the other in
the one: "this is my body, which is given for you" (Luke 22:19).

If the AIDS crisis recalled the relation of sex with politics as a necropol-
itics, a relation that refracted sex through the workings of death and the
negative (Edelman 2004), and thus as something that ought to become the
target of state biopolitical control and regulation in the name of social
reproduction and the reproduction of labour (Chalier and Fœssel 2017), in
the case of "pigsex" enacted in the age of antiretrovirals, the potentially

life-threatening incorporation of the other into the self is lived as embodied fantasy—the self does no longer risk disappearance in its incorporating of the other for antiretrovirals prevent that from happening. And yet,
the political potential is still there to trigger a rethinking of communal
relations, for the self itself has always-already been the product of a self-
narration mediated by imagined and symbolic encounters with alterity. It
is thus that I see, in "pigsex", contemporary molecular technologies of
biopolitical control being used to catalyse or at least mediate new forms
of sexual sociability and relations with alterity that pose a symbolic if not
literal threat to the very autonomy of the self that the production of such
technologies intended to protect in the first place. Through them and by
hacking them for sexual hedonistic purposes, gay "pigs" may just have
opened us a door into thinking how one may come together with an
other in more ethically considerate ways, how to rethink *cummunion* as
an instance of what Helen Hester (2018) called "xeno-hospitality", a
practice of radically opening oneself to alterity and, through that, to take
part in a future-orientated "mutational politics" of solidarity with the
strange and the foreign (4) in an attempt to bring forth a "queerness
[that] is not yet here" (Muñoz 2009, 1). Gay "pig" masculinities invite us
to rethink the queer ethics and worldmaking potential of the ecology of
the sty.

Notes

1
> On baise avec un inconnu. Un corps. C'est-à-dire avant tout, une bite ou
> un cul, que l'on n'aperçoit pas forcément dans la pénombre moite. Un
> inconnu sans identité, sans histoire et sans lendemain. Un rapport à
> l'autre sans autre. Une relation sans nom, ni langage verbal. De la viande.
> Serial, on passe d'un corps à l'autre, puis à un troisième encore, jusqu'à
> plus soif. [...]
> Dans certaines backrooms, les corps vont et viennent, se prêtent et
> s'échangent. Apparaît alors un véritable communisme sexuel. Et même les
> plus vieux ou les moches ont (ou devraient avoir) leur chance. Et tant mieux
> pour eux.
>
> (Rémès 2003, 28)

2 Coincidentally, Weinstein's views haven't changed that much since 2014, as a
recent article he co-wrote and published in the scientific journal *AIDS* evi-
dences. In that article, Weinstein and his co-authors claim that PrEP has led to
increased sexual risk-taking and a consequent rise in rates of diagnosis of other
STIs such as chlamydia and gonorrhoea (see Weinstein, Yang and Cohen
2017). Despite their argument, various other studies have claimed no necessary
causal relation between PrEP uptake and increase in rates of STIs. For
instance, as Werner, Gaskins, Nast and Dressler note in a meta-study review of
20 previously published studies, whilst there has been an increase in diagnoses
of STIs like syphilis, gonorrhoea, and chlamydia amongst PrEP users, that
increase may have been due to the closer intervals between sexual health

screenings that are recommended as part of PrEP follow-up, concluding with a claim that is dramatically different from Weinstein's views: "By offering access to structures that provide regular STI monitoring and prompt treatment, PrEP may not only decrease HIV incidence but also have beneficial effects in decreasing the burden of STIs" (Werner, Gaskins, Nast, and Dressler, 2018). For a similar argument that does not jump to read a causal relation in the correlation between PrEP use and higher STI diagnoses, see Gandhi, Spinelli and Mayer (2019).

References

Angelis, Massimo de. 2017. *Omnia Sunt Communia: On the Commons and the Transformation to Postcapitalism*. London: Zed Books.

Aydemir, Murat. 2007. *Images of Bliss: Ejaculation, Masculinity, Meaning*. Minneapolis: University of Minnesota Press.

Barro, Josh. 2014. "AIDS group wages lonely fight against pill to prevent H.I.V". *TheUpshot*, 16 November 2014. www.nytimes.com/2014/11/17/upshot/aids-group-wages-lonely-fight-against-pill-to-prevent-hiv.html [accessed 5 November 2019].

Bataille, Georges. 1988. *The Accursed Share: An Essay on General Economy*, Volume I. New York: Zone Books.

Beckman, Frida. 2013. *Between Desire and Pleasure: A Deleuzian Theory of Sexuality*. Edinburgh: Edinburgh University Press.

Berlant, Lauren. 1998. "Intimacy: A special issue". *Critical Inquiry* 24 (2): 281–288.

Berlant, Lauren, and Michael Warner. 1998. "Sex in public". *Critical Inquiry* 24 (2): 547–566.

Bersani, Leo. 2010. *Is the Rectum a Grave? and Other Essays*. Chicago: The University of Chicago Press.

Blake, Charlie. 2011. "A preface to pornotheology: Spinoza, Deleuze and the sexing of angels". In *Deleuze and Sex*, edited by Frida Beckman, 174–199. Edinburgh: Edinburgh University Press.

Calabrese, Sarah, and Kristen Underhill. 2015. "How stigma surrounding the use of HIV preexposure prophylaxis undermines prevention and pleasure: A call to destigmatize 'Truvada whores'". *American Journal of Public Health* 105 (10): 1960–1964.

Chalier, Jonathan, and Michaël Fœssel. 2017. "Une revolution sans revolutionnaires?" *Esprit* 436: 34–44.

Chen, Mel Y. 2012. *Animacies: Biopolitics, Racial Mattering, and Queer Affect*. Durham: Duke University Press.

Crary, David. 2014. "Gay men divided over use of HIV prevention drug". *Associated Press*, 6 April 2014. https://apnews.com/c1442585f57b421abe7cc6b0c4f96141 [accessed 5 November 2019].

Crary, David. 2018. "Usage remains low for pill that can prevent HIV infection". *Associated Press*, 8 January 2018. https://apnews.com/845fb524d26440d69bb72fdc8d120e29 [accessed 5 November 2019].

Cronon, William. 1996. "The trouble with wilderness; or, getting back to the wrong nature". In *Uncommon Ground: Rethinking the Human Place in Nature*, edited by William Cronon, 69–90. New York: W. W. Norton & Company.

Daston, Lorraine. 2019. *Against Nature*. Cambridge, MA: The MIT Press.

Dean, Tim. 2009. *Unlimited Intimacy: Reflections on the Subculture of Barebacking*. Chicago: The University of Chicago Press.

Dean, Tim. 2013. "Sameness without identity". *Penumbra*, edited by Sigi Jöttkandt and Joan Copjec, 119–137. Melbourne: re.press.

Dean, Tim. 2015a. "Mediated intimacies: Raw sex, Truvada, and the biopolitics of chemoprophylaxis". *Sexualities* 18 (1/2): 224–246.

Dean, Tim. 2015b. "The art of piss". *Animal Shelter* 4 (2015): 121–129.

Deleuze, Gilles. 1991. *Masochism: Coldness and Cruelty*. New York: Zone Books.

Deleuze, Gilles. 1997. "Re-presentation of Masoch". In Gilles Deleuze, *Essays Critical and Clinical*, 53–55. Minneapolis: University of Minnesota Press.

Deleuze, Gilles, and Félix Guattari. 1994. *What is Philosophy?* London: Verso.

Deleuze, Gilles, and Claire Parnet. 1987. *Dialogues*. New York: Columbia University Press.

Douglas, Mary. 2002. *Purity and Danger: An Analysis of Concept of Pollution and Taboo*. London: Routledge.

Edelman, Lee. 2004. *No Future: Queer Theory and the Death Drive*. Durham: Duke University Press.

Esposito, Roberto. 2010. *Communitas: The Origin and Destiny of Community*. Stanford: Stanford University Press.

Florêncio, João. 2018. "Breeding futures: Masculinity and the ethics of CUMmunion in Treasure Island Media's *Viral Loads*". *Porn Studies* 5 (3): 271–285.

Foucault, Michel, and Jean Le Bitoux. 2011. "The gay science". *Critical Inquiry* 37: 385–403.

Freud, Sigmund. 1989. "Beyond the pleasure principle". In *The Freud Reader*, edited by Peter Gay, 594–626. New York: W. W. Norton & Company.

Fritscher, Jack. 1978. "Upstairs over a vacant lot … the Catacombs". *Drummer* 3 (23): 8–11.

Gandhi, M., M. A. Spinelli, and K. H. Mayer. 2019. "Addressing the sexually transmitted infection and HIV syndemic". *JAMA* 321 (14): 1356–1358. DOI: 10.1001/jama.2019.2945.

García-Iglesias, Jaime. 2019. "Wanting HIV is 'such a hot choice': Exploring bug-chasers' fluid identities and online engagements". *Deviant Behavior*. DOI: 10.1080/01639625.2019.1606617.

Gingerich, John. 2000. "Remembrance and consciousness in Schubert's C-Major String Quintet, D. 956". *The Musical Quarterly* 84 (4): 619–634.

González, Octavio. 2019. "Pre-Exposure Prophylaxis (PrEP), the 'Truvada whore,' and the new gay sexual revolution". *Raw: PrEP, Pedagogy, and the Politics of Barebacking*, edited by Ricky Varghese, 27–48.

Hay, Harry. 1963. Letter to Jim Kepner. 3 August 1963. Harry Hay Papers, Coll2011-003, Box 1, Folder 70. ONE National Gay & Lesbian Archives, Los Angeles, California.

Hester, Helen. 2018. *Xenofeminism*. Cambridge: Polity.

Hocquenghem, Guy. 1993. *Homosexual Desire*. Durham: Duke University Press.

Joseph, Miranda. 2002. *Against the Romance of Community*. Minneapolis: University of Minnesota Press.

Kesel, Marc de. 2009. *Eros and Ethics: Reading Jacques Lacan's Seminar VII*. Albany: State University of New York Press.

Kirchick, James. 2019. "The struggle for gay rights is over". *The Atlantic*, 28 June 2019 [accessed 5 November 2019].

Knight Jr., Richard. 2003. "This Little Piggy". *Chicago Reader*, 28 August 2003. www.chicagoreader.com/chicago/this-little-piggy/Content?oid=913015 [accessed 14 November 2019].

Kristeva, Julia. 1982. *Powers of Horror: An Essay on Abjection*. New York: Columbia University Press.

Lacan, Jacques. 2008. *The Ethics of Psychoanalysis: The Seminar of Jacques Lacan, Book VII*. London: Routledge.

Latour, Bruno. 1993. *We Have Never Been Modern*. Cambridge, MA: Harvard University Press.

Maine, Alexander. 2019. "Bareback sex, PrEP, *National AIDS Trust v NHS England* and the reality of gay sex". *Sexualities*. DOI: 10.1177/1363460719886733.

Menninghaus, Winfried. 2003. *Disgust: The Theory and History of a Strong Sensation*. Albany: State University of New York Press.

Morris, Paul. n.d. "Tom of Finland's Pleasure Park". Unpublished manuscript, typescript.

Morton, Timothy. 2007. *Ecology Without Nature: Rethinking Environmental Aesthetics*. Cambridge, MA: Harvard University Press.

Muñoz, José Esteban. 2009. *Cruising Utopia: The Then and There of Queer Futurity*. New York: New York University Press.

Nancy, Jean-Luc. 2000. *Being Singular Plural*. Stanford: Stanford University Press.

Nancy, Jean-Luc. 2013. *Corpus II: Writings on Sexuality*. New York: Fordham University Press.

Nancy, Jean-Luc. 2016. *Intoxication*. New York: Fordham University Press.

Nancy, Jean-Luc. 2017. "Aux bords de l'intime". *Esprit* 436: 155–162.

Needham, Gary. 2019. "Making sense of *120 BPM*'s digital effects emblem". Paper presented at *120 BPM: A Symposium*, King's College London, May 11, 2019.

Paasonen, Susanna. 2018. *Many Splendored Things: Thinking Sex and Play*. London: Goldsmiths Press.

Pebody, Roger. 2018. "380,000 people on PrEP globally, mostly in the USA and Africa". *aidsmap*, 23 October 2018. www.aidsmap.com/news/oct-2018/380000-people-prep-globally-mostly-usa-and-africa-updated [accessed 5 November 2019].

Preciado, Paul. 2008. "Pharmaco-pornographic politics: Towards a new gender ecology". *Parallax* 14 (1): 105–117.

Preciado, Paul. 2013. *Testo Junkie: Sex, Drugs, and Biopolitics in the Pharmaco-pornographic Era*. New York: The Feminist Press.

Race, Kane. 2015. "Reluctant objects: Sexual pleasure as a problem for HIV biomedical prevention". *GLQ* 22 (1): 1–31.

Race, Kane. n.d. "A lifetime of drugs". Unpublished manuscript, typescript.

Rémès, Érik. 2003. *Serial Fucker: Journal d'un Barebacker*. Paris: Éditions Blanche.

Rubin, Gayle. 2004. "The Catacombs: A temple of the butthole". In *Leatherfolk: Radical Sex, People, Politics, and Practice*, edited by Mark Thompson, 119–141. Los Angeles: Daedalus Publishing Company.

Samuel, Krishen. 2018. "Most PrEP users in Berlin obtained it from informal channels". *aidsmap*, 2 October 2018. www.aidsmap.com/news/oct-2018/most-prep-users-berlin-obtained-it-informal-channels [accessed 5 November 2019].

Sandoval-Sánchez, Alberto. 2005. "Politicizing abjection: In the manner of a prologue for the articulation of AIDS Latino queer identities". *American Literary History* 17 (3): 542–549.

Sullivan, Andrew. 1996. "When plagues end: Notes on the twilight of an epidemic". *New York Times*, 10 November 1996.

Sullivan, Andrew. 2019. "The next step for Gay Pride". *New York Magazine*, 21 June 2019. http://nymag.com/intelligencer/2019/06/andrew-sullivan-the-next-step-for-gay-pride.html [accessed 14 November 2019].

Thornton, Sarah. 1995. *Club Cultures: Music, Media and Subcultural Capital*. Cambridge: Polity.

Treichler, Paula. 1999. *How to Have Theory in an Epidemic: Cultural Chronicles of AIDS*. Durham: Duke University Press.

Tronto, Joan. 2013. *Caring Democracy: Markets, Equality, and Justice*. New York: New York University Press.

Tuhkanen, Mikko. 2002. "Clones and breeders: An introduction to queer sameness". *Umbr(a): Sameness*: 4–7.

Turner, Victor. 1995. *The Ritual Process: Structure and Anti-Structure*. New Brunswick: AldineTransaction.

Tziallas, Evangelos. 2019. "The return of the repressed: Visualizing sex without condoms". In *Raw: PrEP, Pedagogy, and the Politics of Barebacking*, edited by Ricky Varghese, 117–141. Regina: University of Regina Press.

Weinstein, Michael, Otto Yang, and Adam Cohen. 2017. "Were we prepared for PrEP? Five years of implementation". *AIDS: A Year in Review* 31 (16): 2303–2305.

Werner, R. N., M. Gaskins, A. Nast, and C. Dressler. 2018. "Incidence of sexually transmitted infections in men who have sex with men and who are at substantial risk of HIV infection—A meta-analysis of data from trials and observational studies of HIV pre-exposure prophylaxis". *PLoS ONE* 13 (12): e0208107. DOI: 10.1371/journal.pone.0208107.

Zimmerman, Andrew. 2018. "Guinea Sam Nightingale and Magic Marx in Civil War Missouri: Provincializing global history and decolonizing theory". *History of the Present* 8 (2): 140–176.

5 Pig ethics, queer futures

In order to explore the ethics that would ground the potential of "pigsex" to forge different forms of coming together amongst strangers through an opening of the body to alterity and to unforeseen pleasures, in this final chapter I focus on the push and pull between negativity and utopia in "pig" play, drawing from philosophical discussions of hospitality in order to reflect on the structures of sociability and care that ought to sustain the ecology of the "pig" sty approached as a laboratory of queer worldmaking.

When, in 2000, Portuguese filmmaker João Pedro Rodrigues had his first feature film *O Fantasma* screened in competition at the 57th Venice International Film Festival, some audiences and critics at Venice's Palazzo del Cinema were left in a state of shock. The reason for that was not so much the nature of the story Rodrigues had set himself to tell but, rather, the way in which he had decided to film it—explicitly.

O Fantasma tells the story of Sérgio, a young homosexual rubbish collector in Lisbon whose only friend—or, perhaps even, whose alter-ego—is the stray dog that is kept chained outside one of the city's refuse collection centres. Obsessed that he is with satisfying his desires, Sérgio makes use of the invisibility granted to him by the darkness of the night to, as Claudia Morgoglione wrote at the time in the Italian newspaper *La Repubblica*, "immerse himself in the most degraded atmospheres possible" (Morgoglione 2000, my translation). Sérgio is seen having sex with other men, urinating in someone's bed, going through rubbish bins in search of used underwear that he proceeds to sniff and masturbate with, drinking water from dirty puddles, and finishing his days drifting through one of the rubbish dumps on the outskirts of the Portuguese capital, scavenging through the trash in search of food whilst wearing nothing other than a black fetish rubber suit complete with gimp mask, black leather gloves and boots. According to Antonio Pezzuto, another critic who reviewed the film at the time, this use of explicit images placed Rodrigues amongst a generation of young film directors who "are no longer satisfied with ellipses and metaphors", a groups of artists to whom "'pornographic' images become 'common,' 'normal' images" (Archivio Film Rosebud 2009). Explicit sequences, however, are not used in the film for mere shock value. Instead, and as Mário Jorge Torres wrote in *Público* ahead of the Portuguese premiere of the film at the 4th Gay and Lesbian Film Festival in Lisbon that same year:

> Unlike other films where porn appears as undisclosable desire but disappears into mere decorative citation, João Pedro Rodrigues has the courage to take it as a dramatic pole in order to make it implode in the Via Crucis of the lead character, Sérgio, a rubbish man.
>
> (Torres 2000, my translation)

Two narrative angles seem to emerge from the film. On the one hand, *O Fantasma* establishes a very clear relationship between rubbish, the invisibility of the night, and the lives of those who—just like ghosts haunting a dormant city—work to clear away the detritus of our everyday life. From that standpoint, what the film delivers is a story that, despite being fictional, is concerned with unveiling the lives of those who live and work in the invisible background of our contemporary cityscapes, the lives of those whom we never come across but who are, nonetheless, fundamental pieces of our urban ecosystems. On the other hand, the film also establishes a very strong analogy between trash understood as the leftovers of everyday life that must be cleared away out of sight before sunrise, and trash understood as a kind of devalued subjectivity or way of being. Sérgio is, after all, not just a rubbish collector. He is a homosexual and one who, in his hunt for sexual satisfaction, totally disregards the moral standards and norms that guide our contemporary societies. We see that when, after having sex with his female co-worker, he smells her and kicks her out of his room, telling her that she smells "like a bitch". We see it when he attempts to claim ownership of the man he seems to have fallen in love with by breaking into his room and pissing on his bed; we see it when his only friend appears to be the dog they keep at work, the only being with which he appears to be totally at ease. In lifting the veil that covers the lives of those who live on the fringes of society—in exposing that which should remain unseen—*O Fantasma* is, in many ways, a pornographic film. In it, we are faced with a graphic arthouse work that rejects metaphor in favour of an explicit presentation of sex, filth, and excrement on screen.

Of no surprise, then, that according to some critics, the only thing that seemed to save the film from complete doom was its cinematic style and the knowledge of the history of cinema Rodrigues had been able to demonstrate. Its explicit content notwithstanding, Goffredo Fofi, for instance, saw in *O Fantasma* echoes of Jean Cocteau, Louis Feuillade, and Jean Genet, whilst Antonio Pezzuto placed its construction of the cinematic sequences, as well as its organisation of space, in line with the "images of extraordinary rigour" that had become a trademark of Portuguese cinema thanks to Manoel de Oliveira, Pedro Costa, and João César Monteiro

(Archivio Film Rosebud 2009). It is, however, on the explicit content of the film, particularly the ways in which it was used to portray Sérgio as someone who inhabits the threshold between human and animal life, between mind and body, reason and instinct, day and night, cleanliness and filth, that I would like to focus. Whilst Sérgio certainly never calls himself a "pig", the way in which he occupies the thresholds that, as I've argued in previous chapters, define "pig" masculinities, highlights not only the potential but also the challenges of his relationship with both the world and himself. Unlike most of the people and scenes I've drawn from thus far, Sérgio progresses, in *O Fantasma*, into a state of increasing aimlessness and silent disorientation that culminates in scenes of isolation amidst the city's refuse, eating and drinking out of that which society has decided to throw away out of sight. Those are powerful images ending the film without offering any resolution, comfort, or hope. For everything that Sérgio manifests that may, as I've been arguing, constitute an opportunity to forge new allegiances, new modes of queer sociability and relationality, new kinds of embodiment that may just offer an alternative to—or, at least, some respite from—the dictatorship of the self-managed, self-entrepreneurial autonomous subject, his is a story of loneliness and isolation of someone who, failing to abide by the standards of the world in which he lived, living in or as a body that was anything but "proper", found himself excreted to the edges of the city, alone in the company of rotting food, rabbits, seagulls, plastics, broken kitchen appliances, insects, rust, putrefaction. Sérgio's story, even if it is a fictional one, raises therefore questions about the ethics that must accompany the sexual practices and embodiments I've been associating with "pigsex" and "pig masculinities" if they are to serve as springboards for a queer rethinking of our ways of being with one another. If indeed they are to contribute to José Muñoz's (2009) vision of queerness as a "structuring and educated mode of desiring that allows us to see and feel beyond the quagmire of the present" (1).

As I've discussed in Chapter 2, the development of the modern autonomous (hu)man subject happened thanks to the implementation of a set of techniques of the body (Maus 1973) that shaped sanctioned forms of embodiment thanks to the establishment and policing of distinctions of inside and outside, self and other, mind and body, Culture and Nature. Beyond sustaining the ideologies of liberal and neoliberal subjectivity, those distinctions were also responsible for creating the modern idea of Nature as both a bottomless resource pool for capitalist extraction and a mother figure in need of protection. As ecocritical thinkers like William Cronon (1996), Jane Bennett (2010) or Timothy Morton (2007) have argued, this imagining of Nature as a realm separated from Culture has ended up not aiding but, instead, hindering ecological thinking. As an alternative, Morton (2010; 2016) proposed a "dark ecology" that attempts to go beyond the nostalgia of green environmentalism by acknowledging the messy, sticky, dirty and uncertain aspects of contemporary ecosystems.

Inspired by that approach to ecology—by what amounts to a queering of ecological thinking (Mortimer-Sandilands and Erickson 2010)—I want to draw from the previous chapters and use gay "pig" masculinities and their embrace of bodily porosity, toxicity, and *cummunion* as a springboard from where to build a new speculative ethics of co-habitation. Because to think ecologically is ultimately to think about and towards hospitality—about who or what is allowed to share our home with us, who is recognised as the homeowner and who will, instead, forever be seen as a guest—such a speculative ethics ought not to be predicated on a logic of rights, responsible as it is for creating a membership club defined as much by commonality as it is by an exclusion of all those who are seen to have nothing in common (Birch 1993). Instead, the kind of speculative thinking I'm attempting here aims towards an ethics of hospitality whereby the latter is always-already understood as the unconditional welcoming of the other in the self. In undoing the autonomy of their own embodied subjectivities and in enacting forms of sociability based on doing rather than having-in-common—that is, without falling prey to the dominant specular logics of identity and recognition—gay "pigs" can help us think towards new forms of inhuman relationality and develop an embodied ethics, helping us speculate about alternatives to the divides and distinctions that have sustained the European project of modernity, and to the violence that always comes with each and every taxonomy of life and being. For, as Martin Savransky, Alex Wilkie and Marsha Rosengarten (2017) note:

> Speculating is not a matter of determining what is, and what is not, possible, as if possibilities could always be ascertained in advance of events, that is, from the impasse of the present. By contrast, speculation is here associated with a sensibility concerned with resisting a future that presents itself as probable or plausible, and to wager instead that, no matter how pervasive the impasse may be, it can never exhaust the unrealised potential of the present.
>
> (8)

Writing about Russian scientist Vladimir Ivanovich Vernadsky, Lynn Margulis and Dorion Sagan (2000) noted the following:

> What struck him most was that the material of the Earth's crust has been packaged into a myriad moving beings whose reproduction and growth build and break down matter on a global scale. People, for example, redistribute and concentrate oxygen, hydrogen, nitrogen, carbon, sulfur, phosphorus, and other elements of Earth's crust into two-legged, upright forms that have an amazing propensity to wander

across, dig into, and in countless other ways alter Earth's surface. We are walking, talking minerals.

(49)

What has always impressed me about this passage was not just the humility I see it asking from its readers, but also the ways in which it calls into question the distinctions that have sustained the ontological exceptionalism of the human that, in Western thought at least—and as I've already argued—has emerged in association with the privileging of a particular form of subjectivity and embodiment, that of the autonomous male subject of European modernity whom Kant (2009) saw as "the true end of nature" (94). If the embrace of autonomous universal reasoning accompanied by a disciplining of the body understood as the locus of the animal within allowed for humans to raise themselves above the animal (Hengehold 2007; Rasmussen 2011), then Margulis and Sagan's quote seems to argue otherwise. Rather than being autonomous self-enclosed units, our bodies remain fragile and precarious, and the lives that we live are contingent, temporary, and sustained by matter we've borrowed from the world outside. We were born out of chance events and the stuff in our bodies, the stuff that *is* our bodies, isn't ours but merely cuts across us—our bodies are not territories but passageways.

Western modernity, in its phallogocentric logics and imperialist expansion digging for wealth and universal knowledge, has insisted on a single and universalising viewpoint in such a way that embodied differences and local and subcultural knowledges had to either be thrown into invisibility—like Sérgio in *O Fantasma*—or surrender to the centripetal pull of an idealised body and of its idealised subjectivity—like the gay men who, in the aftermath of the AIDS crisis understandably decided to work towards integration into the culture that had excluded them in the first place. That being the case, could an enquiry into the porous nature of "pig" masculinities, their structures of feeling, body schemas, affects, desires, and pleasures help trouble the dynamics of self and other, of belonging and exclusion that have been sustained by the hegemony of the autonomous subject and of its role as the foundational model for the modern body politic? Could "pigsex" and "pig" masculinities not so much negatively push back against the self-enclosed and hermetic body of the neoliberal subject but, instead, be seen as a productive and affirmative praxis, a laboratory where sexual experiments with new "horizons of possibility" (Paasonen 2018) take place that affect not just subjectivities but also the body politic and its relation with its others?

There is a problem raised by Jacques Derrida that is central to my concerns here. In his essay entitled "Foreigner Question", the French philosopher highlighted the dilemma—or, to use his terminology, the aporia—that grounds the status of the foreigner. Drawing from the episode when, in Plato's *The Apology of Socrates*, Socrates, addressing the Athenian judges, declared himself to be foreign to the language of courts, Derrida (2000) noted the tension at the heart of being foreign. He wrote:

> the foreigner is first of all foreign to the legal language in which the duty of hospitality is formulated, the right to asylum, its limits, norms, policing, etc. He has to ask for hospitality in a language which by definition is not his own, the one imposed on him by the master of the house, the host, the kind, the lord, the authorities, the nation, the State, the father, etc. [...]. That is where the question of hospitality begins: must we ask the foreigner to understand us, to speak our language, in all the senses of this term in all its possible extensions, before being able and so as to be able to welcome him into our country?
>
> (15)

This is an increasingly pertinent dilemma. That of the problem we face when, foreigners that we are, we are required to speak the language of our hosts, to put ourselves on their terms as a precondition to enter their homes. That is where, for Derrida, the paradox of hospitality lies:

> If he was already speaking our language, with all that that implies, if we already shared everything that is shared with a language, would the foreigner still be a foreigner and could we speak of asylum or hospitality in regard to him?
>
> (15, 17)

The consequences of this are everywhere to be seen: *if* I speak your language, *then* I am no longer a stranger to you and the question of hospitality is deferred. *If*, however, I cannot translate myself into you, *then* the chance you'll welcome me in your home remains illusory. How can I ask you to welcome me in you without you understanding what I mean? Similarly, why would I want to be in you if being in you means the destruction of what makes us two?

That space between a rock and a hard place: The space of sinking boats in the Mediterranean and of mass shootings in gay nightclubs; the space where only the hissing sound of gas being pumped through pipes is heard above the terrifying and terrified silence of all those who cannot speak; the space of mass graves in the desert, the space of the unclean, the infected, the filthy, the abject, the poor—all of those who aren't you, who don't look like you, don't speak like you, don't desire like you, don't even fuck like you—*tell me who you fuck and I'll tell you who you are!* The space of all those who, nevertheless, inhabit your peripheral vision, the rats—the trash—insistently reminding you of all that which you tell yourself you are not. That space that, with its exclusionary logics, reassures you and lets you sleep better at night (and why should I blame you for wanting a good night's sleep, right?). But what if I could come inside as a stranger? What if I could come as I am, before any possible understanding of what that might mean? What if you could come as you are? (No questions asked; the door has been left on the latch.) What new forms of co-habitation—what new ethics—could that bring about? What can we become when you start welcoming me in you as I welcome you in me without bothering to know your name or what you've come here for? When we open ourselves not just to each other but also to the pauses, the silences, the syncopated rhythms that always haunt all moments of recognition of the self in the other? The edges of the perceptible that always make hospitality a leap of faith, a flirting with death, a duty, a gift, a form of expenditure without reserve, contingency and uncertainty as modes of being and living together. Being as multitude ...

According to Anne Dufourmantelle, whose work on hospitality and exchanges with Derrida helped shape recent philosophical enquiry into the practices and ethics of welcoming strangers into one's homes, "[hospitality], in its essence, is unconditional" (2013, 14). Given the role that, according to Lévi-Strauss's study of kinship structures (1969), incest taboo had in fostering new social alliances through exogamy, "[the] acceptance of the other to the point of the dissolution of self-enclosed tribes or groups [...] is in that sense the condition of the survival of all human societies" (Dufourmantelle 2013, 14). Yet, as Dufourmantelle noted, the dawn of modernity in Europe brought with it a progressive conditioning of the terms of hospitality. Seeking to protect the defining features of the collective national identities that were becoming fundamental to modern bodies politic, political reflections on the place of the foreigner in a space that isn't theirs led to new civil laws being developed to limit the unconditionality that had defined hospitality in pre-state societies. From the fourteenth century onwards, hospitality ceased to be predicated on the "unwritten rule: that the foreigner be received and honored like a king" (14) and started, instead, to be dependent on a series of pre-requisites that the foreigner had to fulfil in order to be welcomed in one's home:

> the intrusion of the foreigner into the "home"—which figures so strongly in the process of unconditional hospitality—would be subjected to certain conditions, rules pertaining to the concept of hospitality: Whom are we going to open our door to, and under what circumstances? How can the one hosting a foreigner protect himself against the violation of his home, or even violence as such? [...] At a time of massive colonial conquests, what hospitality could or should be offered the "savage," the stranger arriving with his or her own unfamiliar codes and culture? What right do we have to ask strangers to abandon their rules and adopt ours?

(15)

That set of questions, which "instigated the moral reflections of Kant as well as of Diderot and the Encyclopedists" (15), is one that is still all-to-familiar to anyone acquainted with the plight of migrants trying to enter Europe or the United States of America in the first decades of the twenty-first century. Those questions, guided by Western political ontologies of the foreigner and epistemologies of asylum, demand from those who try to enter our "homes" that they speak themselves to us in our terms, that they are able to narrate what makes them worthy of being welcomed *here* according to *our* standards and *our* language as their hosts.

A possible way out of such legal curtailing of the unconditionality that both Derrida and Dufourmantelle claimed to be the true essence of hospitality—for "the one who takes in, the host, may well be, from one day to another, cast on the road and in need of refuge him- or herself" (Dufourmantelle 2013, 14)—may pass through a recognition that hospitality—just like the monster (Shildrick 2002), the "pig" (Stallybrass and White 1986) or the cyborg (Haraway 1991)—always concerns, and is defined in terms of, experiences of threshold. In always-already involving the crossing of a boundary—in it being about the foreign entering the familiar, about the other in the self—hospitality proper draws our attention to the contingency of our own existence, to the "exilic condition of humankind as such", for it "is rooted in the experience of death, of letting go, of abandoning everything you have loved, acquired, and imagined" (Dufourmantelle 2013, 17). If the acceptance of our own mortality, coupled with uncertainty with regards to the arrival of our individual death, had been a defining presence in pre-state societies (Benjamin 1999), Western bourgeois modernity was instead marked by an attempt to rationalise "the great metaphysical horror of mortality" and thus make its certainty manageable through practices of hygiene that lodged "an infinitely extendable series of battles against specific diseases" (Bauman 1992, 155). However, the bourgeois obsession with halting death betrayed it as a task doomed to failure. In that context—one in which death is certain and only the time of its arrival is unknown—the thing we are left with is a sense of the contingent ephemerality not only of our own lives but also of the lives of others. In that sense, and to go back to Dufourmantelle (2013), "if hospitality is about a threshold, an act of trespassing, death makes us aware that our finitude confines us to the status of visitors here on earth—a status that, in turn, forms the precondition for hospitality as such" (17). Thus, it "makes sense only if the act of hospitality 'belongs' neither to the host nor to the guest, but to *the gesture by which one of them welcomes the other*" (18, my emphasis).

To my mind, Dufourmantelle's words resonate a lot with the ways in which I've been trying to think about the new corporeal horizons that may be opened by "pig" sex practices and embodied in "pig" masculinities, as well as the ethics of self and other that we may be able to think with and through them. According to "Martin", whom I interviewed in Los

Angeles, group sex encounters in which he is the single bottom—and whether taking place in his personal life or as part of his work in porn—are less about the specific men who top him but more about the gesture of opening himself up to all men who wish to do so:

> I am here to please mankind. You know what I mean? And so in order to please mankind—not you; I don't give a shit what your name is, I don't care what your sign is or what your life story is, I don't wanna fucking know. [...] I am here with my legs up in the air to show the world and anyone who will participate in this energy exchange that I am a bottom. Period.

"Anthony", another gay bottom working in porn whom I also interviewed in Los Angeles, seemed to agree. When I asked him about the kinds of connection established between himself and the men fucking him—whether there is always an individual connection or whether it is just about the cum and not the man who's cumming, he replied:

> It depends on the mindset you're in. I definitely can go into—like—that mindset where I am just a receptacle for cum and then it doesn't really matter what's happening. My job is to—like—milk a load out of this person.

"Martin"'s and "Anthony"'s words strike a chord with the unconditionality of the ethics of hospitality highlighted by both Derrida and Dufourmantelle. For "Martin", being gangfucked by several strangers—by men whom he doesn't know nor does want to know—is a practice of "energy exchange" that does not make his welcoming of others in him a function of the identity of those wanting to come inside him. Instead, to be gangfucked is—I'd argue—framed by "Martin" as a practice of unconditional hospitality. Such approach to sexual hospitality can also be seen taking place in instances of "anon"—that is, anonymous—group sex organised through gay hook-up apps and presented as fantasies in porn videos like Treasure Island Media's infamous *What I Can't See* (1999) and its subsequent sequels—*What I Can't See 2* (2006) and *What I Can't See 3* (2011)—which capitalised on the success and controversy associated with the original video.

Hailed by Paul Morris as "the first bareback gangbang video", a title that made it worthy of being remastered and re-released in 2010, *What I Can't See* was the first video to follow a simple and yet extremely successful premise that made it gain canonical subcultural status: a bottom awaits blindfolded in a room for a group of unknown tops to come in and, one by one—and in what the studio's website describes as a "rawfuck marathon"—cum inside him without him ever removing his blindfold. Writing about the video, Tim Dean (2009) noted how it functioned as an allegory for the imperceptibility of HIV, a virus that, due to its invisibility in sexual encounters, could only be signalled in porn synecdochally, that is, by the presence of ejaculate and its cultural associations with risk. Both the video and Dean's book, however, came out at a time when the visual rhetoric that connected semen with HIV was yet to be broken by the introduction of antiretrovirals and the eventual confirmation of the uninfectiousness of people living with an undetectable viral load. It is with that historical specificity in mind that we must read Dean's words when he wrote:

> It is as if *What I Can't See* were allegorizing gay life before the discovery of HIV—a life not of sexual hedonism as much as of an inevitable yet temporary blindness to exactly what may be entering one's rectum. We might say that the fantasy motivating this movie is that of being able to choose that temporary blindness, rather than being subjected to it by historical circumstances.
>
> (113)

Yet, watching the video today invites a rather different set of readings. Over two decades after its first release; almost a decade after the initial approval of PrEP by the US Federal Drugs Administration; a couple of years after the final results of the PARTNER study presented at the 22nd International AIDS Conference in Amsterdam confirmed zero cases of transmission amongst serodiscordant couples in which the HIV-positive partner had an undetectable viral load; and only one year after the US Centre for Disease Control approved its "U=U" ("Undetectable=Untransmittable") communications, watching a blindfolded man being penetrated without condoms by several men no longer necessarily trigger the chain of meanings that used to take us from semen to HIV and then AIDS. Instead, I would like to contend without detriment to previous readings, that the blindness of the bottom to the tops that penetrate him in *What I Can't See* no longer functions as an allegory for the invisibility of HIV but—when watched in the age of antiretrovirals—it does, instead, speak to the radical ethics of hospitality that I want to associate with "pigsex".

Even if not always enacted every single time gay "pigs" have sex with one another, "pigsex" carries at least the ethical potential to become a sexually intimate form of what Helen Hester (2018) called xeno-hospitality, that is, hospitality to that which is foreign, strange and even "unnatural" and inhuman. Just like Lévi-Strauss highlighted the role of exogamy in the reproduction of societies whilst also, as Dofourmantelle noted, necessarily transforming the societies it reproduced by allowing that which was foreign in, Hester's xenofeminist investment in practices of xeno-hospitality allows us to imagine social reproduction and thus a future, albeit without having to remain dependent on the familiar heteropatriarchal logics of the nuclear family and its dependence on the normative figure of the Child (Edelman 2004). In Hester's (2018) words, "the judicious mobilization of such a future-oriented affect may be necessary if we wish to create conditions that are hospitable to re-engineering what is, for many human and non-human actors alike, an unbearable present" (69). With its potential—if not always actual—radical openness to and welcoming of strangers, I argue that "pigsex" can therefore be understood as a queer form of sexual world-making, a "copyleft" ethics of experimentation with pharmacopornographic technologies (Preciado 2013) that are appropriated and put to use in ways that had not been institutionally sanctioned, in order to bring forth *a* future that veers away both from the temporal coordinates of heteropatriarchy and capitalism, and from normalised and state-sanctioned forms of intimate citizenship (Plummer 2003). Through such a process of radical openness to the bodily fluids of unknown foreign others, intimacy is enacted without subsuming alterity into identity, allowing the subject to be "formed and re-formed through its relation with the other and otherness", thus "leaving otherness intact" (Evans 2019, 112).

If one of the main challenges of morality, as Auschwitz has painfully demonstrated, is that "objects do not go into their concepts without leaving a remainder", that is, that in the move towards identity, something of the body will always-already be necessarily left out—that "the concept does not exhaust the thing conceived" (Adorno 1983, 5)—then ethics ought to start from alterity, from that which will always remain foreign both in the self and in the other, without ever attempting to integrate it back into a shared commonality. Ethics mustn't be dependent on the retroactive identification and naming of single common origins, achieved either through the compulsive breaking down of the other into ever-smaller component parts in the hope that some of them will become recognisable, or through attempting to rewind ontogenetic histories back to a singular primordial moment that can then be conceived as having preceded all individuation. For, if ethics, in Deleuze's reading of Spinoza, is primarily concerned not with what a body is but with what it can do, not with what originated it but with what it can become, "it looks forwards and not backwards; [...] it looks outwards and not inwards" (Buchanan 1997, 80). Rather than departing from a position of recognition of the self in the other, ethics should instead be attentive to the interruptions, syncopations and gaps that, as Ernesto Laclau and Chantal Mouffe (1985) have argued, will always constitute our relationship with both ourselves and others, and that are thus both the conditions of possibility for a pluralistic democracy and signs of the impossibility of its full realisation. Instead of wishing for political tension to be resolved through identity and recognition, it is the radical alterity of the self and the other that allows for a democratic polity to emerge as a horizon in constant negotiation, one in which the principle of identity gives way to alterity "by exposing oneself to expenditure at a loss, to sacrifice" (Lingis 1994, 12). In the words of Laclau and Mouffe (1985), "the logic of equivalence is a logic of the simplification of political space, while the logic of difference is a logic of its expansion and increasing complexity" (130).

It is only through a radical openness of bodies—both individual and collective—to the incommensurably strange alterity of other bodies that a principle of ethical inviolability of the Other can ever be guaranteed. As Lévinas (1969) wrote:

> The Other is not other with a relative alterity as are, in comparison, even ultimate species, which mutually exclude one another but still have their place within the community of a genus [...]. The alterity of the Other does not depend on any quality that would distinguish him from me, for a distinction of this nature would precisely imply between us that community of genus which already nullifies alterity.
>
> (194)

In our present moment of climate emergency and increasing border controls, a time when all bodies have been found to be dangerously entangled and simultaneously estranged from one another, ethics can only emerge as a leap of faith, as a gesture of sacrificial hospitality that welcomes the strange and the foreign in their absolute and unknowable otherness. Even if the "other comes as an intruder" (Lingis 1994, 34) and thus requires an adjustment or even a sacrifice on the part of its host, such a practice of radical hospitality does not have to be seen simply as self-destruction. Instead, it can be conceived as an openness of one's body—of one's home—to new, more ethical, horizons of possibility.

There is a passage in A. A. Bronson's *Negative Thoughts* that got stuck in my mind when I first read it. A catalogue for the eponymous exhibition held at the Museum of Contemporary Art, Chicago in 2001, *Negative Thoughts* is both a book of photographs, a tribute to the late Felix Partz and Jorge Zontal—the two artists who, alongside Bronson, made up the Canadian conceptual art collective General Idea—and a reflection by Bronson, artist and self-described healer, on his own survival as the AIDS crisis took away the lives of his two friends and collaborators. In that passage, Bronson wrote the following:

> I am walking down the beach with Mark on Fire Island. We are not far from the little house in the Pines where Jorge and I spent three idyllic summers. The beach is littered with attractive men, most of them with those deep red-toned Fire Island tans. The waves are high, and men are leaping in and out of the cresting water, drawn in by the drama and romance of the crashing waves. The air is heavy with salt spray, a dense but sparkly mist that obscures our vision and colours the day with a luminous amber glow. I drink in this scene as if I may never see it again, and I realize that this is the way I now relate to the

world: as if I may never see it again. Since Jorge died, since Felix died, I have come to reposition myself in this reality, as a short-term visitor on a visa of unknown duration. I may be deported at any moment, without warning or compassion.

(Bronson 2001, 27)

Deeply moving, Bronson's words are startling in how they allude to resignation and humility in the face of loss and trauma, whilst at the same time positing painful historical events as having—at times, certainly not always—the ability to provide those who have lived through them and survived a certain heightened ability to find beauty and solace in the world around them—to, in short, keep seeking that "luminous amber glow" whilst remaining all-too-aware of one's own finitude.

Whilst I have no intention to build an in-depth critique of Bronson's work here, that passage offers me an incredibly comforting sense of hope. Here I am, a gay man in my early-late-thirties who grew up during the AIDS crisis and, in various ways, been forever affected by it, looking up to the words of one of my elders in search of a sense of futurity, of what living after AIDS may look like. Whilst the Fire Island Pines may have become a highly expensive holiday destination for middle-class gay men, with property developers and recreation and hospitality businesses capitalising on the subcultural memory of a time before the crisis when the island functioned as a sanctuary for gay men wishing to experiment with the wide range of sexual pleasures and sociability available to them, the idyllic walk on a beach populated by carefree men that Bronson describes makes me think of whether such island could be once again inhabited: an island for our times, when trauma and mourning have started giving way to new senses of possibility and social and sexual experimentation with what a queer future may look like.

Yet, the kinds of sexual behaviours and sociability I've described in this book are far from perfect. Gay men are, after all, still men. And men—whether straight or gay—still have a long way to go before we manage to escape the constraints placed upon us by a phallogocentric regime that expects boys to grow up to become men and where our masculinities are obsessively monitored whilst we all continue in various ways to fail to embody the claustrophobic ideal towards which we are all summoned. And yet, despite all of that, what I've encountered throughout my research was a sense that new embodiments of masculinity are being experimented with and given shape in a so-called "post-AIDS" or "post-crisis" conjuncture in which antiretroviral combination therapies, recreational drugs, and new styles of pornography benefiting from the affordances of online media seem to have allowed gay men—the gay men who can afford access to them—to pick up where our elders have left their pursuits of sexual liberation and investigations into "carnal horizons of possibility" (Paasonen 2018, 8). Interrupted as they once were by the onset of the crisis and the deaths of so many of us, today, in the aftermath of PrEP and "U = U", gay men who benefit from the geocorporealities of the antiretroviral age—restricted as the latter nonetheless still are along lines of gender, race, ethnicity, class background, and access to affordable quality healthcare—have been given the chance to rethink and reshape their bodies, their pleasures, and their subcultural structures of kinship.

As I was researching this book, I encountered a variety of gay men all of whom had various histories of struggle, isolation, pain, and, in some instances, ongoing financial difficulties. And yet, amidst all those narratives that are popularly used to explain away gay men's sexual behaviour on account of their traumatic origin stories, the men I encountered had also found ways of feeling content and at ease with themselves at least every once in a while, no longer ashamed by who they were or by the pleasures they enjoyed. In that sense, they seemed to me to be no different from most people trying to forge a meaningful life in the early decades of a century that's increasingly being marked by political unrest, climate emergency, hatred, rising fascism, and impermeability to others, individualism, gentrification, and neoliberal economic models that continue to benefit only a very small minority of the Earth's population. The gay men I encountered seemed to have found strategies to manage any potential risks associated with the pleasures they enjoyed and to quite often look after one another whilst doing so. And still, those pleasures and—to some of them at least—the porn careers that became such important part of their lives continue to be looked down on with suspicion by media exposé after media exposé, tabloid headline after tabloid headline. In the eyes of many—I have no doubts—those are broken and degenerate men. To my eyes, after having spent countless hours in their company, chatting to them, hearing about their lives, laughing, discussing all manner of topics from art to music, politics, or the ongoing environmental crisis, and even at times having sex with them, those men mostly came across as being deeply aware of the world around them, warm, smart, emotionally intelligent, and capable of both laughter and anger whenever the occasion required it. To some people, unfortunately, they will remain risky dangerous unhinged degenerate irresponsible narcissistic hedonistic perverts with a penchant for self-destruction.

I am, however, not deluded and thus do not wish to romanticise a subculture that also carries in itself the seeds of its own destruction even as it may simultaneously point towards new modes of living masculinity and sexuality queerly, and of forging new infrastructures of care beyond the ones sanctioned by the phallogocentric institutions of Abrahamic religions, Western modernity, the state, or capitalism. For, as I researched this book, I've also come across men dropping on club floors whilst overdosing on GHB/GBL; I've heard stories of addiction to crystal metamphetamine, physical and psychological abuse, stalking, doxxing, rape, loneliness. All of those happening within, outside, and alongside porn—porn certainly did not come across as anything exceptional in that regard, no worse and no better than the wider world of life and labour. Yet, I also encountered grassroots infrastructures of care and risk-management. I've attended group discussions about drugs and sex organised by club promoters and hosted by queer health professionals and club performers. I've seen the importance of friendships forged in darkrooms and sex clubs. When some of those gay men had been found to be struggling to manage their drug consumption, I saw friends come to their aid, offering them advice and social environments where they could still feel included without feeling compelled to take whichever substance they had been struggling with. I've seen men resting on other men's laps in clubs, and I've seen them going out for brunch in the early afternoon, heading to movie nights, for a swim in the lake, organising camping weekends away from the city. And so, whilst I do not wish to postulate "pigginess" as the utopia of gay masculinities or sexual sociability, I also do not wish to reduce those practices and subjectivities to the potential risks that may come with them, especially for those who may be less informed and have fewer support networks. But that is exactly why subcultural structures and practices of care have to be highlighted, celebrated, fostered, and protected.

If, as I've been arguing throughout this book, experimenting with the pleasures bodies can afford when they open themselves and become porous to one another is a possible pathway to trouble normative understandings of masculinity; if, through them, one can also interrogate some of the fundamental and naturalised tenets of modern European thought, those practices of experimentation will have to involve a deterritorialisation of the self, a radical dislocation of the ideological gravitational centre of our bodies. And, as Deleuze and Guattari (1983, 1987) have warned us, whilst deterritorialisations bring with them the risk of self-obliteration—for what they called the "Body without Organs" still needs organs to function—carefully managed deterritorialisations can break the subject without actually shattering it. They have the capacity to foster a becoming of the body by exposing it to new sets of orientating principles and relations that may offer some respite from—or point to ways out of—the oedipal structures and symbolic regimes that have heretofore governed and disciplined our world, bodies, and thought.

In approaching "pigsex" as a deterritorialising practice that, when carefully managed, can set gay masculinities into new—and hopefully more ethical—pathways of becoming, I am reminded of Claire Rasmussen's discussion of the troubled relationship between the human and the animal in Western thought. To quote Rasmussen (2011)—and pushing her argument further towards a productive ethics of self-alienation—acknowledging the animal within doesn't "merely [evoke] the strangeness of the other, but also the strangeness of the self" (130). To acknowledge the strangeness of the self—to alienate the self—it is fundamental to experiment with its plasticity as a site of possibility for new kinds of subjectivity, of embodiment, and of ethical relationships with others. To deterritorialise the self involves a destabilisation of the coordinates that have guided and crystallised its formation. Because the latter belong to the register of what Lacan called the Symbolic, the deterritorialisation of the coordinates of one's being is akin to the event that made Antigone a lasting mythical figure. Reflecting on her decision to break Creon's law and bury her brother Polynices, Lacan understood Antigone's law-breaking as something she had to do in order to become the Antigone we've come to know. Despite all the risks associated with breaking Creon's command, which stands as an allegory for Lacan's Law of the Father, it was only in the exact moment in which she broke the law in spite of herself—that is, despite all the likely consequences of her unruly behaviour—that Antigone did, paradoxically, become herself. She became herself by breaking the scripts she had been expected to follow, by opening herself to unknown foreign territories even if that likely meant sacrificing herself. Her action was therefore seen by Lacan as an instance of the ethical act (Lacan 2008; see also Zupančič 2000; Kesel 2009; Ruti 2017). In involving a break away from the law without a guiding map, the ethical act veers away from the reassuring comforts of pre-established paths and moral imperatives, known as they are for deferring one's responsibility for decision-making to the authority of the written law. As such, the ethical act embodied by Antigone "affirms the advent of the absolute individual" (Lacan 2008; 342). Yet, as Mari Ruti (2017) stressed, the autonomy that Lacan associated with Antigone has nothing to do with the autonomy of the modern European subject. Because Antigone acted against the Law and, thus, against the Symbolic order through which she had theretofore existed, "when she [claimed] her 'autonomy' in the sense that Lacan means it, she [did] not become a unitary humanist subject; quite the contrary, she [lost] everything, including her life" (Ruti 2017, 56).

Antigone's death notwithstanding, the ethical act needs not lead to actual physical self-annihilation. Necessary and unlawful—*necessarily unlawful*—the ethical act falls within what Michel Foucault (1990) called an "aesthetics of existence", one that offers the subject not just a pathway to the (symbolic) self-obliteration of sacrifice but also—and most importantly—all the creative possibilities that come with the chance it offers us to then forge ourselves anew (Lacan 2008, 262; Guattari 1995, 1–32, 1996). And even if—and even if, crucially—the Law and the Symbolic will always necessarily return, the ethical act may just contribute to their return in a more liveable manner, as a reterritorialisation that is more bearable to those who have felt trapped, constrained, invisible, buried under the weight of its previous iterations (Ruti 2017, 87–129). In order to unpack the ways in which "pigsex" calls for an ethics that, in being sacrificial, also opens new horizons of being—new becomings—whilst demanding responsibility only to what Derrida (1995) called the "wholly other" found both in the depths of the self and in the irreconcilable strangeness of the other, I would like to make a detour through Kierkegaard's and

Derrida's attempts to grapple with the incommensurability of ethics and morality as it played out in one of the foundational moments of yet another myth, that of Abraham.

Despite the ways in which they have come to shape and serve as models for various laws and guiding principles of the self, the three so-called "Religions of the Book" can be said to have truly begun with one specific episode in the Book of Genesis, one that helps frame ethics as an act of radical openness to the unknown and the unspeakable—the episode in which Abraham not only proved to be but simultaneously *became* the "father of faith". That day, the Biblical story tells us, God called upon Abraham and told him to take Isaac, his only son, to Mount Moriah in order to offer him in sacrifice. Isaac, who was then about twenty-five years old, was Abraham and Sarah's only son, given to them as a gift by God themselves, for both Abraham and Sarah were too old to have children without the help of the Divine Providence. Meditating on that episode, and on the unsurmountable task God required of Abraham as proof of his faith, Søren Kierkegaard noted that, despite Abraham's willingness to sacrifice Isaac, he—Kierkegaard—would never have been able to love his son like Abraham did. Abraham loved his son at least as much as he loved himself and yet he still proceeded with the task God had given him. Resigned, he took Isaac to Mount Moriah and prepared himself to kill him. He did not ask anyone for advice; he did not tell his wife, Sarah, nor his brother Eliezer, nor even Isaac himself, who had no knowledge of what was about to happen until the moment his death became imminent. And despite his love for Isaac, Abraham would have killed his son were it not for an angel of God to suddenly appear at the very moment the father raised a knife in his trembling hand and make him stop. "And he said, Lay not thine hand upon the lad, neither do thou any thing unto him: for now I know that thou fearest God, seeing thou hast not withheld thy son, thine only *son* from me" (Genesis 22:12).

Abraham's willingness to sacrifice his only son disquieted Kierkegaard and became the focus of *Fear and Trembling*, the book he published in 1843 under the pseudonym Johannes de Silentio. How could faith be grounded on a willingness to sacrifice what we most love? How could the three monotheistic religions and the morality that followed them have been born from such an unspeakable will to murder? Kierkegaard (1983) was bewildered; he wrote of Abraham:

> Thinking about Abraham is another matter, however; then I am shattered. I am constantly aware of the prodigious paradox that is the content of Abraham's life, I am constantly repelled, and, despite all its passion, my thought cannot penetrate it, cannot get ahead by a hairsbreadth. I stretch every muscle to get a perspective, and at the very same instant I become paralyzed.

(33)

The Danish philosopher could not understand Abraham; as Sarah wouldn't have been able to understand him either. Because Abraham, Kierkegaard wrote, "speaks no human language [...] he speaks in a divine language, he speaks in tongues" (114). That is why Abraham did not speak to Sarah about the task given to him by God. He did not speak because he was alone in his secret with the Divine. He did not speak because no human language could find a way of explaining what he was about to do. Abraham did not speak because he did not know how to speak, how to grasp and make sense of what God required of him. Therefore, the only thing Abraham could do was to tremble. He did not just fear God but he *trembled*. Sure, fear of God came first; but then Abraham *trembled* and it was his *trembling*—rather than his fear of God—that made him, in Kierkegaard's words, the "knight of faith" (38). For whilst fear paralyses, trembling propels us forward. More often than not—as with Abraham—it moves us towards death, either our own or that of something or someone we love as much as we love ourselves. Abraham trembled and thus he moved, he took the knife in his shaking hand and prepared to take the life out of his son, to offer God what Derrida (1995) called the "gift of death".

In *The Gift of Death*, originally published in French as *Donner la mort in L'Étique du don* ("To give death in the Ethics of the gift"), Derrida noted that trembling is a sign that something always-already unknown is about to happen. Departing from the same episode in the Abrahamic myth, Derrida (1995) wrote:

> Most often we neither know what is coming upon us nor see its origin; it therefore remains a secret. [...] Even if one thinks one knows what is going to happen, the new instant of that happening remains untouched, still unaccessible, in fact unlivable. [...] I am still afraid of what already makes me afraid, of what I can neither see nor foresee. I *tremble* at what exceeds my seeing and my knowing [...] although it concerns the innermost parts of me, right down to my soul, down to the bone, as we say.
>
> (54)

We tremble when we are faced with the "wholly other", with something we cannot grasp despite the fact that it concerns us intimately, "down to the bone" as Derrida noted. And we tremble when, despite our being afraid of it, we have no option other than moving towards it. Because fleeing is not an option; because it is only by being propelled towards it that we, paradoxically perhaps, can actualise our own becoming ourselves.

Putting aside the various religious and moral readings the biblical episode has elicited over the centuries, there is something in the ways in which both Kierkegaard and Derrida have written about it that is useful when trying to figure out the ethics of "pigsex"—or, better, the ethics that

must come with it. Namely, the idea that we tremble when we face a terrifying unknown from which we cannot escape because it is only by moving
towards it that we can open new horizons of possibility for ourselves and
others, even if they demand from us a sacrifice of what we are today.
Unlike fear, which often leads us to flee the threatening scene, trembling—
although still resonating through every inch of our bodies—does nonetheless propel us forward towards an abyss that is unavoidable because, in
Derrida's words, it concerns the innermost parts of ourselves—the
"strangeness of the self" as Rasmussen put it (2011, 130). Further, in
being an instance of absolute responsibility to the absolutely other, the
moment of sacrifice is a moment of "absolute singularity" (Derrida 1995,
84), one that cannot be grasped through existing laws, morality, or principles of being; it can only be tangentially touched on as an instance of
responsibility to alterity—of openness to it—even if that which is other—
God, in Abraham's case—will always remain unknown and unreachable,
just like every other horizon. And yet, the hope is that, in committing to
alterity and being responsible only to it, the move towards the abyss of the
self may not just break us into tiny little particles but that it may also constitute an opportunity for us to put ourselves back together in new, more
ethical and more liveable arrangements, a "will to create from zero, a will
to begin again" (Lacan 2008, 262). Such an ethics of trembling responsibility to alterity brings to mind a passage in Mark Thompson's introduction to the first edition of his landmark edited volume *Leatherfolk*. In it,
Thompson (2004) recalled the first time he went to a leather bar:

> The night I entered a leather bar for the first time marked my own
> escape from those islands of isolated desire. It was the evening of the
> spring equinox, 1975, and with those tentative steps a new journey
> began—one not defined by the values of my oppressors. I met a man
> who invited me home to experience the surrender and release I so des-
> perately wanted. The moment I felt the cool sensation of shackles on
> wrists, something fundamental within me let go. [...]
>
> Radical sex ritual, I learned, is not only about the exploration of
> rage and loss, but can be a way toward joy. At some point in my
> journey the dark became enlightened; preconceived notions were
> turned inside out.
>
> (xvii)

Thompson's words remind us of how moving towards something that
threatens to undo our very being and that is ungraspable because it is not
explainable through the language, laws and "values of our oppressors"—
the language, laws and values into which we were all born—does not have
to simply be an instance of self-obliterating queer negativity. Instead—or,
perhaps, even alongside it—it can also be an affirmative move, "a way
toward joy", as he put it. In that sense, an embrace of sexual practices

that have, at various moments, been conceived as self-shattering—whether BDSM in Thompson's case (Bersani 1986, 1995, 2010) or exchanges of bodily fluids in the case of "pigsex" (Dean 2009; Bersani and Phillips 2008)—can open up pathways to new arrangements and alignments of the body, to new becomings of the subject. More than simply being shattered towards the inorganic *jouissance* of non-being, the subject can re-emerge anew and transformed. Just like with Antigone and Abraham, sacrifice can therefore become the means for a creative practice of the self, enacted through an opening of the latter to the other. In involving an opening, "pigsex" can emerge as an instance of sacrificial hospitality, for welcoming others also always risks the undoing of the self (Dufourmantelle 2013). The hope is that, in undoing the self and fostering a reorganisation of the body, "pigsex" and other practices of sacrificial hospitality may set the embodied subject on a journey towards new "carnal horizons of possibility" (Paasonen 2018, 8). Yet, in order for that to happen, structures of care, solidarity and comradeship will have to be in place so that ripples may open in the seams of the subject, breaking it without shattering it only to then reorganise it into new more liveable arrangements; so that new collective islands of desire and pleasure may be formed in the opening of the self to the other—a "city of Friends", to use Whitman's phrasing in "Calamus". In the "city of Friends", relations of intimate queer comradeship constitute forms of "promiscuous citizenship" (Frank 2011) that are indifferent to state-sanctioned patterns of intimacy and to institutionalised sexualities. As Tripp Rebrovick (2017) wrote of Whitman, in a way that resonates with the creative potential of forms of intimacy that—like "pigsex"—are often reduced to negativity, anti-sociality, and (self-) destructiveness:

> Whitman's queer comrades, however, are not anti-social in the slightest, even as they wrench cities and mock statutes. They create, inhabit, and constantly reconstruct their own social and political orders. [...] Whitman gives us a vision of queers who maintain a critical and negative relation with heteronormativity but still remain committed to the future.
>
> (17)

When sustained by structures of care, solidarity and comradeship, "pigsex" and "pig" masculinities may—just like Whitman's view of comradeship—open themselves to new futures even as they sacrifice or undo pre-coded arrangements of bodies and subjectivities. So whilst there will always be a fine line to be threaded between self-obliteration and creative becoming, it is important that gay men come together not just as sex partners but as true comrades, that we are able to care and look after one another as we take ourselves down cycles of sexual self-fragmentation and recomposition; so that no deterritorialisation is definitive and that we may reconstitute ourselves more ethically, queerly and anew. So that our sacrifices don't kill us but instead propel us forward, hopefully landing us on the shores of new islands of communal pleasure and political possibility.

References

Adorno, Theodor. 1983. *Negative Dialectics*. New York: Continuum.

Archivio Film Rosebud. 2009. "Fantasma Il—Fantasma (O)". Commune di Reggio Emilia. www.comune.re.it/cinema/catfilm.nsf/PES_PerTitoloRB/959E444516B5F BE6C125742E004A4680 [accessed 12 November 2019].

Bauman, Zygmunt. 1992. *Mortality, Immortality and Other Life Strategies*. Cambridge: Polity.

Benjamin, Walter. 1999. "The storyteller: Reflections on the works of Nikolai Leskov". In *Illuminations*, edited by Hannah Arendt, 83–107. London: Pimlico.

Bennett, Jane. 2010. *Vibrant Matter: A Political Ecology of Things*. Durham: Duke University Press.

Bersani, Leo. 1986. *The Freudian Body: Psychoanalysis and Art*. New York: Columbia University Press.

Bersani, Leo. 1995. *Homos*. Cambridge, MA: Harvard University Press.

Bersani, Leo. 2010. *Is the Rectum a Grave? and Other Essays*. Chicago: The University of Chicago Press.

Bersani, Leo, and Adam Phillips. 2008. *Intimacies*. Chicago: The University of Chicago Press.

Birch, Thomas. 1993. "Moral considerability and universal consideration". *Environmental Ethics* 15 (4): 313–332.

Bronson, AA. 2001. *Negative Thoughts*. Chicago: Museum of Contemporary Art, Chicago.

Buchanan, Ian. 1997. "The problem of the body in Deleuze and Guattari, or, what can a body do?" *Body & Society* 3 (3): 73–91.

Cronon, William. 1996. "The Trouble with wilderness; or, getting back to the wrong nature". In *Uncommon Ground: Rethinking the Human Place in Nature*, edited by William Cronon, 69–90. New York: W. W. Norton & Company.

Dean, Tim. 2009. *Unlimited Intimacy: Reflections on the Subculture of Barebacking*. Chicago: The University of Chicago Press.

Deleuze, Gilles and Félix Guattari. 1983. *Anti-Oedipus: Capitalism and Schizophrenia*. Minneapolis: University of Minnesota Press.

Deleuze, Gilles and Félix Guattari. 1987. *A Thousand Plateaus: Capitalism and Schizophrenia*. Minneapolis: University of Minnesota Press.

Derrida, Jacques. 1995. *The Gift of Death*. Chicago: The University of Chicago Press.

Derrida, Jacques. 2000. "Foreigner question". In Anne Dufourmantelle and Jacques Derrida, *Of Hospitality*, 3–73. Stanford: Stanford University Press.

Dufourmantelle, Anne. 2013. "Hospitality—under compassion and violence". In *The Conditions of Hospitality: Ethics, Politics, and Aesthetics on the Threshold of the Possible*, edited by Thomas Claviez, 13–23. New York: Fordham University Press.

Edelman, Lee. 2004. *No Future: Queer Theory and the Death Drive*. Durham: Duke University Press.

Evans, Elliot. 2019. "your blood dazzles m/e": Reading blood, sex, and intimacy in Monique Wittig and Patrick Califia". In *Raw: PrEP, Pedagogy, and the Politics of Barebacking*, edited by Ricky Varghese, 91–114. Regina: University of Regina Press.

Foucault, Michel. 1990. "An aesthetics of existence". In Michel Foucault, *Politics, Philosophy, Culture: Interviews and Other Writings, 1977–1984*, edited by Lawrence D. Kritzman, 47–53. London: Routledge.

Frank, Jason. 2011. "Promiscuous citizenship". In *A Political Companion to Walt Whitman*, edited by John E. Seery, 155–184. Lexington: The University Press of Kentucky.

Guattari, Félix. 1995. *Chaosmosis: An Ethico-aesthetic Paradigm*. Bloomington: Indiana University Press.

Guattari, Félix. 1996. "A liberation of desire: An interview by George Stambolian". In *The Guattari Reader*, edited by Gary Genosko, 204–214. Oxford: Blackwell Publishers.

Haraway, Donna. 1991. *Simians, Cyborgs, and Women: The Reinvention of Nature*. New York: Routledge.

Hengehold, Laura. 2007. *The Body. Problematic: Political Imagination in Kant and Foucault*. University Park, PA: The Pennsylvania State University Press.

Hester, Helen. 2018. *Xenofeminism*. Cambridge: Polity.

Kant, Immanuel. 2009. "Conjectures on the beginning of human history". In Immanuel Kant, *An Answer to the Question: What is Enlightenment?*, 87–105. London: Penguin Books.

Kesel, Marc de. 2009. *Eros and Ethics: Reading Jacques Lacan's Seminar VII*. Albany: State University of New York Press.

Kierkegaard, Søren. 1983. *Fear and Trembling/Repetition*. Princeton: Princeton University Press.

Lacan, Jacques. 2008. *The Ethics of Psychoanalysis: The Seminar of Jacques Lacan, Book VII*. London: Routledge.

Laclau, Ernesto and Chantal Mouffe. 1985. *Hegemony and Socialist Strategy: Towards a Radical Democratic Politics*. London: Verso.

Lévi-Strauss, Claude. 1969. *The Elementary Structures of Kinship*. Boston: Beacon Press.

Lévinas, Emmanuel. 1969. *Totality and Infinity: An Essay on Exteriority*. Pittsburgh: Duquesne University Press.

Lingis, Alphonso. 1994. *The Community of Those who Have Nothing in Common*. Bloomington: Indiana University Press.

Margulis, Lynn, and Dorion Sagan. 2000. *What is Life?* Berkeley: University of California Press.

Maus, Marcel. 1973. "Techniques of the body". *Economy and Society* 2 (1): 70–88.

Morgoglione, Claudia. 2000. "O Fantasma sconvolge il Lido". *La Repubblica*, 7 September 2000. www.repubblica.it/online/mostra_di_venezia/fantasma/fantasma/fantasma.html [accessed 6 November 2019].

Mortimer-Sandilands and Bruce Erickson, eds. 2010. *Queer Ecologies: Sex, Nature, Politics, Desire*. Bloomington: Indiana University Press.

Morton, Timothy. 2007. *Ecology Without Nature: Rethinking Environmental Aesthetics*. Cambridge, MA: Harvard University Press.

Morton, Timothy. 2010. *The Ecological Thought*. Cambridge, MA: Harvard University Press.

Morton, Timothy. 2016. *Dark Ecology: For a Logic of Future Coexistence*. New York: Columbia University Press.

Muñoz, José Esteban. 2009. *Cruising Utopia: The Then and There of Queer Futurity*. New York: New York University Press.

Paasonen, Susanna. 2018. *Many Splendored Things: Thinking Sex and Play*. London: Goldsmiths Press.

Plummer, Ken. 2003. *Intimate Citizenship: Private Decisions and Public Dialogues*. Seattle: University of Washington Press.

Preciado, Paul. 2013. *Testo Junkie: Sex, Drugs, and Biopolitics in the Pharmaco-pornographic Era*. New York: The Feminist Press.

Rasmussen, Claire. 2011. *The Autonomous Animal: Self-Governance and the Modern Subject*. Minneapolis: University of Minnesota Press.

Rebrovick, Tripp. 2017. "A queer politics of touching: Walt Whitman's theory of comrades". *Law, Culture and the Humanities*. DOI: 10.1177/17438721166 88181.

Ruti, Mari. 2017. *The Ethics of Opting Out: Queer Theory's Defiant Subjects*. New York: Columbia University Press.

Savransky, Martin, Alex Wilkie and Marsha Rosengarten. 2017. "The lure of possible futures: On speculative research". In *Speculative Research: The Lure of Possible Futures*, edited by Alex Wilkie, Martin Savransky and Marsha Rosengarten, 1–17. London: Routledge.

Shildrick, Margrit. 2002. *Embodying the Monster: Encounters with the Vulnerable Self*. London: Sage.

Stallybrass, Peter, and Allon White. 1986. *The Politics and Poetics of Transgression*. Ithaca, NY: Cornell University Press.

Thompson, Mark. 2004. "Introduction". In *Leatherfolk: Radical Sex, People, Politics, and Practice*, edited by Mark Thompson, xv–xxiv. Los Angeles: Daedalus Publishing Company.

Torres, Mário Jorge. 2000. "Esse Obscuro Corpo do Desejo". *Público*, 29 September 2000. www.publico.pt/2000/09/29/jornal/esse-obscuro-corpo-do-desejo-149377 [accessed 6 November 2019].

Zupančič, Alenka. 2000. *Ethics of the Real: Kant and Lacan*. London: Verso.

Index